UNIVERSAL ACCESS TO E-MAIL

FEASIBILITY AND SOCIETAL IMPLICATIONS

Robert H. Anderson · Tora K. Bikson
Sally Ann Law · Bridger M. Mitchell

with

Christopher Kedzie · Brent Keltner · Constantijn Panis
Joel Pliskin · Padmanabhan Srinagesh

Supported by
The Markle Foundation

RAND

Those of us who use electronic mail (e-mail) systems extensively to assist in conducting our business or personal affairs understand the significant advantages derived from its key attributes:

- Both parties to the transaction need not be on-line at the same time—e-mail is stored in an electronic "inbox" until accessed.

- The information arrives in a "machine-readable" form such that it can be stored, retrieved, forwarded, cut-and-pasted into new messages, replied to, and reused in flexible ways.

- It is fast, with most messages arriving (worldwide) within minutes of being sent.

- Messages may contain combinations of text, pictures, diagrams, voice annotations, even video clips.

As more of our correspondents obtain e-mail addresses, more of our communication and commerce may be conducted through this efficient medium. To those on-line, e-mail provides a general—often substantial—increase in effectiveness, productivity, and access to relevant information.

What if e-mail were as ubiquitous as telephones, TVs, and VCRs, so that literally *everyone* were on-line, accessible by e-mail, and able to send messages to bulletin boards, news groups, friends, family, and colleagues? Is this technically feasible? If so, at what cost? What would be the personal and societal benefits resulting from "universal access to e-mail?" In particular, in addition to possible economic benefits, could universal access help in creating a more aware and participatory democracy by aiding the formation of interest groups ("virtual communities"), access to current information, and person-to-person contacts?

This is the final report of a two-year RAND study attempting to develop some answers to the above questions. It is designed as a sourcebook on key social, technical, economic, and international issues related to providing universal access to e-mail within the United States. It is our hope that this report will help stimulate public policy discussions regarding the feasibility, desirability, and implications of universal e-mail access. Decisionmakers involved with such public policy issues are the primary audience for this report, but it should also be of interest to academic and business professionals involved with telecommunications policy and its social implications.

The study was sponsored by The Markle Foundation and has benefited greatly from the personal interest and commitment to this study by its president, Dr. Lloyd Morrisett.

The study was carried out under the auspices of RAND's Center for Information Revolution Analysis (CIRA), directed by Dr. Bryan Gabbard.

For further information on this study, please contact, Dr. Bryan Gabbard (Bryan_Gabbard@rand.org), Dr. Robert Anderson (Robert_Anderson@rand.org) or Dr. Tora Bikson (Tora_Bikson@rand.org). This report is also accessible on the World Wide Web at http://www.rand.org/publications/MR/MR650/

CONTENTS

TABLES

One of the most intriguing inventions that visitors see at Monticello—Thomas Jefferson's magnificent home outside Charlottesville, Virginia—is a contraption that allowed him to write on many sheets of paper simultaneously. The device holds several pens in place attached by a series of hinged levers to a central pen. As Jefferson wrote with that main pen, the others moved in unison, providing him several copies of the same correspondence with only a single effort.

Jefferson's writing device was an 18th century high-tech wonder. It freed him from the drudgery of copying. It allowed him to concentrate on composition rather than on production. And it permitted him to mail multiple copies of letters in his own hand as soon as he finished writing.

Jefferson's device never caught on with the public at-large, in part because it could be used by only a small information elite of literate letter writers. Today's technological equivalent, electronic mail—commonly referred to as e-mail—holds that same promise, but it also runs the same risk of catering to a small elite. This time, however, the risks hold far broader implications than in Jefferson's day.

E-mail has swept the communications and information world during the past decade, providing instantaneous global information and data exchange. People who send e-mail via the Internet—the amorphous network that links computers worldwide via telephone lines—can correspond with individuals 10,000 miles away as easily, quickly, and inexpensively as they can with neighbors next door. They can communicate with one or many people at the same time. And they can distribute information to any other user as soon as they create it.

However, even though this revolution has broadened and changed the ranks of people with access to information, it has not altered one fundamental feature: An information elite still exists, made up of those with access to and knowledge about computers and e-mail. And as e-mail becomes more pervasive, as more commercial and government transactions in the United States take place on-line, those information haves may leave the have-nots further behind, unless we make concerted efforts today to provide all citizens with access to the technology.

The topic of universal access to electronic mail has demographic, technical, economic, social, and international perspectives. Our study has touched on all of these to various degrees, resulting in many observations and conclusions. We highlight those we believe to be most important below, followed by a set of research topics whose study could provide additional data about and answers to the questions addressed in this report.

POLICY CONCLUSIONS AND RECOMMENDATIONS

We find that use of electronic mail is valuable for individuals, for communities, for the practice and spread of democracy, and for the general development of a viable National Information Infrastructure (NII). Consequently, the nation should support universal access to e-mail through appropriate public and private policies.

The goal of achieving universal access has two main subgoals: (1) achieving interconnectivity among separate e-mail systems, and (2) widespread accessibility of individuals to some e-mail system.

Universal connectivity among systems appears to be occurring through market forces, although the portability of e-mail addresses and current regulations that distort the prices among potentially competitive communication offerings are likely to remain issues.

Individuals' accessibility to e-mail is hampered by increasing income, education, and racial gaps in the availability of computers and access to network services. Some policy remedies appear to be required. These include creative ways to make terminals cheaper; to have them recycled; to provide access in libraries, community centers, and other public venues; and to provide e-mail "vouchers" or support other forms of cross-subsidies.

The literature reviewed plus information gathered and analyzed in Chapters Two and Five make clear the central role of e-mail in the use of electronic networks; the role of these networks as a social technology is salient. Interpersonal communication, bulletin boards, conferences, and "chat rooms," of course, also provide information and help individuals find or filter information from other sources.

Much study and discussion, both within our government and elsewhere, focus on the content, design, and policies related to an NII. If this report demonstrates anything, it is the importance of person-to-person, and many-to-many communication within such an infrastructure. Therefore,

> It is critical that electronic mail be a basic service in a National Information Infrastructure.

To the extent that public policy guides the evolution of the U.S. NII, it should consider universal access to e-mail as a cornerstone of that policy. Specifically, one-way information-providing technologies—whether broadcasting systems or technologies that provide only search and retrieval—are inadequate. Two-way technologies supporting interactive use and dissemination by all users are key. And everyone should be able to participate:

> It is important to reduce the increasing gaps in access to basic electronic information system services, specifically, access to electronic mail services.

Implementation of such policies should begin as soon as possible, since it will undoubtedly take as much as a decade before full implementation is accomplished, no matter what strategy is envisioned. We recommend that the gaps that are greatest now and that are still widening be addressed first. Specifically, these are deficits in access to computers and electronic networks found in the low-income and low-education segments of the population.

Directory services and addressing mechanisms must be considered core components. Additionally, any obstacles to full connectivity and interoperability must be minimized.

Virtually every study of electronic mail establishes that immediate convenient access is the single most powerful predictor of use. To the extent that national or other policies attempt to redress imbalances caused by the market for electronic access, we conclude that

> *Policy interventions should give priority to widespread home access.*

In addition, and not as a substitute, multiple options for network access located in convenient places (including, for instance, libraries, schools, public buildings, hotel lobbies, business centers, and the like) are important auxiliary access sites. Such common facilities could be considered good locations for help or training centers as well.

Prior studies as well as information presented in Chapters Two and Five show little reason to be concerned that citizens will abandon the needs of their local (physical) communities in favor of virtual communities in cyberspace. Rather, communications are typically addressed to a community of concerned individuals, and either for reasons of subject matter or prior acquaintance, these concerns are often (although not necessarily) geographically bounded. Thus, network access can be expected to enhance rather than detract from community involvement.

> *Provision of community services and activities on-line should be actively supported.*

Local nonprofit providers experience many of the same resource constraints—costs, technical expertise, and so on—that households and individuals face. Engaging people in participatory democracy is not just a problem of giving citizens access but also a problem of enabling the service and information providers. Specific policies might be designed to facilitate and support the development of on-line civic activities offered by government agencies and nonprofit organizations.

Our study of the technical considerations in providing universal access to e-mail concluded that

There are no fundamental technical barriers to providing universal access to electronic mail services.

We concluded that current and evolving Internet standards for e-mail (SMTP and MIME, in particular), although perhaps not the definitive standards for electronic mail, provide a good basis for further evolution of a universal system. To the extent possible, gateways among dissimilar e-mail systems should be avoided, or be regarded as only temporary measures, because information is lost at least one way, and possibly both ways, in such transactions. Therefore, migration of Internet standards down into organization-level systems appears preferable.

We find that access to and the location of physical devices for e-mail use significantly impede universal access. With only about half of U.S. households containing personal computers by the year 2000, a robust set of alternative devices and locations is needed, including keyboard attachments to TV set-top boxes and video game machines, and extended telephones providing e-mail (and likely integrated voice mail) access. Public access is vital, with libraries, post offices, kiosks, and government buildings each playing a role. There might well be a market for "pay" terminals analogous to the ubiquitous pay telephones.

The state of software for "user agents," "knowbots," and similar filtering programs appears capable of handling, sorting, prioritizing, and presenting the large volumes of e-mail that may result from universal access. Similar technologies can give the user sufficient control over content (at least initially using the address or site that is the physical source of the material as an indicator of content; later "filters" may use other cues), so that avoiding objectionable materials should pose no greater problem than it does in other aspects of contemporary life.

We have concluded that e-mail white pages or yellow pages directories will be developed by market forces and therefore conclude that

> *There appears to be no need for governmental or regulatory involvement in the development, or centralization, of directories for universal e-mail addresses (both white and yellow pages).*

In considering the architecture of a universal e-mail system, we were strongly influenced by the recommendations developed by the Computer Science and Telecommunications Board (1994):

> *The design of a universal e-mail system should follow "open data network" guidelines, with a small number of transport services and representation standards (e.g., for fax, video, audio, text).*

Upon this base, a larger but still quite bounded set of "middleware" services such as file systems, security and privacy services, and name servers may be built. An evolving, growing set of applications can then thrive without requiring redesign of the underlying "bearer" and "transport" portions of the network. This model closely resembles that developed over the last several decades within the Internet development community.

Until more is known about appropriate user-computer interfaces for all segments of our society (see our "Recommendations for Further Research," below), we believe that—to the extent inexpensive computing devices can support it—the "Web browsing" model for user interactions, including access to e-mail services, is an important, highly usable, interface model. Within the foreseeable future, it is an important means of access to a burgeoning amount of on-line information and services. Because the cost of computing power continues to drop, we cautiously recommend

> *The "Web browser" model of user-computer interaction should at least be considered a candidate for the minimum level of user interface for e-mail access as well as other hypertext-style access to information.*

This report has considered the need for a simple e-mail address system that gives every U.S. resident a "default" e-mail address by which they can be reached. Such a development would "jump start" a universal access system, because governmental and other organizations could then assume that "everyone" was reachable by this means and design procedures and systems accordingly. The advantages of this approach lead to our recommendation:

> *A simple e-mail address provision scheme should be developed giving every U.S. resident an e-mail address, perhaps based on a person's physical address or telephone number.*

If such a universal addressing scheme were developed, services would then be needed, at least in transition, to "migrate" electronic materials received into paper form for persons not capable of, or not desiring to, access them electronically. Such services could be provided by third-party entrepreneurs or established agencies and companies such as the U.S. Postal Service or one's local telephone service provider.

The economic analysis presented in Chapter Four suggests that economies of scope and scale on the supply side, together with the easy substitutability among messaging and communications services on the demand side, may result in both vertical and horizontal integration—and the formation of strategic alliances—of suppliers in related markets. The growing use of bundled offerings and term and volume discount pricing are consistent with that analysis. The convergence of previously distinct messaging and communications services and the emergence of a unified communications/messaging environment raise a number of significant public policy issues. The following are two major areas in which policy may need to be reformed.

Uniform Regulatory Treatment

It is virtually impossible to distinguish among video, voice, and data services in a modern digital environment. As the discussion of MIME in Chapter Three makes clear, an e-mail message may contain audio and video clips, and might substitute for video-on-demand offered by a cable television provider. However, video services can support data communication. Real-time interactive voice conversations can be carried by the Internet using a variety of commercially available software products, and many consumers access the Internet using modems and ordinary telephone lines.

Nevertheless, given their very different histories, voice, data, and video communications services have been treated very differently by regulators. With the convergence of the communications/messaging market, regulatory distinctions are creating artificial distortions in the marketplace and may be creating incentives for customers to use economically inefficient messaging options. The discussion in Chapter Four about access charges and the enhanced service provider exemption provides one example of artificial cost differences that arise from regulations designed for one application (standard telephony) that must now compete with other applications. We conclude that

> *Policies developed separately for telephony, computer communications, broadcasting, and publishing that create artificial distinctions in the emerging information infrastructure should be reviewed, and a consistent framework should be developed that spans all the industries in the unified communications/messaging industry.*

Address portability provides an example of the need for a consistent regulatory framework. Portability reduces the switching costs of consumers and increases market competitiveness. Chapter Four shows that with the use of bundling, the portability of telephone numbers could be negated through the use of nonportable e-mail addresses.

> *Policymakers should develop a comprehensive approach to address, number, and name portability.*

Efforts at implementing the above recommendation should be compatible with and cognizant of our earlier recommendation that "default" electronic addresses be provided for all U.S. residents. Although there may be some important tradeoffs between address portability and simplicity of routing, policymakers should attempt to make this tradeoff consistently across all competitors.

Open Network Architectures

As technologies converge, each business and residence will have the choice of several access technologies and providers who will offer circuit- and packet-based services. In addition, multiple long-distance and international service providers will offer a comparable range of services.

Given the large sunk costs and the nominal marginal usage costs of facilities-based providers, competition in raw transport is likely to be unstable. Providers are likely to integrate vertically or form alliances that allow them to differentiate their products. Regulations requiring the nondiscriminatory sale of unbundled transport may not be consistent with emerging vertical relationships and competition.

In the near term, regulation should adopt a light-handed approach that specifies minimum capabilities that can be transferred across networks to allow providers sufficient flexibility to develop enhanced features that differentiate their products. In the longer term, when technologies have more fully converged, subscription to multiple networks by each customer may be inexpensive and widespread, and regulations governing interconnections may not be necessary. Providers may then be free to differentiate their offerings based on market demand.

Our study of the economics of e-mail provision concluded that subsidization for current household access could require approximately $1 billion per year, but we have mentioned (in Chapter Four) interesting commercial experiments providing "free" e-mail to those willing to accept advertising; similarly, "near-free" computers might be provided to those willing to subject themselves to additional advertising (e.g., on a built-in "screensaver" display). So the $1 billion amount may possibly be a mid-level estimate, not a minimum required.

Although e-mail penetration is expanding rapidly, some program of economic assistance to marginal consumers may be necessary to achieve universal levels of services. Obligating service providers to offer subscriptions to large classes of customers at low rates that are financed by contributions from other services is unlikely to succeed in the competitive messaging industry. Instead,

> *Any e-mail assistance will require public funding from an industry-wide tax or from general revenues. Subsidies will need to be narrowly targeted to reach consumers who would not otherwise subscribe.*

There are international dimensions to "universal" e-mail within the United States. Policies to influence the development of a national e-mail system should recognize the borderless nature of this technology. Perhaps more than other national systems, an e-mail system will affect and be affected by worldwide standards, policies, and events.

The analysis in Chapter Six leads to the conclusion that democracy in the nations of the world is positively correlated with interconnectivity. For nations emerging into democracy, or attempting to, connectivity is likely to have a positive influence on democratization. We conclude that

> *The United States should support increased interconnectivity abroad, since this may aid the spread of democracy.*

The results of this study support the conclusion that important results and benefits accrue to those becoming internetted, and that the problem to be addressed is the growing disparity among some society segments in access to that internetting. Universal access to electronic mail within the United States is an important solution strategy; achieving universal access will require dedication, focus, and cooperation by individual citizens, commercial companies, nongovernmental organizations, and government at all levels.

RECOMMENDATIONS FOR FURTHER RESEARCH

Our research has uncovered inadequacies in the statistical data describing the phenomena we studied. We encountered other shortfalls in the existing literature or in current field experiments. We therefore recommend that the following research initiatives be undertaken to permit a better understanding of problems and issues related to universal access to e-mail and related interactive information systems.

- Cost-benefit analysis should be initiated to answer the question: What mass of the U.S. population, if it were network-accessible, is necessary to support electronic delivery of major government services (e.g., filing Medicare claims or income tax forms, delivering at least some of the postal mail, or distributing Social Security benefits or disability benefits) in a cost-effective manner? It is possible that the benefits to many government agencies and other organizations could outweigh costs of subsidization, so that a straightforward business case could be made for universal access.

- A sizable and diverse number of grass-roots civic networks (i.e., those not designed, like HomeNet, and supported as field research) should be selected and followed from conception through efforts to raise start-up funding, and so on until they have been operating for some years. Getting comparable information across such activities about what works and what does not through early to later stages in the introduction of these networks (including what proportion of them do not make it), plus the kinds of civic, social, and economic roles they play, would vastly enhance what we have been able to learn from cross-sectional studies and site visits at a single point in time.

- Current Population Survey (CPS) data should be collected on a panel basis to monitor access to and uses and effects of computer networks. In particular, the success of policies and markets to close the identified gaps should be tracked and social benefits assessed. This may require revision or extension of CPS questions and administration schedules.

- Most e-mail systems have been designed for use in academic or business settings. Better understanding of the capabilities and limitations of current user-computer interfaces is needed, especially those related to electronic-mail handling. Existing interfaces rely on metaphors and analogies common to current users: multilevel "filing cabinets," commands to be issued, "Rolodex"-type address files, and forms to be filled out. How should these interfaces (including perhaps modest extensions of Web point-and-click browsers) evolve so that they can serve the entire range of users, including those in bottom-quartile income and education households? Field experiments concentrating on interface design for these prospective user groups are needed.

2SLS	Two-Stage Least Squares
ACM	Association for Computing Machinery
ADMD	Administrative Management Domain
AFDC	Aid for Families with Dependent Children
ANOVA	Analysis of Variance
AOL	America Online
ARPA	Advanced Research Projects Agency
ARPAnet	The Precursor of the Internet
ASCII	American Standard Code for Information Interchange
AT&T	American Telephone and Telegraph
ATM	Asynchronous Transfer Mode
AVT	Applied Voice Technology
BARRNet	A regional, university-based, ISP located in the San Francisco Bay area
BBN	Bolt, Beranek and Newman
BEV	Blacksburg Electronic Village
CAC	Community Access Center
CACM	*Communications of the Association for Computing Machinery*

CCITT	International Telegraph and Telephone Consultative Committee
CD-ROM	Compact Disk-Read Only Memory
CIRA	Center for Information Revolution Analyses
CMR	Commercial Mail Relay
CNRI	Corporation for National Research Initiatives
CPS	Current Population Survey
CPSR	Computer Professionals for Social Responsibility
CSTB	Computer Science and Telecommunications Board
DNS	Domain Name System
e-mail	Electronic Mail
EDI	Electronic Data Interchange
EMMS	Electronic Mail and Messaging Systems
ESP	Enhanced Service Provider
FAQ	Frequently Asked Question
FTP	File Transfer Protocol
GB	Gigabyte (10^9 Bytes)
GDP	Gross Domestic Product
GED	General Equivalency Diploma
GII	Global Information Infrastructure
GUI	Graphic User Interface
HCFO	Hispanic Community Fund Office
IBM	International Business Machines
IETF	Internet Engineering Task Force
IGC	Institute for Global Communications
IP	Information Provider; Internet Protocol
IRS	Internal Revenue Service

ISO	International Standards Organization
ISP	Internet Service Provider
ITU	International Telecommunications Union
KB	Kilobyte (10^3 Bytes)
KIP	Key Information Provider
LAN	Local Area Network
LSCA	Library Services Construction Act
MB	Megabyte (10^6 Bytes)
MCI	Microwave Communications, Inc.
MHz	Megahertz
MIDS	Matrix Information Directory Service
MIME	Multipurpose Internet Mail Extensions
MIS	Management Information System
MUD	Variously defined as Multiple User Dimension, Multiple User Dungeon, or Multiple User Dialogue. It is a computer program allowing users to explore and help create an on-line environment
NAFTA	North American Free Trade Agreement
NCLIS	National Commission on Libraries and Information Science
NII	National Information Infrastructure
NPR	National Public Radio
NSF	National Science Foundation
NTIA	National Telecommunications and Information Agency
ODN	Open Data Network
OLS	Ordinary Least Squares
OSI	Open Systems Interconnection

PC	Personal Computer
PCMCIA	Personal Computer Memory Card International Association
PCS	Personal Communications System
PEN	Public Electronic Network
PSTN	Public Switched Telephone Network
PTA	Parent-Teacher Association
PTW	Playing To Win Network
RAM	Random Access Memory
RFC	Request for Comments
SBA	Small Business Administration
SCN	Seattle Community Network
SES	Socioeconomic Status
SMTP	Simple Mail Transfer Protocol
UNIX	A widely used operating system for computers, originally developed at Bell Laboratories
USC	University of Southern California
USPS	U.S. Postal Service
VAN	Value-Added Network
VCR	Video Cassette Recorder
VT	Virginia Tech
WAN	Wide Area Network
XIWT	Cross-Industry Working Team

Chapter One

INTRODUCTION

Robert H. Anderson, Tora K. Bikson, Sally Ann Law,
Bridger M. Mitchell

Over the last 15 years, the burgeoning use of personal computers has popularized a number of new information services, including in particular electronic mail or "e-mail." E-mail is a form of information interchange in which messages are sent from one personal computer (or computer terminal) to another via modems and a telecommunications system. The use of e-mail began on the ARPAnet[1] (the precursor of the Internet) in the 1960s and 1970s in the United States, gradually spread along with the use of mainframe- and minicomputer-based local nets in the 1970s, and "exploded" along with the rapid growth of personal computers (PCs) and the Internet in the 1980s. E-mail began as a means of information interchange for small, select groups; its use has spread to encompass millions of people in the United States and all over the world. E-mail has given rise to the formation of many "virtual communities"—groups of individuals, often widely separated geographically, who share common interests. The interpersonal linkages and loyalties associated with these virtual communities can be real and powerful.

E-mail has unique properties that distinguish it from other forms of communication; for example, it supports true interactive communication among many participants. For the first time in human his-

---

[1]A brief history of the ARPAnet and Internet can be found in Lynch and Rose (1993), Chapter 1.

tory, we would assert, the means of "broadcasting" or "narrow-casting" are not confined to the few with printing presses, TV stations, money to buy access to those scarce resources, and the like. E-mail is also, unlike telephone calls (with the exception of voice mail and answering machines), asynchronous, so that communication does not depend on the simultaneous availability and attention of sender and recipient. Generalizing greatly, e-mail increases the power of individuals, permitting them to be active participants in a dialog extended in both time and space, rather than passive recipients of "canned" programming and prepackaged information.[2] These characteristics give rise to the question: Can e-mail's novel properties address society's most compelling problems? If so, by what means?

PROBLEM STATEMENT

It is now possible to imagine the arrangement or construction of systems in which nearly universal access to e-mail within the United States could become feasible within a decade—indeed, that is one aspiration of the U.S. National Information Infrastructure (NII)[3] initiative. Since e-mail use is growing rapidly (e.g., within individual corporations, CompuServe, America Online, Internet, and Bitnet systems and on numerous dial-in electronic bulletin boards), the question may be asked: "Why bother? It's happening anyway." Three important answers to this question are: (1) In spite of the growth of these e-mail systems, the majority of U.S. residents probably will continue to lack access to e-mail well into the next century without societal intervention; (2) there is today a significant lack of active participation by many citizens in the dialog that forms the basis for the U.S. democratic process;[4] and (3) some citizens, such as inner-

---

[2]Documentation on this point may be found, for example, in Sproull and Kiesler (1991b).

[3]Introductory materials on plans for the NII may be found at Web page: http://nii.nist.gov/.

[4]Documentation about the decline in U.S. "social capital" and its effect on the performance of representative government may be found in Putnam (1993) and Putnam (1995). Among the data cited in his 1995 article: U.S. voter turnout has declined by nearly a quarter from the early 1960s to 1990; Americans who report they have "attended a public meeting on town or school affairs in the past year" declined from 22 percent in 1973 to 13 percent in 1993; participation in parent-teacher organizations

city minorities and the rural poor, are relatively disenfranchised and constitute groups that will be the last to be reached by commercial e-mail systems that evolve in private markets. Because the properties of e-mail allow individuals to engage in an active civic dialog, with informative and affiliative dimensions, universal e-mail might provide significant benefits in creating interactive communication among U.S. citizens and residents.

The problem, then, is achieving active, responsive citizen participation in our national dialog for all citizens—participation not only in national politics but in local affairs, job markets, educational systems, health and welfare systems, international discourse, and all other aspects of our society.

There are hints that the distinctive properties of electronic mail systems (including access to, and ability to post and retrieve messages from, various electronic bulletin boards) may well be relevant to this re-enfranchisement of all citizens. The civic networks discussed in Chapter Five of this report exemplify these opportunities.

It is also clear that widespread citizen access to an e-mail system could have profound economic implications that might provide new sources of business and revenue to entrepreneurs providing new services; for example, installation of the French Programme Télétel system resulted in a flourishing of electronic services available to virtually all French citizens (and, for that matter, many visitors—through terminals available in hotel rooms and public sites).

It is important to note, however, that the Minitel terminal used by Télétel was not originally conceived of as access to an e-mail system but rather as an "electronic telephone directory." As is often the case, when some facility for communication becomes possible within a system (e.g., ARPAnet, Télétel, and to a growing extent the Dialog system within the United States), its convenience and empowerment of individuals quickly cause e-mail to become an important form of usage. Lack of true e-mail capabilities may be a major contributor to the failure of other electronic service ventures such as

---

dropped from more than 12 million in 1964 to approximately 7 million today; since 1970, volunteering is off for Boy Scouts by 26 percent and for the Red Cross by 61 percent.

teletext experiments, although too many factors may be involved to confirm this assessment.

UNIVERSAL E-MAIL

The initial forays into widespread availability of electronic mail, such as the ARPAnet (and now Internet) experience, Télétel, and growing Prodigy, CompuServe, and America Online usage, lead to an intriguing question: What about "universal e-mail?" What about providing all residents of the United States with access to e-mail service, just as they now all (or almost all) have access to telephone service and postal service? What would be involved in such an undertaking? What are the pros and cons? What are the advantages and disadvantages? Could this have beneficial effects for U.S. society? Greater cohesion? Reduced alienation? Increased participation in the political process? Influence national security? What about beneficial effects for the U.S. economy? Or other productive side effects? And who would pay for the infrastructure and its usage?

More specific questions arise immediately regarding the services and functions to be provided by a universal e-mail system: the required degree of access to such a "universal" service; the provision of privacy; alternative system architectures and implementation schemes; the cost of such a system/service and the method of payment; the likely social and international effect of universal e-mail; and finally, public versus private roles in creating and operating such a service. This report describes our initial study of these and related issues over a two-year period and presents the results of our analyses.

The issue of providing universal e-mail cannot be considered in isolation. As mentioned above, it is part of a larger national debate on a "national information infrastructure" and "global information infrastructure" that is gaining momentum. We hope this report contributes to discussion of the policy and social issues arising from attempts to provide such a service, in addition to technical options regarding implementation of the supporting infrastructure per se, because of these issues' importance in the public policy debate.

SOME DEFINITIONS

Electronic Mail

For the purposes of this report, we have adopted a definition of electronic mail provided in an earlier RAND report (Anderson et al., 1989):

An electronic mail system:

> 1. Permits the asynchronous electronic interchange of information between persons, groups of persons, and functional units of an organization; and
>
> 2. Provides mechanisms supporting the creation, distribution, consumption, processing, and storage of this information . . . .

The words in this definition all have significance. Key among them are the following:

- *Asynchronous*: One defining attribute of e-mail is the ability to send a message when the recipient is not at that moment logged in; the message is placed in an "inbox" for later inspection by the recipient at his or her convenience.

- *Electronic*: The message travels over telecommunication systems at the speed of electricity in copper, of light in a fiberoptic cable, or of microwave or a satellite link (plus additional switching delays). Although some system "gateways" buffer messages for periodic transmission, the result still has a dynamic fundamentally different from postal mail, newspapers, and other traditional media.

- *Interchange of information*: Anyone within the system can send as well as receive messages.

- *Between persons, groups of persons, and functional units of an organization*: Messages may be sent to "mailboxes" representing individuals or groups; "aliases" may be established representing a number of individual addresses, so that a message may be sent to a group of individuals in one action; mailboxes such as "purchasing@abc.com" or "president@whitehouse.gov" may be established that represent a function, to be used by whomever is presently handling that function.

- *Mechanisms supporting the creation, distribution, consumption, processing, and storage*: It must be possible to create messages, send and receive them, store them for future inspection and re-use, and "process" them (e.g., copy portions and paste them into later messages, forward them to others, modify their contents, and reuse them in other applications).

By the above definition, multipart messages containing embedded formatted word-processing documents, video clips, bitmapped pictures, sound clips, and the like are certainly e-mail. Faxes sent from one dedicated fax machine to another, appearing only on output paper are not (because they are not processable in a useful manner), but a "fax" sent from one PC to another meets the definition (because it may be stored for later retransmission, and its contents may be "processed"—e.g., by character recognition or graphics enhancement programs; in fact, some recipients may never get it in paper form). Similarly, using a personal computer to interact with "chat" groups and MUDs[5] usually qualifies as a form of e-mail, because most communication programs through which this interaction is carried out allow the transcript of the interaction to be saved, processed, reused, and so on.

We have tried to use a rather narrow definition of e-mail to focus this report on electronic mail, although it will be clear that most e-mail users will also have facilities at hand to browse the World Wide Web, participate in multiuser simulations and games, and so forth. It is not important to draw too fine a distinction between what is e-mail and what is not; the importance of having *some* definition becomes

---

[5]A MUD is variously defined as Multiple User Dimension, Multiple User Dungeon, or Multiple User Dialogue. It is a computer program allowing users to explore and help create an on-line environment. Each user takes control of a computerized persona/avatar/incarnation/character. The user can walk around, chat with other characters, explore dangerous monster-infested areas, solve puzzles, and even create his or her very own rooms, descriptions, and items. For further information see, for example, http://www.math.okstate.edu/~jds/mudfaq-p1.html.

clearer in Chapter Three's discussion of access devices and their locations and standards and protocols needed.

Universal Access

The other key concept in this report is "universal access." By this, we simply mean e-mail facilities and services that are

- available at modest individual effort and expense to (almost) everyone in the United States in a form that does not require highly specialized skills or,

- accessible in a manner analogous to the level, cost, and ease of use of telephone service or the U.S. Postal Service.

We do not, therefore, envision that every single person will have access, but that e-mail can achieve the same ubiquity that telephones (including the availability of payphones) and TVs have. Table 1.1 shows the penetration of related technologies into U.S. households, for comparison.

Note that the above percentages are not distributed uniformly across various sectors of our society. For example, a recent report (Mueller and Schement, 1995) describes telephone access in Camden, New Jersey, by family income, ethnicity, age, and other demographic

Table 1.1

Availability of Related Technologies
in U.S. Households

Technology	Percentage of Households
Television	95
Telephone	93
Video cassette recorder	85
More than one TV	66
Cable TV	64
Pay-per-view service	51
Video game system	40
Video camera	28
Fax	6

SOURCE: *Times Mirror* (1994).

factors. The report indicates that, overall, only 80.6 percent of households in Camden have telephones; notable disparities include families on food stamps, who lag 20.4 percentage points behind households not on food stamps. For many households, "universal access" means traveling to the nearest working payphone (where receiving incoming messages is sometimes precluded either socially or by the technology). Similarly, universal access to e-mail for many may require using public terminals in shared spaces such as libraries and schools (but where barriers to message reception can readily be eliminated).

ADVANTAGES OF UNIVERSAL E-MAIL

E-mail services can be used both for "telephone-type" messages and for other, usually longer, messages or documents that might otherwise be sent using facsimile or hard-copy postal services, both public and private. Compared with the telephone system, one primary advantage of an e-mail service is that it eliminates "telephone tag." It also provides a content record of the interactions that can be retrieved, printed, studied, selectively forwarded, and in general reused. Other advantages are that it permits (but certainly does not require) more deliberative and reflective, but still interactive, conversational dialogs, as well as one-to-many and many-to-many conversations. These features have led to many new social, commercial, and political groupings of people: the "virtual communities" mentioned above, using e-mail as the linkage.[6] It provides a common context among a set of participants.

Compared with postal services, an e-mail service offers much faster mail delivery—usually minutes between any two locations in the United States (although currently, delays up to a day occur with some Internet access providers), compared with one to several days for postal systems. E-mail systems also afford much more flexibility (both locational and temporal) in that delivery. In the current postal system, a person's mail is delivered to one or two (or at most a few) fixed addresses (e.g., home or office). In most e-mail systems, a person with the proper (portable) terminal equipment can log in to his

---

[6]As one of many examples documenting this, see Klein (1995).

or her "mailbox" from any location that has electronic access to the system. Today, this means that people can pick up their e-mail from their office, their home, their hotel rooms, another office (perhaps in another city) they are visiting, or any site with a phone jack.[7] In the future, as terminal equipment gets smaller and cellular telephones become more ubiquitous, one will be able to pick up or send e-mail while traveling in a car and flying in an airplane. This results in more geographic independence (where one gets mail) and temporal flexibility (when one gets mail).

These advantages are available in any e-mail system. The additional advantage of a universal e-mail system is that since everyone belongs to the system, a user can send e-mail to anyone, not just a limited group, and receive e-mail from anyone. This makes the special advantages of e-mail available for all of one's correspondence, not just a subset. If the costs of such a service permit attractive pricing, it could take over a significant portion of the business of current postal services[8]—especially when next-generation e-mail systems allow the transmission and viewing of multimedia messages containing high-resolution color pictures, "movie clips" of image sequences, and sound, which could, among other things, support a variety of "electronic commerce."

DISADVANTAGES OF UNIVERSAL E-MAIL

The concept of universal e-mail raises serious concerns as well. For example, individual users could get "flooded" with messages, unless some means of "filtering" incoming message traffic is provided. Also, some virtual communities enabled by e-mail could be bad for U.S. society, rather than good; they could conceivably lead to a less-

---

[7]E-mail can also be forwarded automatically to an alternative mailbox (e.g., closer to a vacation spot or sabbatic location).

[8]In this regard, it should be noted that the current U.S. postal services deliver two things: *information* (e.g., letters) and *bulk material* (e.g., packages). A universal e-mail system should, in principle, be able to take over much of the information delivery functions; it obviously cannot handle the bulk material delivery functions. However, some bulk material consists of catalogs and advertising that may, in fact, increasingly become accessible electronically.

cohesive society, rather than a more-cohesive one.[9] It is also clear that within any e-mail system, some users will be "more equal" than others; they will be able to purchase more powerful equipment, giving them more power over their electronic communication. Some will become more knowledgeable in the features and facilities of the system—permitting them, for example, to assemble tailored mailing lists for broadcast of their messages—allowing them to take advantage of those features for their own personal benefit or gain. Special-interest groups may in particular be motivated to become further empowered by use of these communication tools. Some (but not all) would also consider it a disadvantage that national borders become more transparent to international commerce and influences (Ronfeldt et al., 1993).

MOTIVATIONS FOR UNIVERSAL E-MAIL

The apparent advantages of universal e-mail, despite the possible side effects and disadvantages, lead to a number of possible motivations for establishing such a service in the United States, ranging across the spectrum from the utilitarian to the idealistic. At the utilitarian end is efficiency. Electronic mail uses modern information and telecommunications technology to provide a much faster and more efficient means of conveying information from one point to another than current postal systems, which rely on "technologies"— letters written on paper, put in sealed envelopes, and physically transported from sender to receiver—over two millennia old. The increased speed and efficiency of information delivery by e-mail could have many commercial and economic benefits, contributing to increased U.S. economic competitiveness.

At the idealistic end of the spectrum of motivations, the hypothesis is made that electronic mail makes possible much more egalitarian, deliberative, and reflective dialogs among individuals and groups. (See Sproull and Kiesler, 1991b, for supporting evidence.) It might therefore lead to new social and political linkages within U.S. society, reduce the feelings of alienation that many individuals in the United States feel and give them a new sense of "community," revitalize the

---

[9]Potentially even worse could be *hidden* virtual communities—on-line underground communities hiding under encryption or just not advertising themselves.

involvement of the common citizen in the political process, etc., and in general strengthen the cohesion of U.S. society.

Different motivations across this spectrum will appeal to different elements of U.S. society. To achieve widespread appeal—and political/economic support—a U.S. universal e-mail service should satisfy a broad spectrum of these motivations, whether the system is "designed" to meet these objectives (e.g., with heavy U.S. government involvement) or evolves through private initiative and entrepreneurship subject to constraints, incentives, or standards that encourage universal access.

ORGANIZATION OF THIS REPORT

The remainder of this report addresses the key questions raised above. Chapter Two describes our analyses of Current Population Survey (CPS) data collected by the U.S. Census Bureau, not only to obtain a picture of the current state of computer and information service usage in U.S. households but also to determine trends in this usage. It indicates groups and sectors of our society with low rates of electronic information system use, to which particular attention must be paid if "universal" access is to be achieved.

Chapter Three discusses technical considerations in achieving universal access, such as: What are the services that will encourage demand? What are the options for providing physical access, including both the nature of the device (e.g., PCs, TV set-top boxes, game machines, dedicated e-mail devices, display telephones) and the location (home, work, schools, kiosks, and other "common" areas)? What would the demands be for training and support? Are current user interfaces adequate for "everyone"? What about standards for addresses, directories, confidentiality, and privacy? What system architectures are most appropriate?

Chapter Four presents economic and regulatory issues raised by the concept of universal access, treating the provision of e-mail from the perspective of market supply, demand, pricing, and market structure.

Chapter Five explores social issues raised by universal access, using as a basis for this analysis descriptions of site visits to five "wired community" prototypes and experiments planned and underway throughout the country. These visits investigated what works today, what does not, and how these findings might be extrapolated to a nationwide system. They also provide additional insight into training and education requirements and the suite of services that attract users.

Universal access to electronic mail services is not just an idea with national implications. There are significant international implications as well. We have been particularly intrigued by correlations between interconnectivity within countries and their degree of democratization. Chapter Six addresses these topics and argues that the implications could affect the allocation of resources underlying some portions of U.S. foreign policy.

Chapter Seven summarizes our key findings and conclusions.

Appendix A contains further analyses of CPS data for 1984, 1989, and 1993, showing additional trends in computer and information system usage by U.S. households. Appendix B contains descriptions of the site visits made to five "wired-community" projects throughout the United States that form the basis of the discussion in Chapter Five.

Chapter Two

COMPUTERS AND CONNECTIVITY: CURRENT TRENDS

Tora K. Bikson, Constantijn W. A. Panis

INTRODUCTION

The number of individuals who engage in computer-based communications in the United States has increased dramatically in recent years and is expected to continue growing well into the next century. Although its reach at present is far from universal, information technology is already "woven into the fabric of the economic and social life of developed countries," as King and Kraemer (1995) put it.

Converging Trends

The trend toward growing use of computer-based communications stems from two mutually reinforcing influences. First is the often-cited history of improvements in price-to-performance ratios. That is, prices for equal amounts of processing power drop by about half every two years (Tessler, 1991). Having started at least two decades ago, such changes are viewed as the enabling force behind the widespread diffusion of computers to households and offices. Communication technologies are likewise beginning to show price/performance improvements while at the same time shedding their terrestrial and bandwidth constraints (Tessler, 1991; Benjamin and Blount, 1992; King and Kraemer, 1995).

A second and related stream of influence has to do with the convergence of computing and communication technology within an integrated information medium (Eveland and Bikson, 1987). This integration, for instance, permits individuals to communicate information as readily as they create it, to one or many others, sometimes scarcely noticing that generating, editing, storing, and sending are distinct activities (Bikson and Frinking, 1993); conversely, this convergence preserves the "computability" or reusability of what is received via the medium (Steinfield, Kraut, and Streeter, 1993). Steinfield, Kraut, and Streeter contend that this property more than anything else accounts for the benefits of e-mail over other contemporary communication media (e.g., voicemail).

In the past, the advantages of such convergence were generally confined to islands of disconnected interoperability (e.g., within particular organizations). However, the movement toward open systems (discussed further in Chapters Three and Four) has broadened the capability for interconnection, linking larger numbers of geographically dispersed organizations and individuals with heterogeneous hardware and software to one another through a common electronic infrastructure (Bikson, 1994). The result of these lines of influence is perhaps best illustrated by the phenomenal growth of the Internet in the 1990s (see Figure 2.1).

Why Study Technology Trends?

As indicated in the introduction to the report, this chapter provides a detailed look at trends in information and communication technology access for the U.S. population based on CPS data. Specifically, we aimed to learn how evenly computer-based communications capabilities are distributed over the country's varied demographic constituencies and whether those groups exhibit similar trends in access to network services.

Before addressing these questions, however, it is appropriate first to indicate why they are important. That is, are there any reasons to view economic and social stratification of computer and network use differently from the socioeconomic stratification that characterizes the consumption of other goods and services (compare Attewell, 1994). We believe there are at least four important reasons.

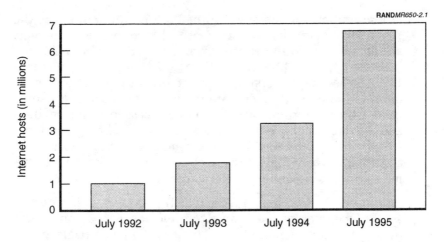

NOTE: Figures for July 1995 are estimates. Each Internet host represents from one to hundreds of users; the total number of individuals it connects is not known.

SOURCE: The Internet Society, file ftp://ftp.isoc.org/isoc/charts/90s-host.txt.

Figure 2.1—Internet Host Growth, Worldwide

•   *Information.* Several well-designed studies have shown that in-
    dividuals who use computer-based communications have more
    accurate information about matters of political, professional,
    and organizational concern than peers who do not. For example,
    a nationwide *Times Mirror* survey of technology in American
    households (1994) indicated that 63 percent of adults who use
    computers and networks scored high on a current events quiz
    administered within the survey, compared to 50 percent of de-
    mographically equivalent computer users without network ac-
    cess and 28 percent of their counterparts who do not use com-
    puters. In another study, Kraut and his colleagues (Kraut, 1993)
    found that otherwise similar employees of a large international
    financial firm differed significantly in knowledge about the
    organization depending on whether they communicated via
    computers; network users knew more (see also Hesse et al.,
    1990).

Different levels of access to computer-based communication
technology, then, may further stratify individuals and create in-

formation have-nots alongside the "information elite," as the *Times Mirror* survey describes those with computers, modems, and access to network services from home. However, the Aspen Institute's Information Bill of Rights (Firestone and Schement, 1995) argues that the emerging information society should have information openly flowing among all individuals and institutions, which in turn requires equitable access to an information and communication infrastructure (see also Denning and Linn, 1994). The policy significance of such potential information stratification can only increase as more public and social information is disseminated electronically.

- *Affiliation.* As Sproull and Faraj (1993) point out, policy discussions of the Internet and other electronic networks assume these media to be chiefly informational in nature. As a correlate, policy discussions cast users as searchers who want effective ways to browse and find the information they desire. Experience suggests a contrasting view of users as social beings who are looking for "affiliation, support, and affirmation" (Sproull and Faraj, 1993). Electronic gatherings, and not just digital documents, are what they seek.

That networks are not just information technologies but also serve as social technologies (or technologies for affiliation) is supported by the well-established tendency of users to turn what were initially designed as media for accessing and using remote data (e.g., ARPAnet and Minitel) into interpersonal messaging media (see Shapiro and Anderson, 1985, Sproull and Kiesler, 1991b; Lytel, 1992). These observations are corroborated by social science research results indicating that network use creates and sustains both strong and weak social ties (Bikson and Eveland, 1990; Feldman, 1987) and that those who use an organization's network feel more positive about their association with the organization than those who do not (Kraut, 1993; Huff, Sproull, and Kiesler, 1989).

This is not to say the two roles for electronic networks are in conflict; on the contrary, people often use other people as providers of information, pointers to information and filters of information (Eveland et al., 1995; Bikson et al., 1995; Sproull and Kiesler, 1991b; Kraut, Dumais, and Koch, 1989; Bikson, Quint, and Johnson, 1984). Rather, it is to underscore that constraints on network access are at the same time constraints on affiliation. To the extent that civic and social alliances increasingly rely on computer-based interactions, constraints on association represented by less-than-universal access pose policy problems—and especially so if the constraints are unfairly distributed over socioeconomic groups.

- *Participation.* Study after study has found that electronic networks are significant predictors of the breakdown of status-based social structures. Networks also are related to increased participation in discussion, decisionmaking, and task processes by those who typically are politically or economically disadvantaged. While explanations for what Kiesler has called the "equalization" effect vary, the results are fairly consensual (see Dubrovsky, Kiesler and Sethna, 1991; Sproull and Kiesler, 1991a, 1991b; Rheingold, 1991; Bikson, 1994; Bikson and Eveland, 1990). That is, for on-line groups, ascribed and achieved status characteristics such as age, race, gender, formal position or title, and socioeconomic level are far less likely to determine interaction patterns, leadership roles, decisionmaking influence, and other outcomes in comparison to groups that meet in person. This finding holds true of professional societies, work groups, and social or political organizations.

  As civic and political groups increasingly rely on electronic networks (see Chapter Five), these media could help them overcome status-linked barriers to full participation in social dialog and public life. However, if access opportunities follow traditional socioeconomic lines, these barriers instead will be strengthened by the emerging information infrastructure (see also the Aspen Institute's Information Bill of Rights, Firestone and Schement 1995, section A-II on nondiscrimination in "the information society").

- *Economic advantage.* There is accumulating evidence that access to computers and communications technology confers economic benefits. At the individual level, for instance, a detailed examination of CPS data from 1984–1989 suggests that workers who use computers on their job earn 10 to 15 percent higher wages than otherwise similar workers who do not (Krueger, 1993). This conclusion rests on a variety of models estimated in the study to correct for unobserved variables that might be correlated with job-related computer use and earnings (e.g., recreational computer use, prior educational achievement, and economic health of the enterprise). Further, an assessment of payoff differentials for specific computer-based activities at work shows the most highly rewarded task that computers are used for is electronic mail (Krueger, 1993).

However, most studies of economic benefits associated with use of networked information and communication technologies have been carried out at the level of the enterprise or firm rather than at the individual or household level (see Computer Science and Telecommunications Board, NRC, 1994). At the firm level, the competitive advantages provided by interorganizational networks are widely recognized (e.g., Quinn, 1992; Rockart and Short, 1991; Malone, Yates, and Benjamin, 1987). More important, for purposes of this project, are findings from a well-designed comparative study of data from hundreds of small, medium, and large businesses in the United States and France carried out by Streeter et al. (in press). The study shows that national interorganizational networks (in contrast to proprietary networks) foster the formation of electronic marketplace relationships among businesses. Further, they diminish large organizations' inherent advantages (size, slack resources) in exploiting new technologies, making it comparatively easier for small- and medium-sized businesses to enter the marketplace and benefit from it. While we do not examine organization-level data in this chapter, these findings mirror some of the equalization effects observed at the individual level. They also call attention to the likelihood that policies affecting universal access to computer-based communications technologies are likely to have a disproportionate influence on the economic well-being of small- and medium-sized enterprises. (Economic effects at the societal level are discussed in Chapter Four in relation to critical mass and network externalities.)

There are significant reasons, then, for policymakers to become involved in the debate over universal access to electronic networks. Networks can influence the public's exposure to information. They can create opportunities for individuals and groups to affiliate and to participate in civic affairs. And they can create or shape economic opportunities and advantages. As suggested by King and Kraemer

(1995), those who lack access to new communication technologies may be at risk of exclusion from the fabric of the nation's social and economic life.

COMPUTER AND COMMUNICATION TECHNOLOGY IN USE

Against this background of converging technology trends and their societal implications, we turn now to a more detailed investigation of access to computers and communication networks in the U.S. population. We rely chiefly on the October 1989 and October 1993 (CPS) data.[1]

The CPS is a large-scale random sample survey of households, conducted monthly by the Bureau of the Census. It is the source for much of the official data published by the Bureau of Labor Statistics. The Bureau of the Census periodically adds supplements to the CPS base questionnaires to gain more insight into topics of interest. In this study, we initially examined the October 1984, October 1989, October 1993, and November 1994 supplements because they include questions on computer use by each individual in the household. The 1984 data are not always comparable to data collected in later years, and the 1994 data were released too recently for careful examination within the context of this project. Consequently we focus here mainly on the 1989 and 1993 data.

Approach to the CPS Data

CPS data are suitable for analysis at the household level or individual level. This report treats the individual as the unit of analysis. Although some outcomes of interest (e.g., presence of a computer at home) are readily interpretable at either level, others (especially behavioral variables such as use of networked services) are not. Exploratory work suggests that for purposes of this study, where both levels of analysis are appropriate, differences between findings at the

---

[1] *Current Population Survey, October 1989 and 1993: School Enrollment* [machine-readable data file], conducted by the Bureau of the Census for the Bureau of Labor Statistics, Bureau of the Census [producer and distributor], Washington, D.C., 1990 and 1994.

individual and household levels are negligible (see, for instance, Figure 2.2).

At the individual level, then, the analyses reported below are based on 289,979 observations (146,850 in 1989 and 143,129 in 1993). The sample consists of noninstitutionalized civilians in the United States living in households. Both adults and children are in the sample, unless explicitly noted otherwise.[2]

Outcome Variables. To represent access to information and communication technology, we employed two binary outcome variables. One, access to a computer at home, is a single-item measure; it receives a positive value if there is at least one computer in an individual's household. At this level of analysis, penetration of computers refers to the percentage of individuals with household access (rather than the percentage of households that have computers).

The other outcome variable, use of network services, represents use of a computer either at home or at work to connect to an electronic

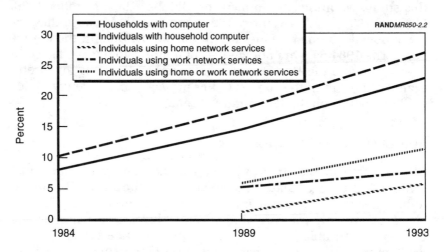

Figure 2.2—Household Computer Access and Network Use

---

[2]The analyses are done using individual weights that approximately equal the inverse of the probability of being in the sample, adjusted for interview response rates and normalized to add up to the sample size.

network. A derived measure, this variable receives a positive value if an individual uses a computer in any one of the following ways:

- at home or at work for electronic mail,

- at home to connect to bulletin boards,

- at home to connect to a computer at work, or

- at work for "communications" (this is distinct from word processing, desktop publishing, newsletter creation, and so on).

An alternative approach would be to define this outcome in terms of having or using a modem (compare *Times Mirror*, 1994). However, preliminary reviews of CPS data and other studies suggest that individuals do not always know whether they have or are using a modem.[3] Further, we decided to include connectivity in the workplace as well as from home in the definition because it provides a more complete picture of the degree to which individuals use electronic avenues to communicate with others. At present, more people use network services from work than from home, often for both work-related and personal or social purposes; and networks are sometimes used by individuals doing part of their work from home (Figure 2.2). Thus, the distinction between work and home use of network services could not be made reliably in the CPS data.

Unfortunately, no questions were asked of students about how they use computers and networks at school. This implies that our network outcome variable underestimates the actual use of network services among students. For most determinants of interest, this underestimate is inconsequential. However, results on variables that are highly correlated with student status (such as age and, possibly, household income) need to be interpreted with this caveat in mind. As background, Figure 2.2 shows home computers as a percentage of both households and individuals in the CPS data; it also shows network use at home and work.

---

[3]Sometimes when computers have built-in modems, the respondents may not be aware of using a modem to access network services. In other cases, respondents are using computers linked to local area networks or hardwired to organization-wide networks that provide access to broader network services (e.g., Internet) without necessitating their use of a modem.

Predictor Variables. Six predictor variables constitute the core of our study: income, education, race/ethnicity, age, sex, and location of residence. Income, a categorical variable defined by quartiles, refers to the total income of the individual's household. Location, another variable defined at the household level, reflects whether the individual lives in an urban or rural area. Remaining predictor variables refer only to the individual. (Each explanatory variable is further defined in the discussion of results below.)

In investigating the CPS data, our goal was to learn whether and how socioeconomic characteristics are correlated with distribution patterns and diffusion trends in access to computers and electronic networks.

Analysis Plan. Figure 2.2 presents aggregated CPS data representing the two outcome variables of interest for the United States population in 1993 and 1989 (and, for access to a computer at home, 1984). The analysis was designed to answer two questions about these outcomes at the individual level.

- In 1993, in comparison to their proportion of the population, are any socioeconomically defined groups significantly underrepresented among those with computers at home and those who use network services anywhere?

- How have recent trends contributed to the distribution of outcomes? That is, have differences between socioeconomically defined groups in access to computers and communications technology narrowed, remained constant, or widened between 1989 and 1993?

Answers to these questions are tested statistically in several ways. First, we examined differences in access to a computer at home and use of network services across socioeconomic groups in the two years separately. These differences follow from cross-tabulations and are shown in bar graphs for each socioeconomic dimension of interest. Because of very large sample sizes, in every cross-tabulation presented, and in both years, the differences between groups are generally statistically significant.[4] (When they are not, we make note of it.)

For purposes of policy analysis and intervention, however, these "gross" differences may be misleading. Socioeconomic status variables are likely to be intercorrelated, meaning that an effort to investigate any one of them should control for the potential influence of all other covariates of interest.[5] Therefore, we held the other socioeconomic variables constant and recalculated computer and network penetration levels to obtain such "net" percentages.[6] Net figures can be interpreted as representing differences between individuals with otherwise equal characteristics (where those equal characteristics are a weighted average of all characteristics found in the data). The same general pattern of findings emerges from the net data but between-group differences are generally reduced.

Appendix A explains the procedure to compute net disparities in detail and provides a table with both gross and net percentage data for

---

[4]Statistical significance is determined here on the basis of the Pearson Chi-square test. Note that all weights are normalized to add up to the sample size.

[5]For example, suppose that equal use of network services across socioeconomic groups is a political goal. As we shall see below, black individuals tend to use network services to a lesser extent than whites. This may prompt policymakers to direct efforts to increase use of network services to black communities. However, as we shall also see below, low-income individuals too tend to make less use of network services than high-income individuals. As is well known, the average household income among blacks is lower than among whites. It may well be the case, then, that part or all of the racial difference is due to income differentials. To achieve equal use of network services across socioeconomic groups, public funds may then be more effective when directed toward poor communities generally, rather than to black communities specifically.

[6]The procedure is explained in detail in Appendix A. For example, consider the effect of household income. We distinguish four income categories, corresponding to four income quartiles. First, we estimate a multivariate regression model for, say, presence of a computer in the household. Then, for all individuals in the sample, we predict the probability he or she has a computer in the household, under the counterfactual assumption that everyone falls into the bottom income quartile. The average, over all individuals in the sample, is the predicted fraction of low-income individuals with a computer, *controlling for all other covariates*. Then we assume that all individuals fall into the second income quartile, again compute predicted probabilities of owning a computer, and average over all individuals in the sample. This is repeated for the third and fourth quartiles, yielding a total of four average probabilities ("net" fractions).

purposes of comparison. It also contains tables of the (probit) regression analyses from which the net percentages were derived. The discussion below emphasizes gross results, but we will point out where and to what extent gross results overstate disparities across socioeconomic groups.

Results of Data Analysis

In what follows, findings from the data analysis are presented first for each of the six predictor variables. We conclude with a discussion of their combined influence on access to computers and communications technology.

Differences by Household Income. Figure 2.3 presents the percentage of individuals who report that there is a computer in the household and that they have access to network services, as a function of household income category. We distinguish among four quartiles; for example, the bottom quartile includes the 25 percent of the population with the lowest household income. In 1993, the quartile cutoff income levels were $15,000, $30,000, and $50,000 per year.

As is immediately clear in Figure 2.3 (left half), there are very large differences in household computer access across income categories.

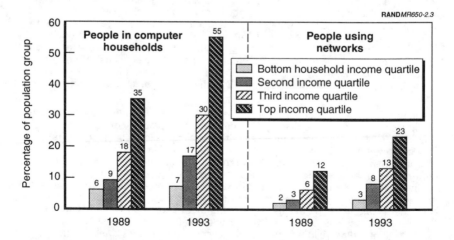

Figure 2.3—Household Computer Access and Network Use, by Income

In 1993, just over 7 percent of the lowest income households had computers, whereas nearly 55 percent of the highest-earning quartile had computers at home. Four years earlier, the respective figures were nearly 6 percent and 35 percent. These data, therefore, reflect highly significant differences in household computer access based on income quartile.

Further, while the income-based gap in household computer access was very large in 1989, it was even wider by 1993. In 1989, individuals in the top quartile were over six times more likely to have access to a computer in the household than individuals in the bottom quartile of the income distribution. By 1993, this gap had widened to well over seven times more likely.

The net disparities, controlling for the other key socioeconomic characteristics, are not quite as large, but they remain substantial. For example, in 1993, on net, individuals in the top income quartile were four and a half times more likely to have access to a computer in the household than those in the bottom quartile (Appendix A, Table A.3). This net income gap is smaller than the gross figure, mainly because low-income individuals tend to have lower-than-average educational attainment. About a third of the income disparity is thus attributable to a concomitant effect from educational differences. The net income gap in 1993 represents a significant widening relative to 1989.

Although use of network services either at home or at work is far less than availability of household computers (see Figure 2.3), generally similar patterns appear for network use as a function of household income level.[7] Again we find large differences between quartiles that are becoming even larger over time. In 1989, close to 2 percent of the lowest income individuals used network services at home or work, whereas over 11 percent of the highest income individuals used them. By 1993, these fractions had increased to nearly 3 percent and 23 percent, respectively. As before, the gross disparities are in part attributable to correlation of household income with other demo-

---

[7]Recall that our measure of network use includes use at home or work, but not at school, since no appropriate questions were asked from students. This implies that we are likely to overstate differences in network use across income categories, because students who live away from their parents tend to have low household incomes.

graphic predictors, notably educational attainment. The net gaps remain very substantial, though, and have widened significantly between 1989 and 1993 (Appendix A).

We conclude, then, that there are large differences in both household computer access and use of network services across income categories. These differences are due partly to other socioeconomic characteristics, but they remain highly significant even after controlling for those other characteristics. The gap between high-income and low-income individuals is not only large, it also widened between 1989 and 1993; higher-income individuals appear to be adopting the new technologies at a faster pace. Interestingly, the net differences are smaller for network usage than for household computer access. This may be due to broader access to network services in the workplace, where no investments in hardware on the part of the individual user are required.[8]

These results are congruent with the *Times Mirror* survey's conclusion (1994) that the spread of technology through American society is quite uneven. While that survey examined data from only one year (1994), it investigated a broad range of technology to find that these disparities are "greatest with respect to computers and on-line capability." Rapidly improving price-to-performance ratios in recent years thus seem not to have narrowed (or even held constant) income-based gaps between information technology haves and have-nots.

Differences by Educational Attainment. Figure 2.4 (left side) shows household computer access fractions for individuals without a high-school diploma, for high school graduates, and for college graduates. (Children under 15 years of age are not included in this part of the analysis.) Persons with some college education, but without bachelor's degrees, are included among high school graduates. As may be expected, there are large differences in household computer access by educational attainment. Among persons without a high school diploma, only about 8 percent had a home computer in 1989.

---

[8]As may be inferred from Figure 2.2, there is no large overlap between use of network services in the home and at work. Use of network services at work by low-income individuals may partially explain why the net disparity in network service use is smaller than in access to a computer in the household.

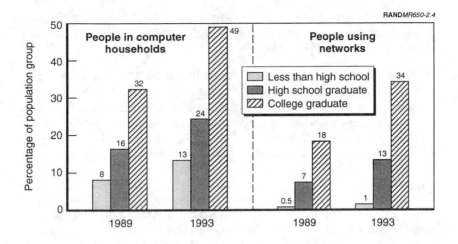

Figure 2.4—Household Computer Access and Network Use, by Education

College graduates, by contrast, had a penetration rate of about 32 percent. All groups experienced an increase in home computers between 1989 and 1993, leading to penetration rates of about 13 percent and 49 percent in 1993 for those without a high school diploma and college graduates, respectively. Controlling for other socioeconomic characteristics, the differences are substantially smaller but still highly significant statistically (see Appendix A) in both years. In the interim, moreover, such education-based differences in household computer access have increased significantly. The disparities parallel, but are less sharp than, the income-based differences in household computer access reported above.

Figure 2.4 (right side) also presents differences in network usage by education category. We find that use of network services is dominated strongly by well-educated individuals. In 1989, a mere half percent of individuals without high school diplomas used network services, compared with over 18 percent of college graduates. Both groups strongly increased their use in 1993, to over 1 percent and about 34 percent, respectively. As expected, the net differences are smaller but still substantial and statistically significant (see Appendix A). The net differences in network use by educational attainment have also widened significantly between 1989 and 1993. Interestingly, the divergence is entirely due to an acceleration of the adoption of network services among college graduates; the gap between high school drop-outs and high school graduates did not change significantly.

In summary, we find large differences in access to information and communications technology by educational attainment that are increasing over time. Given the established correlation between use of network services and knowledge of current political, professional, and organizational affairs cited above (see the introductory section of this chapter), these results suggest that disparities in access to electronic networks may well amplify differential knowledge produced by education differences alone.

The *Times Mirror* survey of technology in American households (1994) yields similar conclusions using 1994 data. It also draws attention to the effect of these patterns of technology access on children's educational opportunities. Among college graduates with children in that sample, almost half reported that the child used a personal computer; but among those with a high school education or less, only 17 percent reported that children used a home computer (*Times Mirror*, 1994). However, while large income- and education-based differences exist in children's access to computer technology, the survey found "virtually no socioeconomic differences in how often and for what purposes children used computers if present in the home." These findings suggest that effects of parental educational stratification could be at least partially offset if it did not result in differential access to information and communications technology for children.

Finally, it should be noted that if more and more jobs at relatively low levels increasingly make discretionary use of network technologies (such as e-mail) available, differences among adults in access to on-line information based on income and education could decrease in the future.[9] At present, such differences are problematic because they exacerbate differences in earnings as well as differences in general level of knowledge (see the introductory section, above).

---

[9]To date, e-mail use in general, and discretionary use in particular, has typically been limited to high-level positions in organizations (e.g., Krueger, 1993). The extent to which organizations in the United States permit or support access to external networks via internal e-mail systems is not presently known.

Differences by Race and Ethnicity. Black community leaders have recently expressed concern that African Americans are lagging behind in the use of computers (*New York Times,* 25 May 1995). At least part of the race-based difference is due to lower average household income and lower average educational attainment among blacks as compared with whites. However, our analysis shows that those characteristics do not account for the entire difference in outcome variables. Rather, racial and ethnic characteristics exert an independent influence on home computer access and network use.

For purposes of this analysis, we combine race and ethnicity into mutually exclusive categories. We distinguish between Hispanics, non-Hispanic whites, non-Hispanic blacks, Native Americans (both Indians and Eskimos), and Americans of Asian descent (including Pacific Islanders). In subsequent comments we refer to non-Hispanic whites as "whites" and to non-Hispanic blacks as "blacks." A small fraction of respondents (0.11 percent) are identified as "other" in the CPS data; we do not reflect the "other" category in Figure 2.5 (or in the table in Appendix A). Figure 2.5 portrays the percentage of individuals with a computer in the household and access to network services at home or at work by racial/ethnic categories.

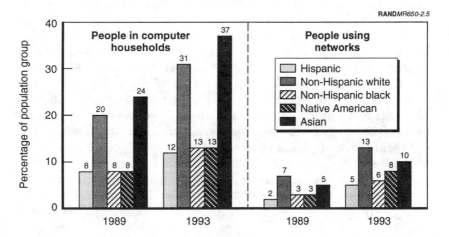

Figure 2.5—Household Computer Access and Network Use, by
Race/Ethnicity

As Figure 2.5 makes clear, the highest penetration rates for household computers are found among whites and Asians. In 1993, over 30 percent of whites and over 37 percent of Asians lived in a household with a computer. Hispanics, blacks, and Native Americans, by contrast, all reported a penetration rate of around 13 percent. As we mentioned above, part of these differences may be due to average differences in other characteristics, notably, household income and educational attainment. Controlling for these characteristics, however, we still find substantial differences. That is, net of other influences, race or ethnicity has a statistically independent and sizable effect on household computer access. In particular, Hispanics, blacks, and Native Americans are currently underrepresented among computerized households. Similar patterns of significant racial/ethnic difference in household computer access are also evident in the 1989 data. However, unlike income- and education-based differences, racial/ethnic gaps in home computer access have not widened over time; instead, they have remained constant.

Differential use of network services as a function of race/ethnicity is also apparent in Figure 2.5. Again, there are significant between-group differences, even when the influence of other socioeconomic characteristics is controlled. Net differences, however, are slightly smaller than for household computer access. Somewhat surprisingly, Asians have the lowest net rate of network use, even though they have the highest net rates of household computer access among the racial/ethnic groups we distinguished. Another striking finding concerns the relatively high use of network services among Native Americans. Controlling for other sources of effect, their net usage rate was not significantly different from the net rate among whites in 1993, despite a much lower penetration rate of computers in their households.[10] Given the results of research on relationships of peripherality to network use (see, for example, Hesse et al., 1990; Huff, Sproull, and Kiesler, 1989), it is worth exploring whether Native American usage rates are at least in part explained by their geographic remoteness. No statistical differences in these patterns emerged from our analyses; that is, the racial/ethnic gap in use of

---

[10]Native Americans are oversampled in the CPS. In 1989, 1,408 Native Americans were interviewed; in 1993, there were 1,703.

network services has remained constant between 1989 and the present.

In summary, we find rather large and persistent differences across race/ethnicity in both household computer access and network services usage. These findings are partially consistent with racial/ethnic differences reported in the *Times Mirror* survey (1994), although that study did not include Asians and Native Americans as separate subsamples. There is no generally accepted explanation for these kinds of differences. For Hispanics, it has been suggested that language barriers may be partly responsible for the differences. For Native Americans, our literature review surfaced what seemed to us a comparatively large number of articles describing on-line educational, library and other information-oriented services targeted to this constituency. For instance, in a recent *BoardWatch* poll of favorite bulletin boards (1994), a Native American entry emerged in the top 20.

In advance, from our literature review, we did not expect to find any race/ethnicity differences other than those that could be explained by differences in income and education and, perhaps, residential location and age. That racial and ethnic differences remain even when the influence of other predictor variables is controlled is a matter that merits further research.

Differences by Age. We now turn to differences by age.[11] For purposes of this analysis we constructed four categories, distinguishing between individuals under 20 years of age, between 20 and 39, between 40 and 59, and 60 years of age and older. Boundaries based on age are admittedly arbitrary, and different studies employ different cutoffs, different numbers of categories or both (see, for instance, *Times Mirror*, 1994; *BoardWatch*, 1994). Particular boundary choices do not, however, appear to affect analytic results in ways that would

---

[11]The treatment of age is determined by the objective of the study. Obviously, the decision to purchase a computer is in part determined by the size and the age composition of the household, but we wish to document socioeconomic differences in *access* to a computer, not in personal ownership or usage. The connection between presence of a computer in the household and access to it requires only the assumption that the computer is available to all household members—a relatively plausible assumption.

affect most policy decisions.[12] Figure 2.6 displays household computer access and network access as a function of the age categories defined here.

As Figure 2.6 suggests, household computer access is distributed fairly evenly across broadly defined age categories up to age 60, where rates of penetration decline steeply. In 1993, around 30 percent of individuals under age 60 had access to a home computer, whereas only about 10 percent of individuals above age 60 lived in a household with a computer. Even when other socioeconomic variables are controlled, this difference is highly significant. The age gap appears to be headed for reduction, though; compared with the situation in 1989, older adults have higher relative penetration rates for household computers. However, this change is not large enough to reach statistical significance in the net figures; as indicated in Appendix A, Table A.1, gaps between those over 60 and others have remained stable.

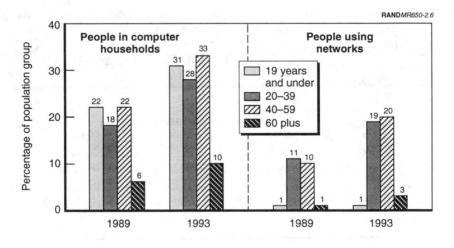

Figure 2.6—Household Computer Access and Network Use, by Age

---

[12]In preliminary analyses, we distinguished as many as eight different age categories. We decided to collapse them into the four categories presented here, because the patterns that emerged were robust to this more parsimonious classification.

Figure 2.6 also reveals the existence of large differences in the use of network services across the age categories defined, with disparities accumulating at both ends of the distribution. In 1993, only 1 percent of children and students under age 20 reported using network services, compared with over 18 percent among 20–39 year olds, over 20 percent among 40–59 year olds, and over 3 percent for people aged 60 and older.[13] In addition, use of network services among very young children (e.g., those too young to read or spell) is likely to be near zero, which further lowers the average estimates for the group under 20 years of age. On the other hand, a special issue of *Communications of the ACM* (CACM) on education reported very little use of networks at school, even in schools where students had access to computers (Soloway, 1993). On balance, then, those in the youngest age category are disproportionately likely to lack network access.

Older adults likewise make significantly less use of network services than younger adults do; the 3 percent access rate reported here coincides almost exactly with that obtained in the 1994 *Times Mirror* survey, in spite of differences in how both outcome and predictor variables were defined. But they may be catching up in the future— the data in Figure 2.6 show that in 1993 older adults were about three and a half times more likely to use network services than in 1989 (net figures in Appendix A show similar change). This growth rate is faster by far than that exhibited in the two other adult age groups during the same period, suggesting that age level per se does not determine either adoption or use of these new technologies. Their rapid diffusion among older adults now may be explained in part by the larger proportion of household income available for discretionary spending among older adults (Bikson et al., 1991). Nonetheless this growth rate has not yet produced a statistically significant reversal of trends; that is, while age gaps have not widened, they also have not yet narrowed significantly between older adults and their younger adult counterparts.

Differences by Sex. There is minor variation by sex in access to home computers and use of network services, as Figure 2.7

---

[13]It should be noted, however, that this measure of network use probably underrepresents students' access to on-line services because no CPS questions addressed network use at school (see above).

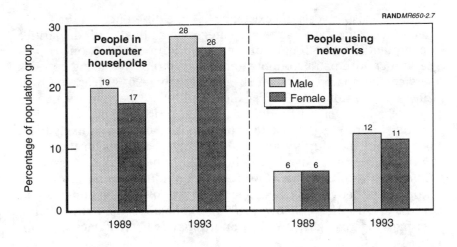

Figure 2.7—Household Computer Access and Network Use, by Sex

illustrates. While the gross percentages shown in Figure 2.7 suggest a two-point difference in 1993, that difference disappears entirely when the influence of other socioeconomic variables is controlled (see the net percentages in Appendix A). This was not the case in 1989; controlling for other variables, men were more likely to have access to a computer in the home in 1989. The difference was small (less than a percentage point), but statistically significant (see Appendix A). Between 1989 and 1993, though, the gender gap has closed. It should be noted that this outcome variable—having a computer at home—does not take into account which household member instigated the purchase of the computer. CPS usage data for 1993 (tabled in Appendix A) show that men in fact make more frequent use of home computers than women; on the other hand, women are significantly more likely than men to use a computer at work (*Times Mirror*, 1994).

Use of network services also exhibits very little variation as a function of sex. We found differences between men and women on this outcome variable to be statistically negligible in both 1989 and 1993 when the influence of other socioeconomic variables is controlled. Paralleling the data for computer use, the *Times Mirror* survey (1994) reported that men engage in on-line activities from home more often than women; but women are more likely to go on-line at work. The reduction of the gender gap among adults, as evidenced in CPS data, seems also to be reflected in the behavior of children in households with computers. *Times Mirror* survey data (1994) show that among all households with a computer and at least one child, one or more children are using the computer in 75 percent of them; and there is little difference between boys and girls in either likelihood or frequency of use.

Further, those survey data indicated that girls may be heavier computer users than boys, at least for applications that assist them with their school work (e.g., word processing). Boys and girls were about equally likely to use a home computer for educational games and art, but boys significantly outpaced girls in frequency of use of the home computer for playing noneducational games. On the whole, our analysis of sex differences in access to information and communications technology provides evidence that the gender gap among adults has decreased; and we concur with the *Times Mirror* conclusion that it could disappear entirely in the next generation.[14]

Differences by Location of Residence. Household computer access and access to network services as a function of residential location, the last predictor variable we explored in detail, are given in Figure 2.8. Location is categorized here as rural or urban, where "urban" characterizes residences within standard metropolitan areas.[15]

Ostensibly, the household computer penetration rate in urban areas is much higher than in rural areas. In 1993, just over 29 percent of individuals living in an urban area had a computer at home, compared with just over 19 percent among rural residents. About half of the difference is due to correlation with other characteristics such as household income or education. The net gap is nonetheless statistically significant and narrowed somewhat between 1989 and 1993 (see Appendix A). There are substantial differences in the use of network services as well. In urban areas, over 12 percent of residents made use of network services in 1993, whereas for rural residents the figure is less than 8 percent. Again, roughly half of the difference is

---

[14]This is not to suggest that sex differences in usage styles and preferences are disappearing. *BoardWatch*, for instance, reports that its own subscriber poll indicates bulletin board usership is still overwhelmingly male (1994).

[15]As defined by the Office of Management and Budget's June 30, 1984, definitions.

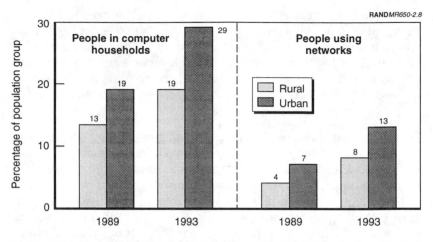

Figure 2.8—Household Computer Access and Network Use, by Location of Residence

due to characteristics such as income and education. The gap has remained approximately constant between 1989 and 1993.

Interestingly, the use of network services is approximately proportional to the penetration of computers in the household; that is, rural residents show no greater deficit in network use than in home computer access when compared with urban dwellers. This finding conflicts with the expectation that "access ramps to the information superhighway" (*Times Mirror* survey, 1994) are likely to take longer to diffuse to rural homes. In contrast to urban modem users, who are often able to dial into the Internet or other networks with a local call (at low or even zero marginal cost), rural telephone connections may well involve nontrivial toll costs. Installation of a second line for computer access may also likely be more costly in rural than in urban areas. Nonetheless, we find no greater urban-rural differences in use of network services than we do in household computer access. Motivation to use network services in spite of such obstacles may be partially explained by geographic remoteness (see Hesse et al., 1990).

Besides urban-rural differences, CPS data also show strong regional differences in distribution of information and communications technology (see Appendix A). For instance, in 1993 about a third of the people in New England and in the Pacific and mountain states had a computer at home, and about 13 percent of people in these areas were using network services; in the east south-central states, by contrast, the corresponding figures are 16 percent and 7 percent. A review of specific cities and towns indicates further disparities that reflect other than regional differences (see also Appendix A). For example, in Michigan in 1993, about two-thirds of people in Ann Arbor had a computer at home and 27 percent of Ann Arbor residents were using electronic networks. In neighboring Flint, 16 percent of the residents had home computers and 5 percent of residents used networks. These differences are likely to be at least partially accounted for by the influence of other socioeconomic variables (income and education, especially). Other factors (e.g., proximity to a major research university) need also to be taken into account in explaining location-related gaps in computers and communication technology.

CONCLUSIONS

Research reviewed in the introduction to this chapter provides evidence that access to computers and communications technology influences opportunities to participate effectively in a range of economic, social, and civic activities. If so, it is important to find out whether parts of the U.S. population are cut off from the emerging information society on the basis of their socioeconomic status. To address this question, the analyses described above sought to learn whether significant differences in access to these electronic media existed in 1989 and 1993 and, if so, what had happened to the size of the gaps over time. Table 2.1 serves as a score card summarizing the results.

Although this score card does not do justice to specific variations along the socioeconomic dimensions studied, it brings to the foreground the main conclusions: There are information society haves and have-nots; membership in these two classes is significantly predicted by income, education, and—to a lesser extent—race/ethnicity, location, and age. Except for gender gaps, these disparities have persisted over a period when the technologies of interest have decreased dramatically in price and increased markedly in user-friendliness.

Table 2.1

Summary of Socioeconomic Findings

	Computers at Home			Use of Network Services		
	Major Gaps in		What Happened to Gap	Major Gaps in		What Happened to Gap
	1993	1989	over Time?	1993	1989	over Time?
Income	Yes	Yes	Widened	Yes	Yes	Widened
Education	Yes	Yes	Widened	Yes	Yes	Widened
Race/ethnicity	Yes	Yes	Constant	Yes	Yes	Constant
Age	Yes	Yes	Constant[a]	Yes	Yes	Constant[a]
Sex	No	Yes	Narrowed	No	No	—
Location	Yes	Yes	Narrowed	Yes	Yes	Constant

[a]Although the results are not statistically significant, the data suggest that those age 60 and older may be beginning to narrow the age gap.

More worrisome still, gaps based on income and education have not merely persisted but in fact have increased significantly. There is nothing in the data, then, to suggest that, without policy intervention, these gaps will close.

These conclusions, drawn from a national sample of the U.S. population, are disturbing because sizable demographic subgroups who remain in the have-not segment may be deprived of the benefits associated with membership in the information society. It is also appropriate, therefore, to inquire whether the quantitative data we have examined provide any evidence that the expected benefits are in fact realized. Most findings about benefits, such as those reviewed in the introduction to this chapter, come either from relatively small experimental research samples or from larger studies carried out at the organizational and international level.

For the most part, CPS data are suggestive rather than conclusive since the survey was not designed to address this question specifically. *Times Mirror* national survey data (1994) more directly bear on it. Results from studies of both datasets, however, tend to corroborate the view that access to computers and communications technology supports informational, affiliative, and participatory outcomes as prior research studies predict.

With respect to information gains, for example, CPS data from 1993 show that 21 percent of adults with household computers use them to access databases (34 percent do so from computers at work). Additionally, 15 percent of adults use home computers for educational programs, as do 39 percent of children with household computers. Even larger percentages of adults as well as children use computers at home to do school assignments (see Appendix A for a table of activities people do by computer). These findings are corroborated by *Times Mirror* data, which show information-seeking to be one of the two most common activities pursued by people with computers and modems at home. This accounts in part for why such people scored higher on a political knowledge test embedded in the survey than a demographically equivalent sample of nonusers (see above). It should be emphasized that such benefits appear not to be restricted to upper socioeconomic levels. Further, the *Times Mirror* survey (1994) also reports that younger children's use is almost entirely a function of access: "Among households with PCs, only modest differences were found across racial or income groups in use of computers by children." Results for the teenage survey were the same. The implication is that provision of the technology could go far toward equalizing information benefits across socioeconomic strata.

A second dimension of interest is affiliation, or the extent to which computer-based media yield social contact and support. Some evidence for this thesis comes from the CPS data, which show that apart from word processing, e-mail is the single activity pursued by the largest proportion of adults with household computers (see Appendix A). More direct evidence on this point comes from the *Times Mirror* survey, which asked more detailed questions about communicative activities. That survey found communicating with other people constitutes a distinct set of activities carried out independently of information-seeking. While acknowledging the importance of information seeking, the *Times Mirror* report concludes: "of potentially equal significance to society is the quieter revolution of computers facilitating communication between people." These findings give strong support to the view that electronic networks are social technologies that serve affiliative needs. It follows that lack of access can constitute a barrier to association in the information age, constraining opportunities for social interaction in ways that universal service policies could remedy. Further, that affiliation is demonstrably an independently significant function of these technologies gives rise to a "right to information" often cited in discussions of computers and connectivity.

A third key question is whether participation in civic and social life is likely to increase along with use of information and communications technology. No CPS items address this point. *Times Mirror* survey data are, however, highly instructive. Comparing computer and modem users with their demographic equivalents, the report notes that, aside from working at home more, the largest difference between them is engagement in groups and organizations. Specifically, the users are significantly more likely than their demographic counterparts to belong to a group in which they regularly take part. Further, controlling for other variables, users belong to more groups and are more likely to have worked for or attended a meeting of a group in the past week. Such measures have long been taken by sociologists (e.g., Havighurst, 1973) as indicators of engagement in civic life. These data are consistent with previous smaller-scale research indicating that computer-based interactions supplement and extend, rather than supplant, social participation (Bikson and Eveland, 1990; Hesse et al., 1990; Huff, Sproull, and Kiesler, 1989; Kraut and Streeter, 1990). Broad access to computers and electronic networks, then, might help reduce if not reverse the trends toward disengagement in civic and political affairs discussed in the introductory chapter.

The congruence of findings between national-sample survey data and social science research studies strengthens the conclusions drawn here. While the social science research projects cited here are well-designed and are better able to support causal conclusions than cross-sectional surveys, questions inevitably arise about whether the results will scale up to the national level. The survey data presented here are national in scope and representative of the U.S. population; but although they can establish clear correlations and reveal strong trends, they shed less light on causal or functional relationships over time. Together, the combined sources should be viewed as a robust policy foundation. Both kinds of information would, however, benefit from studies of real world processes in day-to-day contexts. Understanding how outcomes are distributed over time when entire intact communities are networked with computers and communications technology would richly complement what has been learned from social science and from survey research. Chapter Five represents first steps toward providing that part of the picture.

Chapter Three

TECHNICAL CONSIDERATIONS

Robert H. Anderson, Joel Pliskin

INTRODUCTION

If electronic mail access is to be provided universally within the United States, a set of technical issues must be considered. Among the key ones are providing physical access to e-mail services, providing a user interface that is understandable and usable by "everyone," and assuring that proper standards are in place to allow the evolution of a complex system through the individual activities of entrepreneurs and businesses. Other, related issues, such as creating a demand for such services and providing adequate training and support, are discussed in Chapters Four and Five.

Physical Access

Some in our society will have home or office PCs and modems or other data network links providing access. The data in Chapter Two show that others are unlikely to have such access within the foreseeable future. How do those others obtain or access some physical device by which they can use an e-mail system? There are two subissues: the nature of the physical device (PC, telephone, TV + set-top box, game machine, wireless device, other) and its location (e.g., home, kiosk, library, post office, school, other).

User Interface

Are any of the present user interfaces to e-mail adequate for "universal" access, or do improvements or simplifications need to be made? How can noncomputer-sophisticated users handle potentially large numbers of messages? What tools can be provided for users to filter out objectionable materials (however they wish to define that term) and highlight important messages?

Standards

Given that many competing corporate players are providing services, are standards needed at various levels of interconnect and addressing to allow growth of a truly "universal" system? If so, which standards? The following are areas for standardization considered in this chapter.

Addressing. How do you address messages? Must all addresses be explicitly assigned, or is there a "default" form of address (such as "John_Doe@street.city.state.us") that will (usually) work?

Directories. A variety of efforts are under way to create user directories to make e-mail more accessible. The following are some important questions: How should these directories work? Are existing standards for interconnecting among directories sufficient? Will private enterprise provide these services? Should there be a "default" universal directory, or will regional (domain) directories suffice?

System Architecture. We use the term "architecture" of a system to denote the underlying structure, interfaces, and assumptions within which its components interoperate. What standards and interfaces are required for the information system architecture to support universal e-mail? How do the requirements of universal e-mail correlate with the design and architecture being contemplated for an NII[1] and with international connections leading to a global information infrastructure (GII)?[2]

---

[1]For an overview of governmental aspirations and plans for an NII, see, for example, http://sunsite.unc.edu/nii/NII-Agenda-for-Action.html, or http://nii.nist.gov/.

[2]See http://ntiaunix1.ntia.doc.gov:70/0/papers/documents/giiagend.html.

Security and Integrity Services. For some purposes, users require confidentiality, authentication, anonymity, privacy, and integrity of their messages. What levels of such services must be provided for the system to be used and useful? We place this question within the "standards" category because standard procedures for providing these services must be in place for messages and documents to be exchanged and shared nationwide.

BACKGROUND AND ASSUMPTIONS

We assume that e-mail technology will continue to be disseminated through society by market forces following the fairly standard technology adoption model. Relevant examples of this model are the personal computer itself, as well as VCRs and other consumer technologies. The main assumptions of the model are that

- Technology will be available initially at relatively high prices. Prices will drop at an accelerating rate as the technology achieves wider market acceptance. However, it will be some time before this technology is generally affordable by all segments of society.

- Commercial (i.e., for-profit) applications will generally be aimed at segments of society that can best afford them.

These assumptions imply that, because unaided market forces normally will result in a "trickle down" diffusion of e-mail technology, policies designed to promote universal access should be aimed predominantly at speeding dissemination of e-mail technologies to the lower end of the socioeconomic status (SES). (Later in this chapter, however, we give some reasons why this dissemination may not proceed too rapidly.)

Table 3.1 indicates the pace that related technologies were diffused into U.S. society.

It is worth noting, however, that penetration of various technologies is not evenly distributed throughout the United States. For example, U.S. census tracts still exist with telephone penetrations around 55 percent (Mueller and Schement, 1995).

Table 3.1

Time for Diffusion of Technologies

Technology	Years
Telephone diffused to 50% of households	70
TV diffused to nearly all households	34
VCRs diffused to 65% of households	13
PCs diffused to 30% of households (est.)	20
On-line services diffused to 50% of households	?

SOURCE: King and Kraemer (1995).

The discussion in this chapter is strongly influenced by the current and projected demographics of access to, and use of, personal computers and on-line services. Extrapolating the data in Figure 2.2 and the discussion within the previous chapter, we conclude that, through normal market mechanisms, less than 50 percent of U.S. households by 2000 will have personal computers.[3] Although only about half of these will have modems, the upgrade cost for a reasonable-speed modem for on-line service access (e.g., 14.4 kilobits (KB) per second) will be relatively small (e.g., about $60). We conclude that PC owners will obtain modems (and they will be increasingly built-in as standard equipment) as on-line services become easier to use and more useful. These PCs are more than sufficient for accessing e-mail services. We therefore concentrate in the following discussion on technical issues involved in reaching the "remaining 50 percent," and in particular on bringing e-mail services to the bottom quartile of our society, based on socioeconomic status.

Later subsections of this chapter detail each topic listed in this chapter's introduction. Before addressing those technical topics, however, it is important to understand some of the services related to e-mail that will stimulate demand; without this demand, technical solutions are moot.

---

[3]Estimates of PC penetration into households by the year 2000 vary from about 40–60 percent. For the purposes of this report, whether the actual penetration is at the low, middle, or high end of this range does not significantly affect our conclusions and recommendations. Note that this trend indicates considerably *slower* penetration of PCs into U.S. households than that which occurred with television sets.

PROVIDING SERVICES

Adoption and wide use of e-mail technology will result from the availability of services that users perceive are useful and relevant, or will result from a "critical mass" of use, or both. We distinguish between generic and targeted services.

"Mainstream" Generic Services

This is the class of services that come as part of any e-mail system and should appeal to all users, regardless of socioeconomic status. (Chapter Five provides emerging evidence of this appeal.) Such services include the following:

Electronic Mail. Similar to current Internet mail, a store and forward system for sending messages between users, including the other attributes discussed in our definition of e-mail in Chapter One: creation, distribution, consumption, processing and storage of messages. Among other destinations for e-mail, messages may be posted on "electronic bulletin boards." Initially, this service may be limited to text and, perhaps, simple graphics.

"Chat" Facilities. These services allow nearly instantaneous exchange of typed information (and in the relatively near future, voice and video) among a set of on-line correspondents. These services can catalyze the formation of groups based on common interests rather than common proximity.

Information Retrieval Facilities. This category is intended to encompass all means of gathering remote data. As such, it includes present techniques such as FTP (file transfer protocol), gopher (a file retrieval protocol developed at the University of Minnesota), and portions of Web access. This category might also include soft goods sales,[4] as commerce is increasingly conducted over the net.

---

[4]Soft goods transactions are the sale and purchase of electronic data stream commodities. Soft goods include information purchased from private databases, such as stock quotes from Dow Jones, software, videos, text, and anything else that can be delivered to the buyer in digital format. Soft goods sales can be transacted entirely within the e-mail system. Pricing of these items can be connected to direct measures, such as connect time or volume of information delivered, or they may be priced as individual items just like hard goods. Payment schemes may be similar to that of cur-

Targeted Services

We call "targeted services" those designed specifically to meet the needs of low socioeconomic groups, and thereby to provide incentive for use, creating demand for the e-mail system among the targeted groups. We assume that these services will not be (at least initially) commercially viable and must therefore be either provided or subsidized by some governmental or nonprofit entity.

Use of these services would facilitate several important objectives:

- Increase incentive for commercial service providers to address these segments of society by creating an identifiable user market segment, thus further increasing the diffusion rate of e-mail technologies.

- Increase both general literacy and computer literacy among those now thought to be disadvantaged, thereby increasing their employment marketability.

- Provide potential government savings, if direct computer access to program information increases the productivity of relevant public agencies.

Examples of such targeted services may be found in Chapter Five, which describes five "wired community" efforts in which various such services are being delivered. The following are among the services to be considered:

- Social welfare information—allows users to check on their program status, and file claims, requests, and grievances in such programs as Aid for Families with Dependent Children (AFDC), Medicaid and Food Stamps. E-mail informational access could be tied closely to the use of ATMs or kiosks for the actual distribution of funds for some or all of these programs, as is presently contemplated.

- Provide an "address" (i.e., a stable point of contact) for the homeless or transient.

---

rent computer network services such as CompuServe or to that of telephone companies for 976 calls. Delivery is completed electronically.

- Information about available job training programs, or direct access to relevant training materials; ability to respond to job advertisements.

- Educational programs—such programs could allow people to study for tests such as those for the General Equivalency Diploma (GED) at home, thereby reducing their need for other expensive services such as day care. (However, it is difficult to study or work at home with active toddlers; network access at home is not a panacea.)

- Communication between teachers and parents, and parental access to "bulletin boards" containing homework assignments, school schedules, PTA, etc. (This is especially needed by working lower-income parents whose work schedules prevent them from getting this information during school hours.)

- Social support for older adults or temporarily or permanently handicapped individuals at home.

Perhaps the most common thread running through our studies of "wired community" developments is the importance of e-mail, chat lines, and forums as an "easy entry" service to engage people's interests.

PHYSICAL ACCESS

As mentioned earlier, we assume that about 50 percent of U.S. households will have PCs by the year 2000. A key technical issue, then, is how the remainder of the households—and particularly those in the lower quartile of income and education—will obtain access to cyberspace.

The following devices may be used for access. (In this discussion, we distinguish between devices for access and location of those devices; location options are discussed separately below.)

- Desktop ("personal") computers (either personally owned, or available in a public place).

- Game machines, such as Nintendo or Sega machines that use a television as the display, supplemented by a keyboard.

- TV set-top boxes, such as the cable TV controller device, supplemented by a keyboard.

- Dedicated low-cost devices specialized for e-mail, attachable to either a telephone line or cable TV.

- Wireless access devices (such as Newton and MagicLink).

- Telephone with display screens, supplemented by keyboards.

Some of the above-mentioned devices may not support all of the features we listed in our definition of e-mail, such as storage of messages for later retrieval and reuse. However, such storage can be provided remotely by an e-mail service provider and merely accessed over a telecommunication line by one of these devices.

Below, we outline the pros and cons of each device in light of the various niches each will serve.

Personal Computers

Pros	Cons
• There are existing standards for both hardware and software	• Expensive (new units likely to remain at the $500+ level)—but see discussion of used PCs below
• Powerful enough to handle all technical requirements	• Most low SES groups have had minimal exposure to computers and may therefore be intimidated by them
• Huge installed base ensures continued development, availability	
• Hardware, software, and knowledge to allow training all widely available	

Game Machines (e.g., Sega, and Nintendo)

Pros	Cons
• Many low SES households own television sets and TV-based game machines	• Essentially no interactive software available except for games
• Lower cost than personal computers, because they use TV as display	• No operating system standard to allow development of application programs
• Huge installed base ensures continued development, availability	• Little or no organized training and support
• Family members (especially children) are familiar with their use	• Shared TV use among family members may preclude some e-mail use
	• TV is often not in a good physical location for messaging use
	• Low resolution of current TVs

Set-Top Boxes (other than game machines)

Pros	Cons
• Many low SES households own television sets and receive cable	• No existing standard for either hardware or software[5]
• Lower cost than personal computers because they use existing TV as display	• So far, no standard for keyboard attachment
	• Shared TV use among family members may preclude some e-mail use

Dedicated Device (e.g., Minitel terminal)

Pros	Cons
• Can be optimized for particular services, such as a dedicated e-mail device	• Would require strong and lasting commitment to establish the standard and keep it viable until wide commercial acceptance is achieved
• Can be designed specifically as a low cost "entry-level" device	• Minitel is often viewed as a "dead-end" system without sufficient growth options
	• The display on an inexpensive device is likely to be small for cost reasons
	• No large existing base of programs and third-party software

Wireless Device

Pros	Cons
• Location independence	• With batteries, radio transmission link, etc., cost is likely to remain high (relative to stationary, plugged devices)
• If based on personal computer architectures, there is a large installed base of software, training, etc.	• If a unique architecture, there is no mass market for software applications, training, etc.
	• Display may be small to enhance portability
	• Unless based on PC architecture, no large existing base of programs and third-party software

---

[5]Note, however, that big players are entering the scene and may be bringing substantial standards with them. See *Multimedia Week* (May 15, 1995) and *Multimedia Week* (May 8, 1995).

Telephone with Display Screen

Pros	Cons
• Has multiple purposes (voice, other uses for the display) that could help make it ubiquitous and a "commodity" with reasonable pricing	• Display screen is likely to be small, perhaps noncolor, precluding some uses
• Could have substantial support, documentation, training, etc., from phone companies	• Likely to have a unique architecture, without an initial large installed base of software, training, etc.

Location

Quite independently from the *type* of device used for e-mail access, there are many considerations regarding the *location* of the device. People who routinely use e-mail from office or home, by merely swiveling their chairs to access a handy keyboard and display, know that such "instant" availability is ideal for jotting quick e-mail notes to correspondents, checking periodically for new messages, responding as needed, and so forth. The convenience is also important, for example, for the person with children at home working toward a GED certificate, and for other sustained uses such as parent-teacher interactions, filing Medicare claims, and so on. Unfortunately, many members of our society possess no such "at-hand" devices. For them (and for institutions considering provision of universal e-mail services), location is important.[6] Here are the pros and cons of potential locations:

In Home

Pros	Cons
• Maximum ease of access	• Depending on the hardware system used, may require a high level of subsidization or grants to get systems into the home
• Increases user comfort level, and makes use more likely	
• More likely to involve all family members	• Difficult to provide training and support to such distributed sites

---

[6]This discussion of location assumes the telecommunication cost to be roughly equivalent from the various listed locations. Further discussion of costs related to e-mail is presented in Chapter Four.

At Work

Pros	Cons
• If in normal workplace setting, provides ease of access	• Only relevant for those having jobs
• Equipment costs are usually borne by employer or organization	• Likely to exclude family members without work access
• Training and support usually available	• May exclude personal and social uses

Schools

Pros	Cons
• Children likely to be first to learn this new technology; can bring understanding and use home to parents	• Excludes some family members
• Equipment costs borne by schools; ultimately by taxpayers	• Wiring for communications of school classrooms can be expensive
• Some training and support usually available	• May exclude personal and social uses
• Can be integrated into learning experiences; encourages writing and reading	• Excludes people with no children in school
• Reaches those not in a "household" situation	• Restricted hours of public access
• Shared usage may promote peer helping and shared experiences	
• Requires no phone line, cable, etc., into the home	

"Common" Areas (Libraries, Post Offices, Community Centers, Kiosks)

Pros	Cons
• Does not require a system to be provided to each home; cheaper	• Requires people to come out of the home to use the system
• Shared usage may promote peer helping and shared experiences	• Might require waiting in line
• Easier to provide some training and support	• Hours of access may be limited
• Hardware and software maintained and serviced by others	• Subject to vandalism
• Requires no phone line, cable, etc., into the home	• Not convenient for "spur of the moment" communication
• Reaches those not in a "household" situation	• May not allow continuity of use to carry or "dialog" or "multilog" with others
• Can access when away from home environment	• Not convenient for extended uses over time

It does not take much analysis to conclude that, other than PCs and possibly game machines, none of the other devices mentioned will "sweep the market." The economics of the installed base makes the wide adoption of any other alternative unlikely, absent a strong commitment on the part of government (as in the case of the French Minitel) to establish a new hardware standard. Without such commitment, it is unlikely that the developers of software, training, and support services will be willing to divert resources from the more profitable PC market. The president of Forrester Research Inc., a private research and consulting firm, in a 1995 interview put that viewpoint in stark terms:

> [W]e do not believe that interactive television will be a factor in this century, primarily because of the expense . . . the personal computer will be the primary engine of technology in the home in this decade. (Hill, 1995a.)

Given that market economics point to dominance by the personal computer, location becomes the variable that policy can influence. It certainly will be too expensive to provide every household with a personal computer, but programs could be pursued to make PCs more widely available. For example

- increased tax deductions for donation of used PCs, and

- provision of PCs to libraries and schools.

Used PCs as Entry-Level Access Devices

The option of widespread reliance on provision and support of "used PCs" is an interesting one. On one hand, many corporations and individuals assume that the useful lifetime of a personal computer is about three to four years and have deliberate policies of routine upgrading, making large numbers of well-performing used PCs available. These would certainly be adequate for e-mail access and often for the richer graphical access of Web browsers, etc.[7]

---

[7]As one example of the utility of older PCs, a program called "Minuet" has recently been announced that provides e-mail and gopher access, plus Web browsing, on DOS PCs, even those using DOS 2.1 and with only 512K KB of random access memory (RAM). It is shareware, offered at $50, but with site licenses available. See http://www.MR.Net/~cdh/minuet.html.

On the other hand, used PCs come with a variety of operating systems, hard disks, floppy disk formats, displays, and so forth—making uniform training and service programs problematic and labor-intensive. There is certainly an opportunity for some organization to acquire (e.g., from corporate donations) large quantities of "fairly standard" PCs (e.g., using the Intel chip architecture, that is, "IBM compatible," with at least one 3.5-inch floppy-disk drive), installing a standard suite of software for e-mail access and other basic operations, and making these machines available to targeted households and individuals who could not otherwise afford household PCs.

Convergence of Device Types

One complication affecting our listing of device types arises from the convergence of PCs and game machines. For example, the Apple "Pippin" device has strong Apple Macintosh similarities and compatibilities but uses a TV set as the display device. Current trade press discussion of its specifications indicates that it will include 6 megabytes (MB) of RAM, a quad-speed compact disk–read only memory (CD-ROM), 16-bit stereo sound, and various serial ports and will be available for approximately $500 (Hess, 1995). It will support a keyboard. It will compete mainly in the "game machine" market but will have many PC features although with no built-in floppy-disk drive. It is likely to be completely adequate for e-mail purposes. A recent news report indicates that Sega Enterprises Ltd. will offer an Internet interface to its Saturn 64-bit video game player and is considering offering keyboards for the machine (Standing, 1995). In addition, a series of announcements released as this document was going to press indicate that Oracle Corporation (Pitta, 1995), Sun Microsystems, and Philips Electronics N.V. (Bloomberg, 1995), among others, are preparing to sell low-cost network-oriented computers priced at or below $500. These Internet access devices will support access to e-mail services. These examples illustrate how categories will blur in the next several years and how prices for significant computing technology will fall.

A second blurring of categories comes from the integration of computers with telephones. Recently, an Enterprise Computer Telephony Forum has been formed to promote an open, competitive market for computer and telephone integration. Microsoft has developed a Telephony Application Programming Interface, and Novell has a similar proposal that it developed with AT&T (Cheek, 1995). The marriage of a PC and its display with the telephone will offer features that further integrate telephony, voice mail technology (store, forward, and replay), and personal computing and will further stimulate the use of home PCs. It also leads to the concept of a "universal mailbox" supporting retrieval and submission of voice, video, e-mail, and other information from and to the same mailbox address. As Negroponte (1995a) emphasizes, they are all just bit-streams, hence processable in a uniform manner.

As if the above blurring of categories were not enough, next-generation TV set-top boxes (and then TV sets themselves) will contain significant computing power, leading to digital, interactive television that has many more capabilities than currently (Minoli, 1995). Because the cost of these advanced TV-based systems likely will remain high for approximately the next decade, in this report we do not emphasize their availability and features for the provision of universal e-mail services.

The Cost of PCs

Personal computers have remained quite expensive (e.g., over $1,000) for years, in spite of the drastic increases in computing power per dollar that have been occurring for decades. We attribute this at least to the following factors:

- The technology continues to evolve rapidly, so new features and innovations (e.g., CD-ROMs, high-resolution color displays) are attractive to purchasers and must be written off quickly by developers before they become obsolete.

- There is more profit in high-end machines than in "commodity" machines with significant price competition.

- Software makers continue to compete by adding features, requiring larger and faster machines to operate the resulting software packages.

Negroponte gives similar reasons in a recent article (1995b). In that article he argues that simple but highly usable "commodity" PCs could be produced for $200 each or even given away free:

Today, there are more than 100 million computer screens in the United States. Think of every screen as a potential billboard. Let's assume that each one is turned on once a day and, lo and behold, each day a new advertising message appears—the screen saver for the day . . . . Advertisers would pay to gain access to what turns out to be about 2,000 acres of advertising space (changeable per square inch, per day, or per hour). That money could subsidize the cost of the computer and even pay for you to use it . . . . I am no great fan of advertising, but it does represent a quarter-of-a-trillion-dollar industry, and there must be a way to use its size to make computing affordable to all Americans.

Given the motivation to provide computing access to all U.S. households, such innovative schemes might provide a mechanism to accomplish this goal.

It may be comforting to assume that PCs will become low-cost commodities like telephones, TVs, and VCRs, and that the universal access problem will resolve itself. After all, each of these technologies had "early adopters" that leapt ahead in use of the technologies (just as the top two quartiles of U.S. households in education and income are rapidly acquiring PCs today), but then the rest of the population caught up as price competition brought the technology into the reach of (almost) all.

For the reasons given above, we believe, for the next several decades at least, that this is a false hope. The difference with PCs may be threefold: (1) A "killer app"[8] has not yet emerged for personal computing that makes a PC a "must have" appliance in every household (as, for example, prerecorded movies did for VCRs) such that mass demand would create the market for a "commodity" PC; (2) the technology is not stabilizing so that "commoditization" can occur;[9]

---

[8]"Killer app" is common terminology in the computing field, referring to an application that is so compelling that it drives demand for the relevant device(s) to operate that application. In the early days of the PC, spreadsheets (VisiCalc and Lotus 1-2-3) were such a killer app for business usage of PCs and for some households. Could a killer app for governmental involvement in universal e-mail be submission of income tax returns, Medicare claims, etc., and responses to them electronically?

[9]Just when we think that an "IBM compatible" PC is a commodity, along comes CD-ROM (then double, triple, and quad-speed), laptops and notebooks, virtual reality devices, PCMCIA cards, 28.8-kilobit-per-second modems, software that requires 12 MB minimum to run effectively, and so forth. As an example of "featuritis" keeping the

and (3) there are recurring telecommunication costs, including possible need for a second phone line to avoid tying up the family phone.

However, the new under-$500 "network access terminals" mentioned in the previous subsection can play a vital role in providing inexpensive access.

Assuming some provision of a physical access device and an accessible location for it, we next address the user interface to e-mail services that it provides. .

USER INTERFACE AND TOOLS

Interfaces Usable by "Everyone"

The "interfaces" that software programs present to the user for handling electronic mail range from Spartan command-driven ones to Windows and Macintosh application programs with myriad buttons, menus, "drag-and-drop," and subwindows features.

We have been unable to locate in the social science and "human-computer interface" literature studies of the usability of these existing interfaces for persons in the lowest quartile of income and education in the United States—persons less likely to be "computer literate" and therefore possibly unfamiliar with the many metaphors on which these interfaces are based.

Microsoft's "Bob"[10] and Apple Computer's "Pippin"[11] represent a class of new, "simpler" human-computer interfaces. Corporate research underlying these developments may have resulted in interfaces to such applications as e-mail systems that are usable by

---

price of PCs high, a recent newspaper article indicated (giving as its source, Dataquest Inc.) that in the year 2000, $1,800 will buy: an eighth-generation 600 MHz processor (Octium?), 64 MB of RAM, over 8 gigabytes (GB) of storage, a 14-inch high-quality color monitor, a six-times speed CD-ROM, and a built-in network connection at up to 100 million bits per second. Such a device will offer access to Web offerings including video and high-quality videophone capability and will have voice recognition and speech-to-text transcription on some models (Hill, 1995b).

[10]See http://www.microsoft.com/mshome/showcase/bob/ for an introduction to Bob.

[11]Hess (1995).

"everyone."[12] For now, we believe it is still unclear whether the basic commands required by an e-mail interface (compose and edit a message; file and retrieve messages; send a message, reply to a message, forward a message—all to one or more addressees; organize messages and address lists; etc.) can be made sufficiently natural that their use quickly becomes "obvious," or whether substantial training and education are required for any usefully powerful system.

Some data are becoming available from "wired community" experiments, especially those in lower income and education communities; see, for example, the analyses of some of these experiments in Chapter Five. However, some of these initiatives are only now commencing, and data are still limited on the usability of e-mail systems by persons who are not the primary market for PC-based software application programs.

One of the most promising possibilities for a "universal" interface is the "point-and-click" interface promoted by Web "browsers" such as Mosaic and Netscape. Such an interface is not only appropriate for accessing "pages" of information but also for "fill-in-the-blanks" creation of information (such as messages) for transmission. These browser interfaces, as they continue to evolve, might well be the best candidate for a universal interface to e-mail and many other information services. Further study of the usability of such interfaces in lowest-quartile income and education households is merited.

Handling Volume

Many users of e-mail systems currently receive more than 100 messages a day. After a week out of contact with the system (for example due to travel, illness, equipment malfunction), 500 or more messages may be waiting to be read, organized, responded to, forwarded, discarded—a daunting task for the returning user. Most e-mail systems today are used by businesses to exchange internal information. What if "everyone" were on-line? Would we be deluged with thousands of messages a day? If so, what could be done about it? The bad

---

[12] We put "everyone" in quotes because, of course, no computer interface will be appropriate for all users. We are interested in an interface that can become a "default" interface used by disparate classes of people as a first step up the path of greater computer literacy and control.

news is that volume would be a problem. The good news is that there are reasonable technical means to handle it.

In a universal e-mail system (and at present), each time you send a message there is a likely chance that the recipient will retain for future use your return electronic address. If you post messages to popular bulletin boards or other public locales, it is very likely that someone is collecting the electronic addresses, forming a database, and reusing it or selling it for "bulk" mailings. Similarly, directories will be available on-line (see the discussion of Directories, below, under Standards) with tens of thousands of names, e-mail addresses, and other personal attributes that have either been volunteered by people and organizations or extracted from their transactions. These databases and directories will be used to broadcast messages to thousands of people. The e-mail world could increasingly resemble our present world of "junk" paper mail, unsolicited publications, and some desired (e.g., first-class) mail mixed in with the rest. The problem is exacerbated by the current economics of e-mail, in which the cost of sending messages is insensitive to the volume sent. In fact, one argument for charging per message is that it would hold the volume down.

Computers are powerful tools for organizing such information. E-mail systems now, and will increasingly in the future, provide tools for "filtering" incoming mail based on a set of rules supplied by the user. Mail can automatically be placed in "folders," or even discarded automatically, based on various criteria (sender, keywords appearing in the "Subject" line, or priority) to be read later. Since all of these features are available today,[13] the remaining question is: Can "ordinary" (nonprogramming, noncomputer-literate) persons use such features to maintain control over their e-mail environment and not be overwhelmed? This is a subject that could benefit from more research, especially field research concentrating on lower-SES households and individuals. However, we are quite confident that

---

[13]As one example, the UNIX "mh" mail system, widely distributed with UNIX, has a folder facility and a powerful "pick" command for extracting messages based on Boolean combinations of attributes. When combined with the programming features of the UNIX shell(s), shell programs can be developed to tailor the mail system to the user's specific wishes. Other systems are distributed with what has become known informally as "bozo filters."

contemporary computer software technology is up to this challenge, for example, by using some mix of techniques such as allowing the user to provide illustrative examples of undesirable messages, having a "user agent" program "look over the shoulder" of users as they handle messages, searching for patterns on which rules for handling messages may be based.

In summary, we believe that volume of e-mail is a problem that can be handled straightforwardly by a combination of technical (software) and market responses.

Handling Objectionable Materials

Users may want to filter out material that is objectionable, either to themselves or to other family members such as children. (We note, however, that objectionable materials do not appear to be a problem to date in the civic networks we have investigated, described in Chapter Five.) Technical means exist not only to block access to entire classes of Internet sites but also to facilitate access to selected sites. Users can constrain access to Internet sites by using software that permits packets only to or from preselected addresses or that rejects packets destined for certain other addresses.[14]

Another approach to facilitating user access to Internet information would be to establish content classification and ratings, analogous to those developed for movies or computer games. For example, video stores organize tapes by category (drama, comedy) and provide ratings (G, PG, PG-13) for each tape within each category. If similar categories and ratings were established for content on the Internet, it would be technically straightforward to build browsers and other client software to seek out appropriate content and block unwanted (or unrated) materials. These techniques, however, work best for moderated discussions or other controlled information sources, but not necessarily for e-mail, chat, or unmoderated discussions. Recently, three software industry leaders, including Microsoft, announced their intent to create and implement standards that would

---

[14]One commercially available software package that accomplishes this is SurfWatch; for more information, see http://www.surfwatch.com.

enable users to "lock-out" access to materials they deem inappropriate.

In summary, using relatively straightforward technology, it is possible today to give users greater control of their own access to Internet content without limiting the free flow of information to other users or infringing on the First Amendment rights of content providers.

STANDARDS

In considering the question of standards that might prove relevant to a future national e-mail system, one should first look at standards in use in current networking systems, because they may suffice and they already have a large installed base. Given the extremely large installed bases enjoyed by such current systems (e.g., the Internet) and the difficulty in getting agreement on theoretical standards, it seems most likely that any future national e-mail system will evolve from what currently exists.

Regarding the setting of standards in general, there are two main paradigms: the national and international standards bodies whose committees promulgate standards after considerable discussion and negotiation, and the more informal, practically oriented procedures used by the Internet Engineering Task Force (IETF) over the past decade.[15] The latter are well described by Crocker (1993). A useful feature of the IETF model is that prospective standards, each embodied in a "request for comments" (RFC), are not ratified until they are embodied in working systems that have been tested, evaluated, and found useful.

We discuss below standards for addressing and mail protocols, and directories. We then discuss relevant system architectures for universal e-mail, and standards and other considerations relevant to the provision of confidentiality, authentication, anonymity, privacy, and integrity in messages.

---

[15]Branscomb and Kahin (1995) describe three models for standards development. Their thoughtful analysis considers appropriate government roles in standards setting for the NII.

Addressing and Mail Protocols

Two issues are involved in addressing. The first is the standard by which symbolic addresses are turned into physical addresses. Currently, two addressing standards are in wide use: the Internet Domain Name System (DNS)[16] and the addressing described by portions of the X.400 standard of the International Telecommunication Union (ITU),[17] formerly CCITT. These addresses are in turn embedded in standardized message "headers," with the two primary contenders being the Internet's Simple Mail Transfer Protocol (SMTP)[18] and the ITU's X.400.

It now appears that the DNS, having the advantage of the huge and rapidly growing installed base of the Internet, will dominate future developments. Therefore, any future U.S. system will almost certainly be based on DNS or its descendants. However, X.400 continues to enjoy the support of standards organizations and governments, particularly in Europe. Although simultaneous international use of conflicting standards could cause short-run problems, temporary "gateways" providing (less than complete!) translation between these standards can alleviate the problems. Because gateways lose information,[19] they are not an adequate long-term solution to the implementation of a national and international e-mail system (Stefferud and Pliskin, 1994). As one form of gateway, there exists at least one DNS-to-X.400 (two-way) address converter on the Web, at http://relay.surfnet.nl/index.gb.html. The Internet's RFC 1327[20] specifies mapping between X.400 and Internet mail.

---

[16]The Internet Domain Name System is described by RFC 882, which is available at http://ds.internic.net/rfc/rfc882.txt. Other relevant RFCs are 883 and 973, which are accessible similarly.

[17]The ITU's Web home page is at http://www.itu.ch/. The ITU, which is headquartered in Geneva, Switzerland, is an international organization within which governments and the private sector coordinate global telecom networks and services.

[18]The SMTP, the basic Internet e-mail protocol, is defined in RFC 821, available at http://ds.internic.net/rfc/rfc821.txt.

[19]If gateways did not lose information, at least in one direction, the two standards would be equivalent in all respects. In that case, there would not be two competing standards.

[20]RFC 1327 is available at: http://ds.internic.net/rfc/rfc1327.txt.

The second issue, the *assignment* of symbolic addresses (i.e., the addresses people actually use, for example Jane_Doe@rand.org), has important implications for universal access. To achieve anything close to universal access, particularly among economically disadvantaged groups, either (1) the symbolic addressing scheme must be reasonably intuitive, so that people find and understand the addresses of their correspondents with a minimum of effort or (2) there must be good directory services so that names and other attributes of people can be used effectively to locate their e-mail addresses. (See the discussion of directories, below.)

Affiliation (i.e., domain) structures for those in low-SES groups might be the local community center or housing project. The question in providing access to these groups is what type of affiliation structure, and thus address structure, should be used so that these users will understand it and be able to find counterparts with whom to communicate.

Under the DNS, a symbolic address consists of two components, the user name and the domain name. The address follows the general form "user_name@domain_name." The domain name consists of several subdomain components (for example, "rand.org," "cidmac.ecn.purdue.edu") and is generally assigned to an organization. There is, however, provision within DNS to form domains based on geography; for example, a final suffix of ".us" refers to a domain within the United States, ".fi" refers to Finland, etc. It is possible for more than one addressing scheme to coexist, with both possibly providing access to a common site. For example, The Well in the San Francisco area has the DNS addresses "well.com" and "well.sf.ca.us". Assignment of user names is left to each individual domain.

We believe there should be a "universal" addressing scheme, providing at least a default e-mail address for all U.S. citizens. Such a scheme could be implemented within either the existing Internet Domain Name System or X.400. We use the DNS format in the examples below. Such an address could be derived in a straightforward way from an existing attribute of the person, such as his/her home address: "John_Doe@123_Main_Street.02356-2344.us" or based on some other ID, such as a telephone number.

A disadvantage of this approach, however, is that it removes the advantage of the location-independence of e-mail addressing. With the existing relatively high turnover rates in addresses and telephone numbers in the United States, there would be considerable addressing "churn." Two solutions are (1) use of a "P.O. box" independent of location as an e-mail address (but with less mnemonic value) or (2) use of a "remailer" service that forwards mail to one's current address (such as the new "pobox.com" commercial service discussed in Chapter Four). The topic of address portability (as users change location, and among different e-mail services) is complex. Address portability is discussed further in Chapter Four.

A new white paper is also available from the Cross-Industry Working Team (XIWT), based at the Corporation for National Research Initiatives (CNRI) in Reston, Virginia, on "Nomadicity in the NII" (XIWT, 1995b), which contains a provocative introduction of some of the issues involved because networks are used by "nomads" (people who can easily access services, other people, and content while they are on the move, at intermediate stops, and at arbitrary destinations). Among other points, this document points out that people operate within different contexts (work, home, hobby). People at different locations may share contexts. These contexts can provide focus for e-mail and other interactions and should be taken into account. They also discuss the need for "location coordinators" to keep track of the individuals, devices, and communications system capabilities as changes occur. If the ideas of this working group are fully instantiated in future evolutions of the NII, the problems of address portability may be solved within a larger architectural context.

For those without (or not wanting to be identified by) a physical address, "John_Doe@General_Post_Office.02356-2344.us" might be an option, or even just some identifier to make the name unique, such as "John_Doe_1023.us".

The advantage of using home addresses or telephone numbers is that a correspondent could make an "educated guess" at an e-mail address without knowing it explicitly, given other more familiar information about the recipient. Such educated guesses are handy and already in use; for example, any RAND staff member may receive mail as "firstname_lastname@rand.org". Other organizations use the first letter of the first name followed by the last name, as in "JRogers@company.com".

Any addressing scheme must, of course, allow for (and assume) worldwide addressing, just as postal mail and telephone services are worldwide, but handling of addresses can be deferred to local "domains," just as mail addresses and telephone numbers are today. There need be no universal registration, database, or authority for e-mail addresses, as long as they are assigned within overall naming domains established by some central clearinghouse.

Some services, such as multiple mailboxes per person, might well be considered "extra" features to be provided by third parties, at some cost, as long as they are not precluded by the basic system architecture. (For additional discussion of architectural principles underlying universal e-mail access, see "System Architecture," below.)

Directories

Much about an e-mail system is new and unfamiliar, but the accepted telephone directory metaphors of white pages and yellow pages translate very well into the world of the e-mail system. White pages list subscribers, useful primarily to allow individual users to contact other users. Yellow pages allow businesses to advertise their presence to potential customers. While the white/yellow page distinction may remain the same, the differences between the telephone system and a national e-mail system will cause their implementation to differ.

For white pages, the telephone system offers a directory service baseline. Anyone can obtain basic contact information about any other subscriber (who has not explicitly chosen to be unlisted) by knowing only the subscriber's name and area code, which is a proxy for geographic location. It is the responsibility of each local phone company to maintain its own subscriber database.

This system works because each local phone company is a monopoly having access to information on all the subscribers in a given locality, allowing it to compile and publish a local database that is both complete (for each locality) and self-contained. Long distance companies allow their customers access to the directories of other localities for a fee.

The lack of a usable white pages is a problem in the Internet today. Two potential problems complicate establishing a white pages model in the context of an e-mail system. First, geography is no longer the only, or even the best, criterion by which one person would search for another. Within virtual communities, it may be desirable to list people's coordinates in a multidimensional database with extensive cross-references, including such nontraditional data as profession, organizational membership, and personal interests. Users could determine by which attributes they would like to be listed.

The second, and more important, problem is that the e-mail system is unlikely to be serviced by access providers that are local monopolies. If each access provider maintains only the directory database of its own relatively small number of subscribers, a way of combining directories so that every user has access to every directory must be found if the white pages are to be generally useful. Maintenance and synchronization become important technical considerations. A system modeled along the lines of the current domain name or gopher servers may be appropriate, i.e., each piece is separately maintained, yet the collection appears to the user as a seamless whole. One assumes provision must be made for "unlisted numbers" and other such means of assuring privacy.

The yellow pages model translates into the e-mail world nearly unchanged. The publishers of the current yellow pages (once again, the local telephone monopolies, but with increasing competition from other publishers) sell space to local businesses allowing them to advertise in a directory that is indexed by type of business. However, geography has always been a prime consideration.

In an e-mail system not organized along geographical lines, this distinction becomes problematic. For businesses selling "soft goods" (i.e., goods that can be delivered as digital streams through the e-mail system), geographical location is not a factor. Furthermore, in an age when anything can be delivered overnight, geography is generally much less important. Therefore, the issue becomes one of how large can the yellow pages become and who, if anyone, will publish and maintain a global yellow pages? Will the yellow pages be useful at all if it is not reasonably comprehensive?

It seems certain that several yellow pages will be set up by competing businesses and, over time, mergers and cooperative agreements will cause consolidation.

A standard for directories has been defined by the ITU as X.500. A good introductory description of X.500, with links to other sources, appears at http://www.earn.net/gnrt/x500.html. It states in part

> X.500 is a protocol which specifies a model for connecting local directory services to form one distributed global directory. Local databases hold and maintain a part of the global database and the directory information is made available via a local server called a Directory System Agent (DSA). The user perceives the entire directory to be accessible from the local server. X.500 also supports data management functions (addition, modification and deletion of entries).

> Each item (entry) in the X.500 directory describes one object (e.g., a person, a network resource, an organization) and has a unique identifier called a Distinguished Name (DN). The entry consists of a collection of attributes (e.g., for a person this might be last name, organization name, e-mail address). The entries are found by navigating through a Directory Information Tree (DIT). At the top of the tree is the World, which is subdivided at the next level into countries, and at the next into organizations. Information on people, resources, etc., is stored within organizations . . . .

> X.500 is an OSI (Open System Interconnection) protocol, named after the number of the CCITT (International Telegraph and Telephone Consultative Committee) Recommendation document containing its specification.

It appears that, as the main extant specification for a distributed directory system, X.500 will continue to emerge as the standard for implementing linked network directories.

System Architecture

We believe the essential principles of a system architecture within which universal e-mail services can flourish are best described in a recent publication by the Computer Science and Telecommunications Board (CSTB) of the National Research Council.[21] We call particular attention to its Chapter 2. Using their terminology, an open data network (ODN):

> is one that is capable of carrying information services of all kinds, from suppliers of all kinds, to customers of all kinds, across network service providers of all kinds, in a seamless accessible fashion. (P. 43.)

The CSTB report provides a number of challenging technical and organizational objectives for an ODN:

- technology independence,
- scalability,
- decentralized operation,
- appropriate architecture and supporting standards,
- security,
- flexibility in providing network services,
- accommodation of heterogeneity, and
- facilitation of accounting and cost recovery.

The above list is based primarily on successful experiences with the Internet architecture and policies to date, although it diverges in some details.

To implement an ODN, the CSTB describes a four-layer architecture as a conceptual model:[22]

---

[21]CSTB (1994).

[22]The reader should be aware that there is also an International Standards Organization (ISO) Open Systems Interconnection (OSI) seven-level architecture model. Its layers are physical, data link, network, transport, session, presentation, application. See, for example, Rose (1989), section 2.3.

1. *Bearer Service.* At the lowest level, there is an abstract bit-level transport service that implements a specified range of qualities of service to support. At this level, "bits are bits, and nothing more."[23] This bearer service resides on a network technology substrate, which may comprise a variety of communication links (copper, fiber, microwave) and switches (packet or ATM switches, store-and-forward switches, circuit switches).

2. *Transport Layer.* Services at this level typically include reliable, sequenced delivery, flow control, and end-point connection establishment. Also included are conventions for the format of data being transported across the network.

3. *Middleware.* These functions are a toolkit for application implementors. Such tools would include file system support, privacy protection, authentication and other security functions, storage repositories, name servers, and directory services of other types.

4. *Applications.* At this level resides e-mail, airline reservations systems, interactive education programs, etc.

The bearer service is central for an ODN. The CSTB report argues that services at this level must be priced separately from the higher-level services so that higher-level services can be implemented by providers different from those of the bearer service. The bearer service must also be independent of any specific technology choice. The authors remark that "The [Internet Protocol]'s decoupling from specific technologies is one of the keys to the success of the Internet, and this lesson should not be lost in designing the [ODN]."[24]

The relationship among these levels, and examples of the services provided by each, are captured in the book's Figure 2.1, which provides examples of services at each layer. The "hourglass shape" is meant to indicate the relative sparseness of services and protocols at each level (see Figure 3.1).

Note that portions of a universal e-mail service are "middleware" (e.g., directories, connection services) and other portions are "applications." With a proper ODN architecture, a universal e-mail

---

[23]CSTB (1994), p. 47.

[24]CSTB (1994), p. 54.

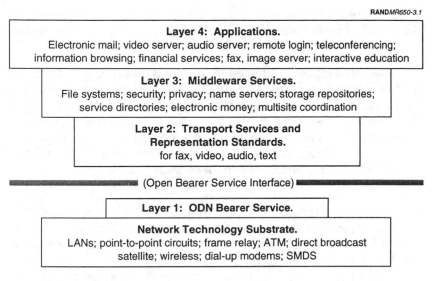

RAND*MR650-3.1*

Layer 4: Applications.
Electronic mail; video server; audio server; remote login; teleconferencing;
information browsing; financial services; fax, image server; interactive education

Layer 3: Middleware Services.
File systems; security; privacy; name servers; storage repositories;
service directories; electronic money; multisite coordination

**Layer 2: Transport Services and
Representation Standards.**
for fax, video, audio, text

(Open Bearer Service Interface)

Layer 1: ODN Bearer Service.

Network Technology Substrate.
LANs; point-to-point circuits; frame relay; ATM; direct broadcast
satellite; wireless; dial-up modems; SMDS

SOURCE: CSTB (1994), Figure 2.1.

Figure 3.1—A Four-Layer Model for the Open Data Network

service can be independent of particular network technology substrates, such as telcos, satellite, cable, and microwave.

The "pinched middle" of the hourglass shape in Figure 3.1 is also consistent with a point made repeatedly by an expert consultant in e-mail technologies, Einar Stefferud. He argues that in decentralized systems such as nationwide e-mail provision, it is essential to have simplicity at the core of the system (e.g., particularly in the transport layer), with whatever complexity is necessary pushed to the "edges" of the system (e.g., in the application layer, residing in desktop PCs).[25] The Internet community's adoption of MIME (Multipurpose Internet Mail Extensions)[26] for multipurpose mail is a case in point in proper use of this paradigm: All that is required for MIME's use by two correspondents is their use of MIME-compatible software in

---

[25]Stefferud (1995).

[26]MIME is described by RFC 1521, which is available on the Web at http://ds.internic.net/rfc/rfc1521.txt. This RFC is updated by RFC 1590, which is accessible similarly. See also Borenstein (1993). In addition to its other features, MIME was designed to be compatible with both the Internet's mail system and X.400.

their computers (at the "edges"). No change whatsoever is needed in the "core" of e-mail transmission on the Internet (i.e., use of the basic SMTP protocol).

The interested reader is directed to the CSTB report in its entirety for further details on an appropriate architecture for nationwide (or global) service such as universal access to e-mail. The report captures the best of what has been learned from the Internet experience, generalizing it as needed for more commercial and robust applications. It also delineates the key roles that government, industry, and other players can provide within an evolving services system based on an open architecture in which no one provider is dominant.

A recent white paper developed by the XIWT, based at CNRI in Reston, Virginia, also addresses an architectural framework for the NII (XIWT, 1995a). It contains conclusions and recommendations similar to those above but chooses to describe an architectural framework in three layers: physical infrastructure, enabling services, and applications. It argues that each layer must be considered from three related aspects: functionality, trust, and control. This white paper is apparently the first of a planned series on NII architecture. Persons interested in this topic should consider monitoring the XIWT web site (http://www.cnri.reston.va.us/xiwt) for updated postings.

This section has concentrated on physical infrastructure and software, but it is important to remember that a "service infrastructure" is equally important for success of universal access to e-mail. Chapters Four and Five provide more information on services required and the market dynamics involved in providing them.

Security and Integrity Services[27]

Electronic mail is different from traditional mail, and direct application of methods used to alleviate security and privacy concerns about paper mail require alteration in the e-mail environment. What measures must be taken for e-mail to provide a level of trust at least as great as the public's confidence in the U.S. Postal Service (USPS)?

---

[27]This subsection was written by Mark Gabriele, based on an extended outline provided by Willis H. Ware.

Before considering these measures, however, it is useful to clarify some terminology. These definitions are taken from Ware (1993):

- *Confidentiality*—a status accorded to information to indicate that it is sensitive for stated reasons, that it must be protected, and that access to it must be controlled.

- *Privacy (informational privacy or data privacy)*—a broad term referring to the utilization, sometimes even exploitation, of information about people for various purposes. It is an information-use issue, although the word is sometimes used loosely as a synonym for confidentiality or even secrecy.

- *Security*—the totality of safeguards in a computer-based information system that protects both it and its information against some defined threat, and limits access to the system and its data to authorized users in accordance with an established policy. Hence, system security contributes to the assurance of confidentiality, and to conformance with access restrictions, and is obviously a precursor for honoring privacy restrictions.

Differences Between Postal and E-Mail. In considering security, integrity of messages, and so on, some relevant differences between postal and electronic mail are the following:

Legal Status. USPS mail is protected by a number of different legal safeguards. Postal statutes, case law, and long experience all reinforce each other and the concept of paper mail as a virtually inviolate and safe method of transmitting information. For example, the USPS and its agents cannot legally divulge enveloped mail to any third party, except as may be specified by a court order or federal search warrant. No such statement can be made about e-mail at the present time. Case law provides methods for the use of USPS mail for legally binding commercial transactions. The only statute directed at providing some legal protection for e-mail is the Electronic Communications Privacy Act, which falls far short of the extensive coverage provided by the postal statutes. There is almost no case law establishing a framework for e-mail as a commercial medium.

Infinite Duplicability and Monitoring. An unlimited number of identical copies of any electronic message can be produced. Such copies could be made invisibly, by unknown parties, and very selectively. At present, very few e-mail systems incorporate the analog of a "sealed envelope" for mail, leaving the contents of the e-mail message legible at all stages of message transit. Even if the message contents are not legible (e.g., because the sender had encrypted the text of a message), the e-mail message is marked with the sender and the recipient addresses, allowing a third party to monitor the traffic to or from a specific individual. When performed by the USPS, this is referred to as a "mail cover" and is carried out only with proper administrative authorization. There is no effective difference between performing a "mail cover" and tracing the sender of each item of e-mail addressed to an individual; however, there is a tremendous difference in the level of effort required to do the job.

Ability to Identify the Sender. In conducting commerce via mailed communications, it is particularly important to establish and verify the identity of the sender. Recipients of USPS mail can recognize either the signature of the sender or the letterhead on the paper or can obtain partial assurance from the return address or postmark. In e-mail, there is no signature or letterhead in the traditional sense. Instead, a cryptographic technique called a "digital signature" is sometimes used to provide near-perfect assurance that the person who claims to have sent an electronic message actually did send it, if both the sender and the recipient agree in advance to use this method. Most current e-mail systems provide some information about the originator of the message; however, this information is not necessarily reliable and can be tampered with.

Because e-mail is unlikely to be provided to all as a free service, there may need to be some (as yet undetermined) electronic equivalent of postage.[28] (See the discussion of costs in Chapter Four.) This could take the form of an account against which charges are accrued and billing is performed, or a paid-in-advance service similar to the "farecards" in use on some transit systems. Such accounting systems

---

[28]However, simple e-mail riding on top of other services may be "too cheap to meter" and bundled in at a fixed low monthly net access rate, therefore not requiring the accounting mechanisms described in this paragraph. In addition, some services have recently been announced that plan to provide free e-mail in conjunction with advertising. See Juno at http://www.juno.com and Freemark at http://www.freemark.com.

may provide strong evidence regarding the sender of a given message, but the recipient cannot have much confidence in that information, because standards for identification and authentication vary widely from system to system and because the message may have been altered either at the source or in transit.

Given the above uncertainties, electronic commerce and other activities requiring authentication and integrity of messages will initially be conducted within electronic "enclaves" in which users share common systems, authentication mechanisms, and so forth.

Integrity. The sealed envelope in which paper mail is contained gives a reasonably high level of assurance that the contents are exactly what was sent. Most e-mail systems do not provide an analogous mechanism, although encryption schemes can be used among consenting parties to ensure integrity of message contents.

In summary, as typically implemented, e-mail systems lack strong safeguards to ensure the confidentiality of message contents, uniform mechanisms to establish the authenticity of the sender, a commonly accepted way to ensure integrity of the message, anything to prevent the unauthorized duplication and sending of a message to other parties, and features resembling any of the special USPS mail services (e.g., certified, insured, return receipt).[29] Nonetheless, e-mail is widely accepted by a broad class of people who use it for many business and personal purposes. Further, except for the very limited use of cryptographic techniques, e-mail systems today operate quite successfully on faith, good will, and mutual trust.

Privacy. The difficulties inherent in current e-mail systems, described above, involve a threat posed by a malevolent third party external to the electronic mail discourse. This third party may wish to read private mail, divert it, forge it, etc. However, distinct from such a threat, there are issues relating to the privacy of e-mail communications and how these communications are treated by their recipi-

---

[29]The USPS plans to introduce relevant electronic services, however. A March 1995 briefing on USPS "Electronic Commerce Services" listed the following products and services as ones they intend to offer: (1) public key certificate authority management, and (2) electronic correspondence services: Postmark and Seal, Archive, Authenticate. The briefing has been given to various groups by Robert A.F. Reisner, Vice President for Technology Applications, USPS.

ent. These privacy issues involve how information freely given by a person in the context of a written communication may be used.

Case law has established that an item mailed via traditional USPS mail is legally given to the recipient by the sender as soon as it is placed into the mailbox; that is, senders relinquish their rights to ownership of the physical items (e.g., the paper on which letters are written). The author of a message does not relinquish all rights to the words written on a piece of paper and the order in which they are arranged; that is protected to some degree by copyright law.

Electronic mail sends the message without sending the paper. The exact applicability of existing statutes to this new paradigm is uncertain; however, presumably the recipient is free to share the item with anyone, subject to legal constraints such as copyright, defamation, or violation of trade secrets. While there is no specific privacy law broadly governing how all received USPS mail can be used or shared with others, many laws constrain divulgence to third parties based on the content of the material. There are also social customs and general expectations of personal behavior that combine to suppress privacy concerns about USPS mail. It should also be noted that many persons use e-mail through the facilities of their employer, and many employers assume the right to monitor and restrict such uses—sometimes as part of a written corporate e-mail policy—for example, restricting use to valid business purposes. Such policies are an additional factor in a user's choice of location for e-mail access, as discussed above.

Electronic mail, however, implies a ready ability for the recipient to duplicate, share, or publish for the world to see anything that is sent. Because of this, there may be a latent privacy issue for e-mail that must be addressed to support its wide acceptance. The recipient of a traditional letter is simply not able to press a button and make the contents of that letter known to millions of people, as is entirely possible with e-mail.

Additional considerations and discussion of case law regarding privacy and intellectual property rights in electronic media may be found in Branscomb (1994).

Anonymity. Anonymous remailers are unique to the e-mail environment. These services accept an incoming message (which contains information indicating its originator), remove all identifying characteristics from that message, and remail it to the intended recipient. We are unaware of the existence of such services for postal mail; people apparently feel sufficiently comfortable with the anonymity achieved by more conventional methods (e.g., sending letters without return addresses).

With e-mail, however, there is no convenient and entirely reliable method of concealing the identity of the sender without using an anonymizing service. Many such services exist today, usually operated as a public service by a privacy-conscious individual or group. These anonymous remailers can play a useful role: They allow people who might feel stigmatized or uncomfortable by being personally identified with the contents of their messages (e.g., victims of sexual abuse or harassment, whistleblowers).

Some e-mail anonymous remailers discard the records of incoming messages as they arrive, so a reply cannot be sent using records of the remailer. Most anonymous servers currently operate as "two-way," in that they are able to establish a link between in- and outbound messages. This requires keeping a database, so the users must trust the remailer—and the remailer operator—not to reveal their identity.

The legal status of anonymous remailers—what records they must keep, what information they must furnish to law enforcement authorities—is completely unsettled. In at least one instance, the operator of an anonymous remailer cooperated with law enforcement and revealed the identity of a single user of the service. Situations like this become especially obscure legally when the anonymous remailer is in a foreign country under a different legal jurisdiction.

What Is Needed? This discussion leads to a set of questions rather than answers: Are the following technical features essential in an electronic mail system having wide societal appeal and acceptance:

- an electronic "envelope" (with verifiable "postmark" and date/time stamp)?
- digital signatures?
- a feature ensuring the integrity of the message content?

The fact remains that electronic mail systems are widely used for many purposes today, and they run more or less successfully on trust and good faith. But there is no reason to believe that the status quo will prevail over the long term, when there is much wider use of e-mail by people who are less grounded in the traditions and etiquette of this unique communications medium, the scale factor of more users, increased sophistication of threats from computer "crackers," and much greater use of the Internet and e-mail for "electronic commerce." For example, many initiatives are under way to provide secure commercial transactions, and even "electronic money," on the Internet;[30] these initiatives will inevitably lead to additional facilities for security, privacy, and authentication of e-mail and other transactions in cyberspace.

Assuming that some action must be taken to improve upon the security and privacy offered by electronic mail systems that exist today, policymakers must determine the priority in which the technical features noted above must be included in any officially sanctioned e-mail system. As it happens, using currently available technology to implement an electronic envelope or digital signature can also provide assurance that the integrity of the message has not been compromised (or, more accurately, that if the integrity of the message has been compromised, it will be immediately evident to the recipient).

THE TECHNICAL "BOTTOM LINE"

The primary message of this chapter is that *there are no fundamental technical barriers to the provision of universal access to e-mail within the United States.* In particular, the standards that have evolved over 15 years within the ARPAnet/Internet for electronic mail (SMTP, DNS, MIME) provide a robust, proven backbone for a set of core services adequate for the evolution of a nationwide e-mail system.

Other conclusions and recommendations that have been mentioned above are summarized with those of other chapters in Chapter Seven.

---

[30]As one example of many recent articles, see Holland and Cortese (1995).

Chapter Four

ECONOMIC ISSUES

Bridger M. Mitchell, Padmanabhan Srinagesh[1]

This chapter examines the economic characteristics of e-mail service and the regulatory and policy issues that are raised by universal access. Economic factors strongly condition the unregulated development of communication services. Understanding their influence and direction is essential in determining the potential need for public intervention and formulating appropriate policies to promote effective, widespread e-mail service.

Our approach is to examine e-mail as part of a larger communications market. For this purpose, e-mail is considered to be a service that allows any location with a valid e-mail address to exchange information, in accordance with a common e-mail standard, with any other location with a valid e-mail address. The key elements defining e-mail are the set of reachable addresses and the permitted forms of information exchange; see also our definition of e-mail and universal access in Chapter Three.

The e-mail market is young, fast-changing, and growing rapidly. In the first section, we examine this market's basic characteristics, comparing them with more mature communications services and the universal service issues they have faced. In the next sections, we take up the particular demand and supply features of e-mail service.

---

[1]The views expressed in this report are not necessarily those of Dr. Srinagesh's employer, Bellcore. Nor are the views expressed in other chapters of this report necessarily those of Dr. Srinagesh.

Although the e-mail market is evolving rapidly, we examine recent trends to venture tentative predictions of the emerging equilibrium, industry structure, and range of supply prices for basic service. This leads to considering potential market failures that may need to be addressed by policymakers.

THE E-MAIL MARKETPLACE

To focus on the distinctive characteristics of e-mail, we first review the development of two communications technologies that have achieved nearly universal levels of service—the telephone and (within business) facsimile.

Telephone Service

Alexander Graham Bell was granted his first patent in March 1876, and the first Bell Telephone Company was formed the next year. From this beginning, a worldwide communications system made up of public telephone networks has developed in four distinguishable phases.

Launching a New Service. In its initial years, local exchange businesses linked a community of business subscribers within small central-city areas. From a single telephone, only subscribers to that local network were reachable. Network operators competed side by side for subscribers, and businesses with broad communities of interest had to maintain separate telephones for each network to reach most of their correspondents.

Widening the Network. Local telephone exchanges began to interconnect with distant cities, extending their reach by long-distance lines. Competition between local networks disappeared as exchanges were merged or acquired by AT&T.

Deepening the Network. With nationwide connectivity achieved, federal policy (in the Communications Act of 1934) proclaimed the goal of universal service and telephone companies emphasized expanding the number of subscribers and extending service to high-cost and remote areas.[2] Monopoly supply, regulated by government commissions, guided developments. Policies, such as geographic averaging of rates and the residual pricing of the monthly charge paid by residential consumers, were used to promote universal service.

Restructuring for Economic Efficiency. Competition policy led to the breaking up of AT&T into separate long-distance and local businesses in 1984. Price structures that favored broad customer classes were replaced by programs to assist marginal subscribers, and barriers to entry of competitors and new technologies were dismantled.

The costs of telephone service in the unified Bell system were almost entirely in the network infrastructure, the distribution cables and local switching facilities in particular. With these large fixed costs and other large network costs common to supplying both business and residence service, the industry had many elements of a natural monopoly—wherein the costs of production by a single firm fall below the total costs of two or more firms. At the same time, customers placed widely different values on obtaining service. These factors together allowed telephone companies to charge systematically higher prices for business service and for long-distance calls to keep basic residential rates low. For decades this practice was the cornerstone of the broadly successful universal service policy guiding the operation of the telephone network.

Fax Service

Modern facsimile service provides a different example of a widely used communications service that is nearly universal in the business sector.[3] Fax is a value-added service provided via the telephone infrastructure. No additional network infrastructure or network service is required. Instead, the service depends on users having compatible fax terminal equipment from which to transmit and receive

---

[2]The notion of universal service has evolved with changing circumstances from maximum interconnectivity among independent network providers to maximum penetration of the potential market. This evolution is discussed further below.

[3]To date, only 6 percent of households have fax capabilities, a much lower penetration than the 27 percent of households with computers (*Times Mirror*, 1994).

images over regular telephone lines. With the telephone network in place, the development of widespread fax service depends only on acquisition of fax terminals by consumers and standardization of manufacturing protocols. The importance of the telephone network as a critical factor in the success of fax cannot be overstated. Alexander Bain invented the fax machine in 1843, one year before telegraph services were deployed, but the service was not widely used. According to one observer: "Since the phone wasn't invented until 33 years later, the system proved to have limited appeal" (EMMS, 1994, p. 3).

Common protocol usage has evolved through market experience. Standardization, while assisted by international technical organizations, is not regulated. Elements of the fax service continue to evolve. Terminals and protocols provide for higher-speed and finer-quality image transmission, while maintaining compatibility with the most widely used basic standards. Service providers develop mailbox and broadcast capabilities. Manufacturers have added elemental scanning and transmission capabilities to personal computers, printers, and wireless notebooks. These developments are simultaneously extending the fax network's market penetration and broadening its usefulness and value to consumers.

Both telephone and fax are also platforms for additional services. The telephone system, under development for more than 100 years, now supports data transmission, fax, and switched video. The fax network has also expanded, from user-attended bilateral exchange of single sheets to unattended document exchange and broadcast distribution. Fax can be transported over data networks as well as voice telephone networks.

Economic Characteristics of E-Mail

What are some salient economic characteristics of e-mail?[4]

- E-mail, like fax, is supplied by an overlay network service that depends on other communications infrastructure for transport

---

[4]Cost characteristics and most demand characteristics are discussed separately below. This discussion concentrates on relevant general factors.

and routing. Current e-mail systems depend on packet-data networks and frequently use telephone lines for local access. E-mail access can also be provided over cellular or other wireless networks, and over cable television cables.

- Most e-mail systems use "packet switching" technology that makes efficient use of network capacity. As a consequence, network use is quite cheap.

- An individual e-mail transmission is one-way, communication need not occur in real time, and messages are storable. As a result there may be less of a peak-load problem than in telephony.

- E-mail user communities are geographic, but only to a degree. Business demand for e-mail is initially concentrated on internal communication and is particularly useful for messaging between geographically separated plants and offices. Business demand extends next to communications with suppliers and then to customer relationships. Consumer demand is oriented toward communities that share common interests, with only limited geographic emphasis; some of the "wired community" developments discussed in Chapter Five, such as LatinoNet, exemplify this. Increased demand to communicate outside the organization—growth in collaborative ventures as well as links to suppliers and customers—raises the value of interconnection of e-mail systems and the use of common protocols and addressing standards.

The addressing and message protocols of basic e-mail service are developing into a platform for additional communications services (see Chapter Three). E-mail "user-agent" programs can automate the search for and retrieval of information from remote databases. Besides point-to-point communication, e-mail is well suited to broadcast distribution of messages and electronic conferencing. Multimedia (audio, video) components can be included in, or appended to, e-mail messages.

Alternative Market Structures

The supply of a network communications service is compatible with several quite different organizations of the market. Public ownership and operation of the network has been the rule for postal services and was widely used outside the United States for telephone services until quite recently. In the United States, telephone service was begun by competing private companies, competition that eventually proved unsustainable. The emergent territorial monopoly structure, dominated by AT&T, realized the advantages of economies of scale and the balance of political power. Then in the 1970s and 1980s, technological changes, procompetitive public policies, growth in demand, and almost full penetration again made multiple networks possible. Today, the U.S. telecommunications sector is firmly on the path to open competition.

Technological and regulatory changes have driven the transformation from monopoly to competition. The cost structure of much of the pre-1970s telephone network had strong elements of natural monopoly. However, the existence of substantial economies of scale for producing telephone terminal equipment was doubtful and when that market was deregulated, the successful entry of a variety of suppliers marked the first step toward disintegration of the broader monopoly of network infrastructure.

Beginning in the 1950s, microwave radio proved a superior, lower-cost technology for long-distance transmission and greatly reduced the incumbent's scale and right-of-way advantages in intercity markets. By exploiting microwave technology, the newly formed Microwave Communications, Inc. (MCI) company became a powerful national competitor. More recently, fiber optics and digital switching have enabled new competitors to enter formerly monopoly markets. Competitive access providers such as Teleport and MFS connect large business locations in urban areas with the facilities of interexchange carriers, using fiber rings for high-speed data and telephone service. New wireless technologies, such as those envisioned by the newly licensed Personal Communications System (PCS) operators, and the development of telephony over cable television networks (described in Carroll, 1995) are likely to result in additional competition in the local exchange.

Procompetitive public policy developments have grown as technology has changed. Policy increasingly has recognized the economic benefits of competition when alternative communications technologies are available. As political power shifted from states to the federal government, the regulatory barriers facing new entrants have been lowered. Regulators have explicitly adopted competitive instruments in important cases. In 1995, the federal government conducted the first use of auctions to allocate radio frequency spectrum for personal communications systems.[5] Competitive procedures also have been used to encourage innovative approaches to common standards for advanced television equipment and protocols.

Telecommunications firms use many communication technologies to supply markets. Economies of scope and scale lead firms to integrate "vertically" in two separate dimensions—over two or more service layers (transport, switching, and provision of information services) and over hierarchical levels of network switching and control (local, long-distance, and international service). Similar economies provide incentives to integrate "horizontally" across geographic areas as well as across nonsubstitutable services such as cable TV distribution and switched-voice telephone services. The landscape of the local telecommunications sector is changing rapidly. Local and long-distance companies are racing to enter each others' markets, cable television operators are experimenting with switched telephone service and Internet access, and wireless suppliers are expanding into mobile data and fax messaging services (see Vogelsang and Mitchell, 1996).

Rules governing interconnection can affect the ways in which network service providers compete with one another. Consider, first, an entrant who obtains an interconnection agreement with the incumbent and supplies a technically comparable service. The incumbent and the entrant will offer the same reachability, and competition will likely focus on price and service quality (as measured, for example, by billing accuracy and refunds for billing errors). Next, consider a new supplier whose network is not connected to the incumbent's network. In this case, the entrant will have significantly less reach than the incumbent, and must offer a different product that will induce at least some consumers to buy its services in addition to the services of the incumbent. Producers of software that permits individuals with multimedia computers to talk to each other over the Internet fall in this category: Their customers can talk to each other

---

[5]This action finally introduced the economic efficiency advocated by Ronald Coase over 35 years ago (Coase, 1959).

but not to individuals who possess an ordinary phone. Although telephony over the Internet has begun to grow, it offers considerably less reach than the public switched telephone network. The main attraction of the software is that a few calls placed over the Internet (which charges most users a usage-independent fee) saves enough in phone charges to recover the cost of the software. In addition, the interface provided by computer-based telephony is preferred by some consumers to using the standard telephone.

In the case of e-mail and other services provided over virtual networks, some degree of competition is possible without interconnection. By subscribing to multiple networks, consumers can communicate with correspondents who are not members of the same e-mail system. In effect, users with multiple subscriptions can serve as e-mail gateways between unconnected systems. Where e-mail network providers offer service at low monthly fees and usage charges, these arrangements could persist in an equilibrium of less than fully interconnected systems.

It is clear that the terms and conditions of interconnection dictate the nature of competition and play a central role in the evaluation of the telecommunications market. Incumbent carriers initially argued that they could not supply the same quality of access to outsiders that they provide within their own network. Thus, MCI's first customers had to dial many extra digits to reach their supplier over the old Bell system, and it took over a decade and substantial investment in upgraded switching equipment to achieve equal access. Furthermore, after providing interconnection, incumbent carriers have often successfully charged high access prices that replace contributions lost to the entrants in the retail markets.

Does competition hinder universal service? In the telephone network, entry of new competitors has largely removed the opportunity to support low-price network access and subscription services by contributions from high-value services elsewhere in the network. If some services had made disproportionate contributions before competition had arrived, market entry would have forced a rebalancing of rates, lowering the prices of competitive services. The final effect could increase or decrease overall penetration.

Policies to promote universal telephone service have shifted from maintaining regulated monopolies and disproportionate contributions from some services to developing broader-based industry funds for use in targeted subsidy programs for defined classes of users.

To summarize this section: U.S. communications networks will be supplied by competing providers. Public policies to promote universal service, e-mail or otherwise, cannot be based on a monopoly model of a network.

Concepts of Universality

In modern usage, universal telephone service has come to mean *maximum penetration* of the potential market of all subscribers.[6] As discussed in Chapter One, this is the meaning we use throughout this report. This goal is often attributed to congressional intent in enacting the 1934 Communications Act, whose purpose is to

> make available, so far as possible, to all the people of the United States a rapid, efficient, Nation-wide, and world-wide wire and radio communication service with adequate facilities at reasonable charges.

Although the words "universal service" do not appear in the act, since 1934 federal and state regulators increasingly invoked the goal of universal service to justify policies that restricted competition and encouraged price structures that promoted maximum penetration (Mueller, 1993).

Where does e-mail fit in this picture? E-mail connectivity for basic text messaging is growing rapidly (see the section, below) and the transport infrastructures on which it travels are effectively universal. E-mail penetration is at a middle level for business users and quite

---

[6]In the expansionary phase of local telephone systems at the turn of the century, Theodore Vail first used the term "universal service" with respect to the telephone network in AT&T's 1907 annual report. Vail articulated the goal more explicitly in 1910 as one of *maximum connectivity*—enabling a telephone user, by subscribing to one network, to reach as many other telephones as possible (Vail, 1910).

small for households. The state of e-mail penetration in the United States is discussed more fully in Chapter Two.

DEMAND FOR E-MAIL SERVICE

This section first discusses the major segments of the e-mail market. We then take up two central features of the demand for e-mail: the network externality that affects demand and the relationship (complementarity and substitutability) between e-mail and other messaging and communications services.

Major Market Segments

Small businesses, large businesses, and households use e-mail to satisfy a range of messaging and communications needs. Until recently, large and medium-sized businesses with local area network (LAN)-based computing environments used e-mail primarily as a tool for internal communications and placed a premium on reliability, security, and confidentiality. According to one study, about 70 percent of all e-mail remains within a given work group, 20 percent is between different company locations, and only 10 percent is between different companies or individuals (EMMS, 1994, p. 79). Households continue to use e-mail as an adjunct to information services and not as a ubiquitous communications service. The needs of the different market segments vary, as do their willingness to pay. These differences are clearly revealed by data on subscription rates and prices.

Traditionally, most households have obtained e-mail connectivity from an on-line service provider. The four major on-line services— GEnie, America Online, Prodigy, and CompuServe—offer an e-mail box as part of their basic packages. In addition, all four now exchange e-mail with the Internet. Worldwide on-line subscriptions for these providers are summarized in Table 4.1.[7]

---

[7]For commercial e-mail accounts, monthly payments by subscribers presumably indicate active use or an option value of maintaining service. This is in contrast to noncommercial networks described in Chapter Five in which the number of active users may be considerably smaller than the number of subscriber accounts.

Table 4.1

Worldwide Subscriptions for Key E-Mail
Providers (in millions)

Provider	As of	
	12/31/94	3/31/95
CompuServe	2.66	2.8
America Online	1.5	2.2
Prodigy	1.2	1.3
GEnie	0.1	0.1

SOURCE: *MacWeek*, July 10, 1995.

Business users subscribe to some of these e-mail services (particularly CompuServe). The number of residential users was estimated at about 2.7 million in 1993 (Winther, 1994). As of March 1995, it is estimated that there were 6.7 million consumer mailboxes, with CompuServe, America Online, and Prodigy being the only providers with more than 1 million mailboxes (EMMS, April 3, 1995, p. 3). Each of those three services currently charge $9.95/month for the first five hours of use, then $2.95 for each additional hour, with some discounts for frequent users (Clark, 1995).

Six major providers of e-mail services target businesses: GE Information Services, IBM Mail, SprintMail, MCIMail, AT&TMail and CompuServe. The worldwide annual revenue from e-mail (almost all from the companies listed above) is estimated to be about $568 million per year in 1993 and growing at 17 percent per year (Michel, 1994, p. 23).

The computed price for representative e-mail messages varies from a high of 27.5 cents per thousand characters (GE Information Services) to 2 cents per thousand characters (CompuServe) (EMMS, 1994, p. 183). The average mailbox generates about $20 per month (Michel, 1994, p. 24).

Network Externalities and Interconnection

E-mail shares an important economic characteristic with a larger family of electronic messaging and communications services: Call and network externalities are an important determinant of demand (Mitchell and Vogelsang, 1991, pp. 55–61). *Call externalities* arise because a communication between two parties is typically initiated by one party, whose decision is guided by its private benefit. But benefits (which in some cases could be negative) are conferred (or inflicted) on the other party. In this case an individual's decision about using a communications service may not be consistent with maximum social welfare because the individual benefits of decisionmakers do not coincide with social benefits. *Network externalities* arise because an individual's decision to join a network is typically guided only by the benefit to that individual of communicating with others on the network. This private benefit differs from the social benefit, which includes the benefits others receive from being able to communicate with the individual in question. The traditional view is that these externalities will result in networks that are too small in comparison to the optimal (social welfare-maximizing) network (Mitchell and Vogelsang, 1991, p. 55). The lack of interconnection among early e-mail services (discussed below) likely resulted in virtual networks that were too small.

Until quite recently, neither the interoperability of LAN-based e-mail offered by different vendors nor the interconnectivity of wide area network (WAN)-based e-mail systems could be assumed. E-mail networks were disconnected islands, largely because important users did not conceive of e-mail as the basis for ubiquitous public switched telephone network (PSTN)-like connectivity. As a consequence, the addresses (or people) that could be reached by any individual depended on the address/service provider of that individual: CompuServe's customers could exchange e-mail with one another, but not with the customers of Prodigy.

Early interconnections among public e-mail providers resulted from a patchwork of bilateral agreements. One of the first was the link between MCIMail and CompuServe, established in February 1986 (EMMS, 1994, p. 207). In February 1993, the original proprietary interconnection protocol (MEP2) was replaced with an X.400 gateway, and CompuServe eliminated its surcharge for messages sent to MCIMail users. While details of interconnection continued to evolve, the fact of interconnection soon became unremarkable. In March 1993, according to one report: "AT&T EasyLink . . . interconnects with seven additional Administrative Management Domains (ADMDs), and it does not even bother to ask for press attention." (EMMS, 1994, p. 196). The proliferation of interconnection arrangements increases the value of e-mail to the network service providers' customers through an increase in the reach of their networks.

The e-mail market has continued moving from a fragmented to an integrated model. The primary force responsible for this change has been the growth of the Internet, which clearly demonstrated the benefits of the integrated model. The Internet concept originated independently at RAND (Baran et al., 1964) and at Bolt, Beranek and Newman (BBN) in the early 1960s, took seed as an Advanced Research Projects Agency (ARPA) project in the late 1960s, and transitioned to commercial status by the early 1990s. As mentioned in Chapter One, Lynch and Rose (1993) provide a brief history of the Internet.

The key feature of the Internet is openness. This is partly a matter of technological capability and partly a matter of business necessity. On the technical side, the Internet was designed to run over a variety of underlying network substrates and from the outset served an important "gateway function" (as described by Bunn and David, 1988) that allowed communication across incompatible lower-level protocols. On the business side, the relatively low cost of entry (discussed below) together with a liberal interconnection policy developed under the National Science Foundation's (NSF's) leadership ensured that no one firm could capture a large market share. As all network users were accustomed to full connectivity, at least among university sites that dominated the early Internet, competing Internet service providers (ISPs) could not disconnect from other ISPs and retain customers.

The interconnection of commercial e-mail services with the Internet was initially accomplished by Commercial Mail Relay (CMR), a gateway operated by the Information Sciences Institute in Marina del Rey, California. CMR interconnected the Internet with MCIMail, Tele-mail and DIALCOM (NNSC Report on the Internet, Section 5.20). Currently, as discussed in Chapter Three, the Internet has become the de facto means of interconnecting a variety of e-mail systems.

To summarize: E-mail services have moved quite rapidly to maximize connectivity. Interconnection to the Internet is now a requirement for any service provider who wishes to serve the mass market. Thus, the market has largely solved the problem of universal service, when it is defined as maximum reach/connectivity. As a consequence, consumers do not currently have to ask: "How many e-mail networks should I join?" Instead, they can ask: "Should I get e-mail service, and if so, which provider should I use?" This latter decision may still be influenced by network externalities, and hence the free market may form networks that are too small. It is also possible that future entrants will not be fully interconnected, and public policy may need to address the fact that universal service may require subscription to multiple networks. Thus, unregulated markets may on their own produce insufficient penetration. Below we address the policy issue of public interventions to extend service to additional users.

Substitutes and Complements

Electronic mail is part of a spectrum of complementary and competing communications and messaging services, but with some unique features. These services include telephone calls, faxes, voice mail, and letters (regular mail and courier services). The market for electronic services in this group is growing substantially.

Fax phone calls in the United States accounted for $11 billion[8] per year in 1993 and $25 billion worldwide (EMMS, 1994). In the United States, nearly 20 percent of all business telephone lines are connected to a fax machine. Enhanced fax services (Fax Mailbox, Automatic Retry, Never Busy Fax, and Fax Broadcasting) are small by comparison to basic fax calls and accounted for $15 million to small businesses and residences in 1993 (Winther, 1994).

Voice messaging services to small businesses and residences generated about $220 million in 1993 and are projected to generate about $1 billion in 1998 (Winther, 1994, p. 2).

There is some evidence that patterns of substitution may be unexpected. It might be thought that e-mail, voice mail and fax are close substitutes: All three are noninteractive, store-and-forward applica-

---

[8]Unless otherwise noted, the dollar amounts in this section represent gross revenue to service providers resulting from these specific services.

tions where real-time response is not critical. However, an early (1986) study cited by Huber (1987, p. 11.2) suggested that 55 percent of e-mail is diverted from the telephone, 10 percent from Telex, and 5 percent each from first class mail, courier services, and other electronic transmission techniques. The remaining 20 percent represents new demand. Whether these patterns are found in the current market is not known, but the growth of answering machines and voice mail suggest that telephone calls often turn out to be store-and-forward messages, for which e-mail might be an acceptable substitute.

While we did not discover any empirical studies that directly address the substitutability and/or complementarity of voice, e-mail, and fax services, commercial initiatives over the past few years suggest a strong complementarity between the services (Markus, Bikson, El Shinnaway, and Soe, 1992; Sproull and Kiesler, 1991b; Bikson and Eveland, 1990; and Culnan and Markus, 1987). Traditionally, fax machines communicated with other fax machines, telephones communicated with other telephones, and e-mail users communicated with e-mail boxes. Each service had a reachability determined by the penetration rate of that service. Interoperability across services would increase the reachability of each service and increase the value of each service to every user. This is a natural consequence of the network and call externalities described above. Subsequently, several vendors have announced initiatives to provide integrated service. For example, AT&T and Lotus have formed a strategic alliance to integrate AT&T's INTUITY AUDIX voice messaging system with both cc:Mail and Lotus Notes. The system will contain a text-to-speech synthesizer to permit e-mail to be read to the user by a mechanical voice (Probe Research, 1994). Lotus is also developing an integrated voice/e-mail messaging system with Siemens; the joint effort will be based on Siemens' Phone-mail, Lotus Notes, and cc:Mail (EMMS, February 6, 1995, p. 4).

Gateways connecting fax and e-mail services have long been a staple feature of the high-end e-mail systems (such as SprintMail and MCIMail) aimed at business users. More recently, fax/e-mail gateways have been demonstrated on the Internet. Carl Malamud and Marshall Rose were responsible for the first implementation (http://www.town.hall.org). A current version of their approach can be found at http://bond.edu.au/Fax/faq.html (Bond University in Australia). Numerous commercial implementations also exist, including InterFax and FAXiNET (http://www.awa.com/faxinet/).

Further off in the future is unified messaging, which uses a single mailbox for voice, fax, data, and video; manages all messages with common tools; and permits retrieval from the user's terminal of choice. Applied Voice Technology (AVT) has described its vision of unified messaging, which allows for seamless integration of the four major media (EMMS, 1994, p. 361). AVT currently sells products that offer limited integration of voice mail, fax, and e-mail through a single mailbox accessible through a graphic user interface (GUI) on a PC.

Developments in e-mail technology reinforce this trend toward convergence. The initial standard for Internet e-mail was the SMTP, which supports aliasing and mailing lists, both of which can be used to provide multicast service to the users. (See also Chapter Three.) Although SMTP limits the content of the message to simple American Standards for Information Interchange (ASCII) characters, this restriction may not be as prohibitive as it appears: uuencode and binhex formats, and Postscript files, can be included in SMTP messages. (These formats permit binary files including images to be sent as SMTP mail.) In addition, the MIME standard permits Internet mail to contain multimedia data including image, audio, and video.[9] Although not all gateways among e-mail systems currently support various encoding and MIME protocols, the SMTP and MIME protocols form an appropriate basis for universal e-mail systems supporting multimedia messages. See Chapter Three for more details on these protocols and standards.

In sum: E-mail has evolved from a limited role as an adjunct to information services for households and an extension of LAN-based intracorporate communications to a broadly accessible messaging and communications service that is more like the public telephone network. Technological developments point toward the convergence of previously distinct messaging and communications services into a closely integrated communications environment. The implications for universal service are twofold: Electronic messaging service will

---

[9]MIME is compliant with both the SMTP and X.400 addressing standards.

likely be supplied by several technologies, each capable of providing widely available, addressable message exchange. A universal service policy can be geared to a common-denominator service: plain text message exchange to and from the Internet (or possibly Web browsing as a basic standard) in the near to mid term, and access to a ubiquitous information infrastructure offering voice, video, and data services in the longer term.

THE SUPPLY OF E-MAIL SERVICES

E-mail is a communication and computer service provided over two large infrastructures that support many communications services and computer applications. The communications infrastructure includes the public switched telephone network, public data networks (such as the Internet), and cable television networks. Other services that use this infrastructure include voice, fax, and video communications and broadcast entertainment. The computer infrastructure that is used to support e-mail consists of many terminal devices, including individual personal computers and LANs connecting members of organizations. This infrastructure is also used for database, spreadsheet, and word processing applications and for computer games.

The two infrastructures vary in some important dimensions. Many users share large portions of the communications network, which spreads the cost of infrastructure investment. In contrast, many elements of the computing infrastructure do not possess this property, and the cost of an individual user's computer hardware and software is high. However, households use PCs for a variety of purposes (such as computing, communications, education, and entertainment), and users may find that the incremental cost of any one application is small.

E-mail, as it is currently constituted, also requires a service infrastructure. Individuals need to have mail stored for them when they are not on-line, they must have their outgoing messages correctly routed, and they need access to a directory of addresses. This infrastructure, which is supplied by the firms described above, is the focus of this section. Brief consideration is given to terminal devices, since their cost may be an important barrier to widespread penetration of e-mail.

Given the joint use of the communications, computer, and e-mail service infrastructures, the difference between the total cost of supporting all the communications and computing needs of an end user and the incremental costs of providing e-mail can be substantial. While the fixed cost associated with the communications and computing infrastructure is extremely large, the incremental cost of providing e-mail (the service infrastructure) may be relatively small.

The relative importance of fixed and variable costs of e-mail provision vary among service providers and vary with the type of customer being served. These variations are captured in some of the published data reviewed below.

The Costs of Traditional E-Mail Service Providers

In 1987, e-mail was used primarily by business customers. "While entering the office automation market would require heavy capital expenditures, adding software to provide an electronic mail capability in existing computer products would require only modest expenditures" (Huber, 1987, p. 11.1). Huber's study supports the notion that there are substantial economies of scope between e-mail provision and other computer-based services. It reports that a typical e-mail service bureau would have the cost structure shown in Table 4.2, at two different information system capacity levels.

Table 4.2

Cost Breakdown in a Typical E-Mail Service
Bureau

	Message Volume at	
Input	25% of Capacity	100% of Capacity
Computer hardware and maintenance	59%	40%
Software	12%	8%
Packet networks	10%	22%
Sales/marketing	10%	21%
Local access lines	5%	2%
Support/other	3%	7%

SOURCE: Huber (1987), Table EM.6, p. 11.16.

The computer hardware, access lines, underlying packet transport, and sales and marketing, which account for more than 85 percent of all service bureau costs, potentially can be shared with other services provided by that firm, generating scope economies for the e-mail provider. In the short run, the legacy of past investment and integration decisions will be an important factor in determining scope economies. Over time, the fundamental economies of scope will determine the optimal form of investment and the degree of integration. Huber points out that companies like GEISCO, that began as computer time-sharing firms, use the same hardware to provide e-mail and generate economies of scope through the efficient sharing of computer hardware. AT&TMail and MCIMail, which started out as e-mail services, used dedicated computer hardware and did not obtain these economies of scope at that time. Thus, different firms realized different degrees of scope economies. However, fundamental economies of scope (deriving from the joint use of hardware and other inputs) has led to greater integration over time. AT&T EasyLink, for example, currently offers a variety of enhanced messaging services, electronic data interchange (EDI) services and information services (Gonzalez, 1995, p. 179).

For a provider that owns the underlying network (e.g., MCI), the incremental cost of the packet transport would be close to zero if the packet network were underused, and the sunk cost would be substantial. For an unintegrated provider of e-mail (such as CompuServe) that leases facilities on which it built its packet transport network, the incremental cost of transport would be determined by the prices of leased lines and packet switches. To the extent that lines can be leased at large volume and term discounts, the cost of transport may look more like a fixed cost than a variable cost. In contrast, e-mail providers who purchase packet transport from value-added networks (VANs) will have a cost structure that reflects the price structure of packet transport. These prices have traditionally not offered steep volume and term discounts, and so e-mail providers in this category have a greater proportion of variable costs, compared with providers in the other two categories. This suggests that owners of facilities-based networks may have greater economies of scale (high fixed and low incremental costs) than owners of VANs, and VAN owners may have greater economies of scale than purchasers of packet transport. These cost advantages of facilities-based networks have led to expansion through greater vertical integration, often through acquisitions. For example, AT&T acquired the largest provider of e-mail services, EasyLink, from Western Union in 1991.

The economies of scope in marketing and sales costs arise when providers bundle distinct services into packages that are developed for specific market segments. For example:

> In a number of announcements over the past two years, [network service providers] have begun to target new and potentially less technologically advanced users by offering simplified access to multiple services . . . . [T]he move will lead to new categories of services—of which mail services are just a part (Michel, 1994, p. 28).

A recent example of this approach is MCI's decision to offer members of its Friends & Family Program a free electronic mailbox (*Wall Street Journal,* November 11, 1994, p. B3).

In sum, traditional providers of e-mail appear to have considerable economies of scale and scope. These economies have consequences that are discussed below.

The Costs of Internet Service Providers

ISPs vary greatly in many dimensions, including target market served, area of coverage, and organizational form (nonprofit versus for profit). The costs of ISPs vary with their positions in each of these dimensions. There is some scattered information on the costs of providing Internet access (MacKie-Mason and Varian, 1993, and "Internet Costs . . . ," 1995).

BARRNet,[10] a regional, university-based, ISP located in the San Francisco Bay area, posted its budget for 1993 on its FTP server. Its expected cost allocation for 1993 was

---

[10]BARRNet was purchased by Bolt, Beranek, and Newman and is now known as BBN Planet. See Web site http://www.barrnet.net/ for details.

Personnel (mainly for network management, consultants)	54%
Equipment and maintenance	18%
Office/general expenses	12%
Backbone data circuits	16%

These costs reflect two important strategic decisions. First, its decision to offer services primarily in the Bay Area meant that its customers were quite close to one another. BARRNet did not need to purchase long backbone links to establish nodes near its customers. Second, BARRNet did not provide a great deal of customer support or market its services actively. It described its early business approach in the following terms:

> BARRNet was conceived and implemented as a network of networks. It connects "sites" or "campuses" rather than individual computers. Our assumption has been generally that our member sites operate their own networks, and support their own users. BARRNet is then more a provider of "wholesale" network service than "retail" service . . . .

Thus, customer support was not a significant portion of BARRNet's expenses.

A broader examination of publicly available information on other large ISPs suggests that approximately 25 percent to 40 percent of the expenditures related to Internet access flow through to providers of underlying transport ("Internet Costs . . . ," 1995). There is little information on the relative shares of hardware, software, network management, customer support, general administrative expenses, and overhead. However, all of these major inputs can be shared by e-mail, newsgroups, browsing tools such as gopher and Netscape, and other Internet applications. In consequence, e-mail is rarely sold as a stand-alone service by ISPs.

There has been a consolidation of mid-sized regional ISPs such as BARRNet. Recently, in addition to its BARRNet purchase, Bolt, Beranek and Newman (which designed the first packet switches on the ARPAnet) acquired NEARNET (a regional provider based in Boston) and SURAnet (a regional provider covering the Southeastern United States). Although this development may be consistent with the presence of large economies of scale in the provision of Internet access, an explosion in the growth of agile, small resellers calls into question the advantages of size. According to Joel Maloff, these resellers represent the fastest growing segment of the ISP market. (Maloff Company, 1995). This latter development has been driven largely by the low entry costs. According to one recent entrant, Smoot Carl-Mitchell: "The total cost of the hardware to get into the business was less than $15,000 . . . . Maybe you should not let that out . . . or everybody and his dog will be setting up as Internet service providers in their kitchens." (Lewis, 1994a, p. D1). The article talks about a 15-year-old high school student who sells Internet access out of a spare room at home.

The simultaneous growth of large and small firms, and the vanishing middle, may initially be puzzling, as they seem to suggest opposite conclusions regarding underlying economies of scale. However, a more careful analysis of the record suggests that small entrants face major problems in scaling up their enterprises and may be viable only as small niche players. The Inet Access FAQ[11] by David Dennis (http://amazing.cinenet.net/faq.html) provides a partial description of the economics of entry by small providers: "Finally, if your only reason is to make money, you probably shouldn't do it. You'll be beaten out by those of us who love the net and who are willing to work utterly ridiculous hours to make our system a success."

The economic viability of this approach is not assured. As the FAQ points out, a reseller with a 56 KB[12] connection to the Internet can support 100 users and make a profit of $500 per month. Although a reseller with a T1 connection can support many more dial-up customers and be more profitable, the ability of the entrepreneur to deal with routine business activities will be strained.

Thus, although there appears to be rapid growth among resellers, there is reason to believe that the enthusiasm of net-lovers is not supported by the fundamental economics. Economies of scope and scale will favor larger providers with distinct cost advantages. As the Internet matures and the explosive rates of growth fall, ISPs will focus their marketing efforts on each others' customers, and

---

[11]FAQ is a common abbreviation for a file containing answers to frequently asked questions.

[12]"KB" is a unit of communications bandwidth representing thousands of bits per second. Fifty-six KB is the bandwidth of a voice grade telephone line.

economies of scale and marketing clout will count. The growth of small ISP resellers may well be a transitory phase. If bandwidth-intensive uses of e-mail (via MIME or other standards) become very popular, then facilities-based carriers may have a decisive cost advantage, depending on the equilibrium that emerges in the market for raw transport, to be discussed below.

In sum: There are considerable economies of scope at all levels of output, and there are considerable economies of scale. In the long run, the industry will move to a few large providers who offer packages of computer and other communications services. The potential oligopolistic structure, and the attendant dangers of inefficient pricing, may be a public policy concern. However, the continued opportunity for niche-player entry may temper this concern, and the potential role of niche players in introducing new products to the market may provide for dynamic efficiency. A continuing fringe of small and innovative players at the leading edge of the market may alleviate the concerns usually associated with relatively high degrees of concentration.

Terminal Costs

Chapter Three describes different devices that individuals use to send and receive e-mail. Personal computers, game machines, set-top boxes, wireless handheld access devices, screen-based telephones, and dedicated devices were considered and their advantages and disadvantages described. An important determinant of the appropriate choice of access device is the consumer's ability to use it for multiple purposes. Consumer valuation of a multipurpose device would be determined by the sum of the values placed on all uses of the device. A heterogeneous population may value a particular application, such as e-mail, in quite different ways, resulting in small adoption rates for special-purpose devices. However, the sum of values placed on a variety of uses is more likely to result in a greater proportion of the population with valuations above a critical value. This can combine with the economies of scope present in the use of major hardware and software components to result in deeper penetration rates for e-mail service.

A multipurpose device, such as a PC, may also be compatible with a greater variety of network substrates and support a greater variety of access modes and speeds. PCs are currently used over the phone network, cable TV networks, and wireless data networks, and significant economies of scale and cumulative production continue to drive prices down. Devices that run only over a single network (such as a wireless network) may never achieve the scale economies of PCs.

The history of computer and telecommunications terminals is one of rapid and nearly continuous cost reduction and expansion of features, driven by fast-paced technological improvements in semiconductors, fabrication and manufacturing, and economies of large-scale production. The markets supplying terminal equipment are highly competitive, ensuring that these advances are soon translated into lower prices and products with differentiated features to more closely match users' preferences. (But see the discussion in Chapter Three of reasons why PC prices may remain relatively high.)

Basic e-mail capability can be added to a general-purpose terminal at small incremental cost. The additional components needed in a PC are a modem and interface software; in a TV set-top controller, some interface software, plus possibly a keyboard and additional memory; in a fax machine, a keyboard and software. The upgrade needed for a voice telephone could be minimal, if voice messaging is handled centrally by a network, or it could require a display screen, keyboard, and software. The capabilities of different types of terminals will affect the costs and architectural requirements of the e-mail service provider. When a PC is the e-mail access device, it can readily provide message storage, filtering, and editing functions. Voice and portable data access devices, in contrast, will need to have these services supplied by a network service provider or possibly a supplementary piece of terminal equipment.

In sum: The costs of basic e-mail terminal capabilities are dropping rapidly, allowing a larger number of potential users to economically add e-mail features to equipment they may acquire for entertainment, computation, or other communications uses. Lower costs, combined with growth in network services and the rapidly growing network community that can be reached, will lead to rapidly rising e-mail penetration among households. Nevertheless, the costs of acquiring a basic terminal will remain a deterrent for some potential users with limited resources and for others who expect only small benefits from an e-mail connection. As mentioned in Chapter Three, the cost may be offset or covered by various advertising offerings, but this option remains quite speculative. Public actions to encourage universal access will need to address this barrier. We examine possible strategies below.

THE EMERGING EQUILIBRIUM MARKET STRUCTURE

This section reviews trends in messaging services and network infrastructure markets. We also identify important economic factors that are leading toward an equilibrium market structure composed of predominantly national, vertically integrated suppliers with resellers and niche suppliers occupying secondary roles.

Economies of scope in the provision of electronic messaging services suggest that providers may offer a range of messaging alternatives. These alternatives likely will be packaged in various ways to meet the needs of different market segments. This means that revenues from each customer will be relatively constant even if the mix of e-mail, fax, and voice mail used changes dramatically. Customers will benefit from less variable bills and the greater convenience and reachability of messaging services that interoperate.

Marginal Costs and Congestion

The trend toward bundling messaging services may be strengthened by other fundamental economic forces in the communications industry. These include the large sunk costs and excess capacity in underlying transmission links, and oligopolistic competition among a few large companies that invest in the underlying physical communications infrastructure. AT&T, MCI, Sprint, and Wiltel each owns a national fiber optic network that connects all major cities. Each has substantial excess capacity. The cost to provide transmission links include high sunk costs of construction and the variable costs of digital cross connects, multiplexers, and the optoelectronics needed to operate the fiber. Providing switched service requires additional investments in switch hardware and software. In addition, firms incur costs associated with customer acquisition (marketing and sales), turning service on and off (provisioning, credit checks, setting up a billing account, etc.), maintaining and monitoring the network to ensure that customer expectations for service are met, terminating customers, and general administration.

The incremental cost of carrying traffic over the infrastructure network is zero, as long as there is excess transmission and switching capacity. During periods of congestion, when additional traffic is offered it imposes a social cost that can be measured by the degradation in quality of service. In traditional telephony, congestion can result in delay in getting dial tone, a fast busy signal, or a recorded announcement requesting that the user try placing the call later. Delayed dial tone arises when the originating switch is congested and the fast busy signal denotes the unavailability of trunks.

Reduced service quality can be measured by the delay imposed on the user. Economically efficient approaches to dealing with congestion for local calls are discussed in Park and Mitchell (1987) and Koschat, Srinagesh, and Uhler (1995). One finding of quantitative studies is that the benefits of peak-load pricing[13] are quite small when there is sufficient capacity in the network to keep blocking probabilities low.

The economic analysis of congestion in data networks is quite similar. Congestion at the packet level may result in slower throughput at the application layer, and this may not be perceptible to the consumer, just as a small delay in getting dial tone may be imperceptible. Congestion can be reduced by overprovisioning capacity, using real-time pricing mechanisms (MacKie-Mason and Varian, 1993), offering multiple qualities of service (Cocchi et al., 1993), or using peak-load prices (Park and Mitchell, 1987). The application of congestion pricing to data networks is a topic of ongoing research, and no definitive answers regarding optimal price structures are available. Present practice is to offer users free e-mail until a fairly generous limit is reached, at which point use charges begin to apply. Current prices are virtually unrelated to congestion. The widespread use of multimedia mail, which can more easily congest the network, may move price structures toward greater

---

[13]Peak-load pricing recognizes that investment in capacity is driven by the need to accommodate peak traffic, and that reductions in peak traffic can result in reduced capacity costs. Premium prices during peak periods are used to reduce peak traffic and realize capacity cost savings.

reliance on a mix of use charges and multiple grades of service (e.g., priority, standard, economy).

Pricing Trends

The history of leased-line prices in recent years reveals a strong downward trend. According to *Business Week*, private-line prices fell by 80 percent between 1989 and 1994, and this is consistent with competition that drives prices to marginal costs (*Business Week*, September 12, 1994, p. 90). During the same period, the use of term and volume discounts increased dramatically. AT&T offers customers a standard month-to-month tariff for T1 service and charges a nonrecurring fee, a fixed monthly fee, and a monthly rate per mile. Customers who are willing to sign a five-year contract and commit to spending $1 million per month are offered 57 percent off the standard month-to-month rates. Smaller discounts apply to customers who choose shorter terms and lower commitment volumes: A one-year term commitment to spend $2,000 per month obtains a discount of 18 percent.

The overall trend toward lower prices masks a more complex reality.

> There are two types of tariffs: "front of the book" rates, which are paid by smaller and uninformed large customers, and "back of the book" rates, which are offered to the customers who are ready to defect to another carrier and to customers who know enough to ask for them. The "front of the book" rates continue their relentless 5 to 7 percent annual increases (Hills, 1995, p. 32).

In 1994, AT&T filed over 1,200 special ("back of the book") contracts, and MCI filed over 400.

Nonstandard commercial contracting is one means for sharing risk between the producer and consumers (Williamson, 1988, pp. 159–161). In addition to risk reduction, long-term contracts reduce customer churn, which often ranges from 20 to 50 percent per year in competitive telecommunications markets. According to data submitted by AT&T, "consumer churn is running at the remarkable annual rate of 30 million" in 1995.[14] Since service activation and termination costs can be high, reduction of churn can be an effective cost saving measure.

Some tariffs for fast packet services filed by local exchange carriers offer term and volume discounts, and the economic forces that give rise to term/volume commitments for private lines have probably resulted in term/volume commitments for long distance fast packet services as well. There is little published information on long distance fast packet prices. According to one source, none of the long distance carriers or enhanced service providers (e.g., CompuServe) tariff their frame relay offerings (Toth, 1995, pp. 23–24).

The effect of term/volume commitments in private lines and fast packet services affects the cost structures of VANs that do not own their own transport infrastructure. It may be expected that large VANs who lease their transport infrastructures will sign multiyear contracts, possibly on an exclusive basis, with a single carrier. These VANs will have sunk costs. Competition among VANs will therefore be similar to competition at the lower level, and we may expect to see term/volume contracts emerge for messaging services offered by VANS, including Internet Service Providers. A quick survey of Internet providers shows this to be the case. For example, in January 1995, AlterNet offered customers with a T1 connection a 10 percent discount if they committed to a two-year term. Global Connect, an ISP in Virginia, offers customers an annual rate that is 10 times the monthly rate, amounting to a 17 percent discount for a one-year commitment. There are many other examples of this sort on the Internet.

The Internet is beginning to resemble the private-line market in one other aspect: Prices are increasingly being viewed as proprietary. ISPs that used to post prices on their FTP (file transfer protocol) or Web servers now ask potential customers to call for quotes. Presumably, prices are determined after negotiation.

To summarize: The market will move increasingly toward vertically integrated or allied firms, tied together by long-term, exclusive

---

[14]*Ex Parte Presentation in Support of AT&T's Motion for Reclassification as a Nondominant Carrier*, CC Docket No. 79-252, April 20, 1995, p. 34.

contracts, together with a competitive fringe of resellers/innovators who offer leading-edge solutions. The distinctions between e-mail, voice mail, and fax may not always be discernible to customers. Customers will face a variety of optional price structures and will be encouraged to purchase bundles of services with inducements to stay loyal (term commitments, frequent flyer tie-ins, cash back every quarter, etc.). Consumers without stable jobs, incomes, or housing, and therefore not qualified for special discounts tied to long-term contracts, may face relatively high prices.

POLICY ISSUES

As described in this and previous chapters, e-mail is supplied largely through conventional market arrangements that use well-established communications infrastructures to physically transport and route messages and administrative traffic. These infrastructures—the public switched telephone network, packet-switched data networks interconnected to the Internet, and cable television distribution systems—have nearly ubiquitous coverage across the United States.

Universal connectivity of e-mail systems, while not as far advanced, is within sight. User interest in widely reachable messaging has impelled commercial service providers to establish gateways and develop protocol conversion software to allow proprietary messaging systems to exchange plain-text e-mail messages. These forces will be sufficient to ensure quite widespread connectivity for basic messaging.

What remains to be achieved, then, is widespread subscription to and use of e-mail service. In the business sector, universal penetration will be approached when the messaging services provide high-quality support for financial transactions and sensitive commercial communications, which in turn require e-mail privacy and integrity and the ability to verify identity and authenticity of correspondents (see Chapter Three for a technical discussion of these issues).

The extent of residential penetration will depend to a great degree on quite different factors. Demand for e-mail is likely to be quite price-elastic for many consumers who have relatively good substitutes (postal mail and telephone service) for many messages. For other messaging, as emphasized in Chapter Five, such as participation in school and civic activities and interest-group discussions, e-mail may evolve into the dominant communications medium. Low first-time costs, especially for a user terminal, and low recurring charges for e-mail service could substantially expand residential penetration. Because most users may obtain e-mail service as a by-product of a multipurpose terminal device, the market success of set-top television devices and home computers will be an important determinant of penetration. Equally important may be new mass-market applications, such as financial transactions and home shopping.

To summarize: Many of the economic prerequisites for universal e-mail service are either in place or are developing rapidly through market processes. The principal gaps in achieving a universal standard of service are a limited number of issues concerning interoperability of e-mail systems and common addressing, as outlined in Chapter Three, and a program to provide financial support to marginal consumers who would not otherwise subscribe to an e-mail service. We turn to these matters in the next subsections.

Network Supply Conditions

Without public intervention, market forces are rapidly extending the availability of e-mail to broad segments of American business and consumers. Nevertheless, the market structure that is now developing raises concerns in the following areas.

- Any market that contains a few large firms may not approximate the theoretical model of competition, and economic efficiency may not be maximized (but this arrangement may still be preferable to government intervention). Competing firms may try to create added value by differentiating their services. In the process, seamless interoperability and interconnection may be lost so that consumers who can afford to purchase access from only one provider may be restricted in the functionalities available to them as they communicate with individuals on other networks.

- The trend toward integrated service and bundling may introduce unexpected switching costs (costs associated with customers switching providers), and these costs may hamper innovation and competition.

Standards, Interoperability, and Interconnection. The convergence of e-mail, fax, and voice messaging may be hampered by difficult technical and business issues.

On the technical side, standards or gateways may be necessary to permit different systems to interoperate, at least for a core set of functionalities. The industry has taken various approaches to interoperability in different messaging markets. E-mail interoperability appears to be evolving rapidly through the use of gateways. A discussion of specific gateway programs that enable interoperability between LAN e-mail systems and the Internet is contained in Lipschutz (1995). Fax interoperability has been achieved through the relatively wide acceptance of a common set of standards (G3 and G4 Fax). In contrast, voice mail interoperability does not exist; with few exceptions, voice mail saved on one system cannot be forwarded to a voice mailbox on another system.

Interoperability of e-mail systems, fax machines, and e-mail/fax gateways appears to be developing in the market in response to competitive pressures. Voice mail interoperability has not developed in a like manner. However, recent announcements of integrated messaging may result in the development of a de facto standard. These solutions may have to compete with alternative approaches, such as MIME and X.400 e-mail standards. The market has not yet settled on a de facto standard for the converging electronic messaging industry.

As providers seek to differentiate their service, the market may settle on multiple standards and incompatible service definitions. Gateways between the different services may enable interoperation of only basic features (such as ASCII-based plain text mail). By subscribing to multiple services, businesses that rely on electronic messaging and some households may be able to communicate with others using advanced features all or most of the time. But consumers who can afford only one software interface or one service provider may find that advanced features often do not work, since most of their messages go through gateways that translate only core functionalities. Will these core functionalities provide capabilities that are envisioned by current definitions of universal e-mail? At this writing, the appropriate government role may be to wait and see what the market does.

Longer-run policy options cover a wide spectrum. At one end, the government may decide to adopt a laissez faire attitude. The argument for this option is that government regulations, and the proceedings necessary to develop and enforce them, cannot keep pace with rapid technological change in the computing and communications industry. At the other end of the spectrum, the government could establish requirements governing the degree of interoperability among e-mail networks. A light-handed regulatory approach could specify minimum capabilities that will be transferred across networks (perhaps plain text mail and some basic directory capabilities), while leaving providers free to offer optional enhancements to their customers.

In between these two extremes, the government could attempt to promote open standards by using its clout as a large purchaser. For example, the federal government could announce that its contract for electronic messaging services would be awarded to multiple firms (just as FTS2000 was awarded to two firms) and require all bidders to provide services that interoperate with each other for a specified set of functionalities. However, the federal government's record in setting standards that are then extended into general commercial practice is poor. The use of the ADA computer language and standardized protocol layers for computer communication have not been widely adopted. We recommend that instead of attempting to mandate economywide e-mail standards through government procurement, the more effective role is to facilitate cooperative approaches to standard setting, as federal agencies did with the development of high-definition television specifications.

Terms of Interconnection. The business issues that stand in the way of rapid convergence of different messaging technologies arise from difficulties in formulating the proper mix of competition and cooperation among competitive networks. Seamlessly interconnected networks are of greater value to consumers than fragmented or partially interconnected networks. Cooperative interconnection arrangements may therefore be attractive to all network providers. However, if networks are seamlessly interconnected, large network providers with substantial investments in international facilities may look no different to the consumer than a small local reseller of e-mail service. If the terms of interconnection favor the smaller network, the small reseller, with almost no sunk cost, may be able to consistently undersell the large provider from whom it obtains interconnectivity. But, if interconnection terms are too unfavorable, new entrants may not gain a toehold, and effective competition may not develop. The terms and conditions of interconnection present a difficult bargaining problem. A regulatory framework may be necessary to ensure that interconnection arrangements are fair to all competing networks. (The economics of interconnection and proposed regulatory frameworks are discussed in Arnbak et al., 1994.)

The convergence of electronic messaging systems may strain existing interconnection arrangements. Currently, a consumer who makes a long distance telephone call and then leaves a voice mail message will pay for the call. The price for the call typically varies with the distance, the time, and the duration of the call. A significant component of that price is the access charge paid by the long distance carrier to the local exchange carriers who originate and terminate the call. The framework of access charges is set by regulators as part of the terms and conditions of interconnection between long distance and local telephone companies.

E-mail (including e-mail that contains a voice message in digital form) escapes the access charge when the originator calls a local number to reach his e-mail provider and only local service charges apply. Even though the e-mail message is destined for a distant location, and may travel over facilities of the long distance carrier who carried the voice mail, the suppliers of e-mail, fax, and voice mail as well as other enhanced service providers (ESPs) are exempt from access charges. The exemption creates an artificial cost differential between traditional voice messaging (which imposes a high cost on the sender) and e-mail (which imposes a smaller, often zero, cost). The cost differential is based on an increasingly arbitrary distinction between interexchange carriers and ESPs. Ideally, a consumer's choice of messaging service should be based on economic costs and not on artificial regulatory distinctions; this is not the case today.

These distortions have several implications for universal service. In general, as messaging technologies become closer substitutes for each other, regulatory policies that systematically advantage a particular type of service should be closely examined. Pricing distortions are usually undesirable public policy, because they lead to higher-cost methods of production when consumers and product developers choose among alternatives using prices that are not based on costs. Pricing that advantages one messaging technology over another will artificially promote the development of the favored service. To be sure, such pricing distortions will promote more widespread use of the preferred services, and to that degree perhaps contribute to universal service for that type of messaging technology. However, universal telephone service is partially funded by toll and access services that contribute toward the sunk costs of network facilities. A policy that artificially depresses the price of e-mail (as the ESP exemption does) may indirectly weaken the funding of universal telephone service. This will have a negative effect on universal e-mail to the extent that e-mail rides over the telephone network: A household without telephone service will have fewer alternatives for access to its e-mail provider. The tradeoff between preserving universal telephone service and achieving universal e-mail service needs more careful analysis.

Number and Address Portability with Bundling. The trend toward bundling communications and messaging services highlights other inconsistencies in the regulatory treatment of traditional telephony and ESPs. Different rules govern number portability and address portability. "Equal access" requirements now in place for telephone carriers permit virtually all consumers to select a preferred long distance carrier while retaining "1+" dialing capability. Number portability extends to 800 numbers. Customers can retain their 800 number when they switch providers. Number portability is being considered for customers who are served by competing local exchange carriers; trials are now under way, and a request for proposal for the required database technology has been issued by a group that includes NYNEX, Rochester Tel, AT&T, MFS Intelenet, Teleport Communications Group, and Sprint (Vittoro, 1995). Direct inward dialing trunks and call forwarding are being used as interim solutions.

The rationale for number portability is to reduce customer switching costs and reduce the barriers facing potential entrants. Without number portability, businesses would be reluctant to switch carriers and change their number, as they would have to replace their existing stationery and their employees' business cards, change their advertisements, and undertake costly efforts to ensure that their customers and suppliers knew about the change. Residential customers may have smaller absolute switching costs, yet the costs might be substantial in comparison to their potential savings from changing providers. Switching costs can pose a significant barrier to competition. A firm seeking to enter the market must offer equal service at a sufficiently lower price to offset the potential customer's switching cost, or offer a sufficiently higher-quality product to obtain the business at the same price.

While telephone number portability is driven by a combination of industry efforts and regulatory requirements, there is no similar initiative to make e-mail addresses portable. Thus, a consumer who obtains e-mail from Prodigy might have an e-mail address of the form jane@prodigy.com. If the consumer switched to another provider (e.g., to PSI), her e-mail address would also switch (e.g., to jane@psi.com). Consumers can avoid this problem by purchasing their own "vanity" domain name (e.g., jane@joe.com), but this service costs between $100–$200 per year, which may exceed the switching costs for many consumers (Berlin and Kantor, 1995). Alternatively, a user can maintain a single e-mail box for all incoming correspondence and redirect that mail to a service-provider mailbox. (One service providing such mail redirection services is "pobox.com," described at http://www.tgc.com/70011.html.)

The consequences of no address portability can be larger than expected in a market where communications and messaging services are bundled. Consider, for example, MCI's offer of a free e-mail box to members of its Friends & Family program (*Wall Street Journal,* November 11, 1994, p. B3). Customers who join the program receive an MCI mailbox. If the address is of the form jane@mcimail.com, customers will not have a portable e-mail address. Since the e-mail account is bundled with the long-distance package, customers will incur a switching cost if they decide to change long distance providers: The free mailbox will no longer be available, and a monthly charge for e-mail will apply if the consumer continues to obtain e-mail service from the same provider. If the consumer decides to accept a package, including e-mail, from another provider, then switching costs associated with the new e-mail address will be incurred. The friction in the e-mail market will be felt in the voice market as well.

The implications of these supply conditions for universal e-mail are principally that public legislative and regulatory policy should adopt a broad view and aim for consistency across the entire range of communications and messaging services. In this way, resource costs, and not arbitrary regulations, will guide consumer choice and will permit the full benefits of competition to be realized.

Support of Marginal Consumers

If e-mail is to reach the vast majority of the population, marginal consumers—those who would not at current prices subscribe to an e-mail service—will need economic assistance to participate. Two approaches could be considered. The first would place requirements on service providers to offer below-cost service to consumers as a condition of doing business. The alternative approach is to provide funds directly to consumers with which they can purchase e-mail equipment and services.

The regulatory approach of imposing *universal service obligations* on service providers has been the prevailing practice in the telephone industry (OECD, 1991). As a condition of obtaining a franchise, or license, to supply local telephone service, a carrier is required by its state regulator to construct its network in all areas of its service territory and to offer basic services at standard tariffed rates to all consumers. In areas that are especially costly to serve (e.g., because they are remote, topographically difficult, or thinly populated), the costs of satisfying these obligations exceed the revenues the carrier can expect from the customers it gains. In other areas, rates for the basic access service to residential consumers may be set above the incremental cost of providing access and make a partial contribution toward recovery of fixed or sunk costs. Remaining costs are then recovered through higher contributions in other areas and for other services.

Such price structures, which result in disproportionate contributions from some customers or services, are sustainable so long as the supplier does not face competition. But when the profitable segments of the market are open to entry, other suppliers are able to capture the profitable business with lower prices or better service while avoiding the obligation of producing unremunerative service. With reduced revenues from profitable services, the original monopolist is less able to maintain services to marginal subscribers and high-cost areas. Ultimately, competition is incompatible with maintaining universal service by cross-subsidies.

This experience from the telephone industry indicates that a policy of promoting universal e-mail service that keeps basic subscription prices low by generating high contributions from other services will be infeasible in the openly competitive information services industry.[15] If an obligation to provide below-cost service were imposed on particular e-mail service suppliers, they would find themselves losing profitable markets to other firms that do not have the cost of those obligations. In principle, entry into the e-mail service provision business could be regulated and a service obligation imposed on each licensed entrant. However, regulating entry would go strongly against the dynamic of the innovative computer networking industry. Indeed, erecting successful barriers to entry appears improbable. The history of innovation in digital technology is one of an increasing number of alternative ways of representing and transmitting information. Bootleg messaging systems would likely circumvent any regulatory effort.

The alternative policy approach is to provide purchasing power directly to marginal consumers. A program of e-mail service vouchers would enable consumers to shop for terminal equipment, user training, and e-mail service in competitive markets. A voucher program would require several policy decisions about funding and eligibility. The program could be funded by a "tax" on a defined segment of the communications and information services industry, included as a surcharge in prices that e-mail service providers charge other firms, or from general revenues.

- Industry-tax funding has been successfully used to support federal and state voucher-like programs for basic telephone

---

[15]It is not clear how one would impose equal obligations on all providers. Suppose a company argued that some proportion of its customers were being served below cost, and it was meeting its obligations, and that the existence of unserved customers meant that the other providers were shirking their duty. A regulator would have to do a customer-by-customer analysis of all carriers to find out whether that was true. With only one provider, there can be no shifting of blame. With many providers, the information needed to find out who, if anyone, was shirking their obligation would be hard to get and easy to falsify.

service.   The tax is levied by regulatory authorities on the licensed telephone service providers. For example, the California universal telephone service program is funded by a tax on gross revenues of final service providers. Alternatively, a broader-based value-added tax on all communications industry providers has been proposed by Noam (1993).

- Raising funds to support universal service subsidies through access charges also has been successfully used in the telephone industry since the breakup of AT&T into separate local and long-distance companies. The practice has transferred revenues from long-distance carriers to local carriers. However, this approach is now encountering difficulties as competing fiber-optic access providers divert much high-volume business traffic from local carriers and bypass the access charge system. Similar difficulties would confront access charges that would subsidize e-mail services. For the most part, e-mail service providers themselves do not control a bottleneck that limits access to the customer. Instead, that access is limited by several facilities-based network operators — telephone, cable TV, wireless, and alternative access providers.[16]

General revenues have been the source of funds for broad social welfare programs, including education and library services. Vouchers have been used in some public programs, notably food-stamps, to put purchasing power directly in the hands of marginal consumers. However, proposals to use vouchers more widely, for energy subsidies and choice of schools, have received only limited support.

What might the costs of basic e-mail service be? The costs of serving low-use telephone customers are instructive. According to AT&T, its "basic schedule rates do not cover the direct costs of serving the one-third of consumers who make under $3 per month in calls. These costs not only include AT&T's network costs, but also universal ser-

---

[16]If e-mail subtracts business from "retail" telecommunications services, it may have to make more than a marginal contribution to network costs—becoming more expensive, which may in turn jeopardize universal service.

vice costs of $.52 per customer and bill rendering costs ranging from $.33 to $.88 per customer."[17]

This suggests that an unregulated market may charge a minimum monthly fee above $3 for subscription to a basic e-mail package. Current prices appear to be in the range of $10 per month for a range of information services and e-mail, with monthly usage allowances that are quite generous. Individuals who make very limited use of e-mail and other communications/networking services (spending less than $5 per month) may not be able to find a provider who is willing to serve them. The amount of the subsidy necessary to induce the marginal consumer to subscribe (and thus be reachable by others) will depend on the difference between his willingness to pay for local and long distance service, e-mail, and other messaging options, and the price of a bare-bones package of these services. This subsidy could, conceivably, be higher or lower than current subsidies offered to telephone subscribers. If the additional value of e-mail to the marginal subscriber is greater than the incremental cost of providing e-mail service, the necessary subsidy will be smaller. If the additional value of e-mail is less than its incremental cost, the necessary subsidy will be greater.

The potential costs of subsidizing universal e-mail service are considerable. To obtain a sense of the magnitude that might be involved, consider a minimum-cost basic e-mail service that might cost $5 per month, or $60 per year, in competitive markets. Amortizing modest terminal and training costs over five years could add at least $40 per year. Thus, $100 per year would be a conservative estimate of the amount required to underwrite basic service for marginal consumers. In a mature industry, unsubsidized e-mail penetration could perhaps eventually approach the levels achieved in the telephone system. In 1994, about 94 percent of U.S. households had access to a telephone. If e-mail subsidies of $100/year were required for 10 percent of the approximately 100 million U.S. households, this would require an annual budget of $1 billion. (But recall the discussion in Chapter Three of possible "free" e-mail services and terminals becoming available through the bundling of ad-

---

[17] *Ex Parte Presentation in Support of AT&T's Motion for Reclassification as a Nondominant Carrier,* CC Docket No. 79-252, April 20, 1995, p. 51.

vertising with services and devices, which might materially lower this amount.)

Eligibility for e-mail service subsidies would need to be tightly defined to avoid potentially large cost overruns or unfunded mandates. To the extent that marginal consumers will not purchase e-mail service because of limited resources, eligibility for subsidies should be defined in financial terms. To avoid establishing a separate administrative bureaucracy to determine eligibility, qualification for voucher assistance could be linked to eligibility for other public-assistance programs, although this could make the program subject to considerable variability across the states. To assist other citizens unlikely to subscribe on their own, outreach programs based in community organizations such as libraries and senior centers—exemplified by "wired community" efforts described in Chapter Five—could qualify for per-user subsidy payments. See Johnson (1988) for additional analysis of the costs of lifeline telephone programs per supported subscriber.

The universal-service policies considered here have been consciously confined to basic e-mail service. Multimedia messaging will undoubtedly grow in popularity and evolve in directions yet to be established. But designing policies to support standardization of such services and financing access to them are premature when those technologies are still being discovered.

CONCLUSIONS

Several overall conclusions emerge from this chapter's discussion.

*   The convergence of communications technologies provides a variety of infrastructures over which e-mail services can be delivered. The wide availability of alternative telephone, cable television, and wireless networks will broaden the reach of e-mail services. At the same time, regulatory conditions governing interconnection and charges for access can increasingly bias the use of particular supply arrangements. Government efforts should strive for neutral policies that avoid pricing distortions among messaging systems.

- Compatibility and standardization will remain important for interconnectivity. That is, "universal service" in the sense of Vail (1907, 1910) and Mueller (1993)—achieving the greatest connectivity among disparate systems—is likely to be a precursor to universal service in the sense of reaching "all" U.S. citizens. Market developments that increasingly bundle communications services may reduce the portability of e-mail addresses and increase consumers' costs of switching among suppliers.

- Although e-mail penetration is expanding rapidly, some program of economic assistance to marginal consumers may be necessary to achieve universal levels of services. Obligating service providers to offer subscriptions to large classes of customers at low rates that are financed by contributions from other services, a policy that was successfully used in the telephone industry for many years, is unlikely to succeed in the competitive messaging industry. Instead, e-mail assistance will require public funding from an industrywide tax or from general revenues. Subsidies will need to be narrowly targeted to reach consumers who would not otherwise subscribe.

Chapter Five

CIVIC NETWORKS: SOCIAL BENEFITS OF ON-LINE COMMUNITIES

Sally Ann Law, Brent Keltner

INTRODUCTION

The network of hundreds of thousands of electronically connected computers, which is expected to become a key element of an NII, already has revolutionized the way people work, live, and do business (King and Kraemer, 1995). This network enables reliable, fast, asynchronous point-to-point information exchange over small and large geographic distances. The scope of the future effect of access to an NII is still somewhat uncertain (van de Donk, Snellen, and Tops, 1995). However, its potential to improve formal and informal communication among individuals and groups, provide access to important information sources, facilitate business transactions, shape government process, and simplify access to and delivery of public services is becoming clear (e.g., Bikson and Law, 1993; Sproull and Kiesler, 1991b; Steinfield, Kraut, and Streeter, 1993).

Currently, individuals access electronic networks in two main ways. First, a large number of people directly access the Internet (described in more detail in Chapters Two through Four) through computers and accounts associated with their school or work. Second, also as described in Chapters Two through Four, an increasing number of individuals access electronic networks via one (or more) of several commercial on-line services, including Internet service providers (e.g., America Online, CompuServe). Common to both access mechanisms is the provision of e-mail, which prior research indicates (e.g., Bikson and Law, 1993; Eveland and Bikson, 1987) acts as the "hook" causing users first to realize the advantages of networked technologies and gradually to experiment with more advanced features and services. Many such features facilitate interactions beyond the boundaries of the United States to the GII—extending users' horizons both literally and figuratively (see Chapter Six).

Yet, as Chapter Two has shown, access to computers and computer networks is not evenly distributed throughout the population. Specifically, computer access and use is positively related to higher levels of education and income. Also, race is independently related to computer and network access—whites being significantly more likely to have access to both than blacks and Hispanics. Probably most significant for this study of the implications of countrywide access to e-mail is the fact that income- and education-based gaps between these groups are widening over time (again, see Chapter Two for more discussion of these data and trends). Apparently, if current trends continue without intervention, access to electronic information and communications technologies (and associated benefits) will be skewed in favor of traditionally advantaged groups.

Against this background, we turn in this chapter to the issue of extending network access to currently underserved populations. By "underserved populations" we mean groups often referred to as the "have-nots" in the popular press (e.g., Schrage, 1993; Shiver, 1995; Williams, 1995). These groups include those with low levels of income and education, ethnic minorities, the elderly, and the physically challenged. Further, we examine how on-line access to people, groups, and relevant information can—and is—helping nonprofit and public sector organizations operate more effectively. Finally, we explore how on-line access to local and federal government representatives, as well as to nongovernmental organizations, may increase citizen participation in government affairs and whether such access offers benefits to community members.

We examine these issues in the context of the increasing number of "civic networks" emerging countrywide. What principally distinguishes civic networks from other organizations that provide network access and services is their objective: to use network technology to serve public interests and increase public access to information. Most civic networks typically aim to reach underserved populations described above. "[I]n general terms, a civic network improves access to information of all kinds to the general public or to targeted members of the local community who are traditionally underserved" (Vu et al., 1994).

This chapter will describe the range of information services that civic networks can and do provide to their constituents. The chapter also will discuss implementation strategies (e.g., location of computer terminals, delivery of user training) that are undertaken to ensure that target populations are reached effectively. Further, given e-mail's significance as a catalyst for other on-line computer use, and thus as an important influence on universality of network use, we particularly examine the role of and access to e-mail in populations served by civic networks.

The results reported here are based on in-depth studies of five civic networks. By synthesizing findings across the five networks, we offer preliminary answers to two questions: (1) What are the individual, group, and societal benefits (and potential disadvantages) of access to networked communication technologies, especially for tradition-ally underserved individuals and groups and (2) what can we learn from the implementation of civic networks that will help us under-stand what it takes to deliver on-line access to all groups in society? Both questions are central to this study's overall research questions: Is it feasible to provide universal access to e-mail in the United States, and what are the likely societal benefits?[1]

STUDY APPROACH

The research reported in this chapter follows a case-study-like ap-proach that RAND researchers have used successfully in other set-tings where contextual characteristics are complex and where there is a paucity of prior research on which to build (e.g., Bikson and Law, 1994; Stasz et al., 1991). Because civic networks have been in exis-tence only a relatively short amount of time, few systematic data

---

[1]The benefits discussed in this chapter are restricted to domestic issues. The many, often related, international implications of electronic networks are considered in Chapter Six.

have been gathered about them.[2] We believed that observational visits and in-depth interviews with key stakeholders at a selected group of sites would yield a rich source of qualitative information from which to learn and draw conclusions about the kinds of issues raised above.

Site Selection

In selecting sites for in-depth study, our goal was to devise an illustrative rather than a representative sample of civic networks. They were chosen from a larger group of similar organizations operating around the country using network technology to support a wide variety of publicly oriented activities. The final sample reflects an attempt to include networks aimed at reaching underserved communities—such as poor, inner-city residents and ethnic minorities— as well as networks whose goal is to promote "electronic democracy" and facilitate the on-line delivery of government services.

The resulting sample comprised five civic networks:

- The Public Electronic Network (PEN), Santa Monica, CA

- The Seattle Community Network (SCN), Seattle, WA

- The Playing to Win Network (PTW), Boston, MA

- LatinoNet, San Francisco, CA

- The Blacksburg Electronic Village (BEV), Blacksburg, VA.

The main features of each are outlined in Table 5.1. Syntheses of interview information from each site visit are in Appendix B, along with a copy of the semistructured interview protocol. Following is a brief glance at the distinguishing characteristics of each network.

The Public Electronic Network in Santa Monica was founded in 1988 with the primary goal of increasing citizens' awareness of and participation in local government affairs, i.e., promoting "electronic democracy." Impressed with how e-mail had improved

---

[2]A notable exception is the previously cited Columbia University study prepared for the U.S. National Commission on Libraries and Information Sciences.

Table 5.1

Key Features of Civic Networks

	Background	Funding	Main Objectives	Challenges Faced by Network
Public Electronic Network	*Location:* Santa Monica, CA *Started Operations:* Feb. 1988 *No. of Subscribers:*[a] 6,700	*Host Equipment:* private sector donation *Operating Budget:* covered by City Hall	Facilitating political access Improving delivery of government services Promoting community dialog	Deciding on appropriate-use guidelines Getting city officials to participate interactively
Seattle Community Network	*Location:* Seattle, WA *Started Operations:* May 1994 *No. of Subscribers:* 3,500	*Host Equipment:* private sector donation *Operating Budget:* fundraising and volunteers	Facilitating community-building and peer support Getting community information on-line	Keeping a volunteer organization operating Raising funds through private donations
Playing to Win Network	*Location:* Newton, MA *Started Operations:* Nov. 1993 *No. of Subscribers:* 56 nonprofits	*Host Equipment:* paid for by nonprofits *Operating Budget:* NSF grant	Creating a nonprofit support network Bringing technology to low-income communities	Arriving at common goals and purpose Finding resources in "nonprofit budgets"
LatinoNet	*Location:* San Francisco, CA *Started Operations:* Nov. 1994 *No. of Subscribers:* 80 nonprofits	*Host Equipment:* private sector donation *Operating Budget:* membership and user fees	Supporting community-building Streamlining nonprofit organizations Raising political awareness	Resistance to use of new technology Nonprofits' skepticism about benefits
Blacksburg Electronic Village	*Location:* Blacksburg, VA *Started Operations:* Oct. 1993 *No. of Subscribers:* 10,000	*Host Equipment:* University's infrastructure and private sector donations *Operating Budget:* University supported, Library Construction Services Act (LCSA) grant	Facilitating community-building and peer support Supporting commerce Improving delivery of city services	Soliciting equipment from Bell Atlantic Enlisting volunteers to post information

[a]Reported number of subscribers represents the best estimates of the network organizers. When asked to distinguish subscribers from active users, administrators acknowledged that such statistics are difficult, if not impossible, to track.

communications and responsiveness within City Hall itself, officials aimed to extend the model and the technology to facilitate more effective communication between local citizens and their government. Their secondary goal was to allow citizens to conduct increasing amounts of local government-related business on-line, e.g., payment of parking tickets or application for business licenses.

Organizers of the Seattle Community Network, founded in 1994, view it primarily as a mechanism to foster community-building by providing a forum for idea-sharing among Seattle community residents. They aim to reach all residents, including the urban poor and ethnic minorities. A secondary goal of SCN is to give local organizations a venue to promote activities and events.

The Blacksburg Electronic Village was started with a goal of creating a "virtual community" where all activities that take place within a normal community—from politics to business and social organizing—could be conducted via an on-line network. BEV was established in 1993 with the involvement of all the major institutions in the community, including Virginia Polytechnic Institute and State University, social service organizations, businesses, and City Hall.

Both LatinoNet, founded in late 1994, and the Playing to Win Network, begun in 1993, focus network outreach and service delivery at organizations rather than individuals. The Playing to Win Network is an outgrowth of a larger project aimed at bringing computers to nonprofits and inner-city residents. That project, called Playing to Win Inc., is in New York City. The headquarters of the Playing to Win Network Project is in Boston, MA. See Appendix B for details.

Both these networks promote interaction among organizations with similar goals and needs. LatinoNet was founded to develop better channels of communication between Latino nonprofit organizations throughout the nation. The Playing to Win Network was established to allow administrators at community and social service organizations to draw on the knowledge and accrued expertise of colleagues facing similar challenges throughout the United States.[3]

---

[3]Whereas LatinoNet has played an important role in bringing network and telecommunications resources to the nonprofits with which it works, many of the nonprofits

Combined, the five sites provide a rich source of information on ways that civic networks are structured to provide on-line access to underserved populations, the kinds of services they offer, and how they help support and reshape personal, business, and government interactions.

Information Gathering

Our data collection goal was twofold. Our first objective was to understand how different civic networks use network technology to accomplish varied missions. We wanted to find out what types of services each offers and the benefits (and potential disadvantages) these services bring to individuals, groups, and public and private sector organizations. Second, we wanted to understand the strategies the networks use to ensure that their target populations have access to and take advantage of available services.

Semistructured interviews served as the primary method for gathering contextual information on the characteristics of the five civic networks, their range of services, and delivery strategies. The interviews were guided by a protocol to ensure that information relevant to key research questions was collected systematically across all sites. However, the protocol was designed to be sufficiently open-ended to accommodate each organization's different objectives and to allow unanticipated themes to emerge and be explored (see Appendix B). At each network, the aim was to interview at least one individual in each of the following five categories:

- a project director or senior administrator
- an operations manager
- a technical support specialist
- an employee involved in community outreach
- one or more representative users of the network.

in the Playing to Win Network had integrated network communications into their operations before joining Playing to Win.

In practice, the number of interviews at each site varied. Differences in the number of interviews stemmed primarily from the size of each operation and the level of penetration into the communities each one serves. In total, we conducted around 30 semistructured interviews across all five sites. Two additional data-gathering techniques complemented our semistructured interviews. We informally solicited information on usage from users of the different civic networks during training sessions and open-use hours at public access sites. We also collected, where available, published papers and reports on the demographics and frequency of use from project organizers (see Appendix B for detailed information).

FINDINGS

We present our study findings in two main sections. First, we describe what we learned about how access to e-mail and other on-line services is affecting the ways people live, work, and do business. Second, we discuss the major implementation implications associated with delivering e-mail and on-line services to various target populations, particularly the traditionally underserved.

The Benefits of Access to Electronic Networks

We found that there are four main categories of benefits associated with access to e-mail and other on-line services such as are provided by civic networks. These benefits are similar to many described in various research articles and in the trade press. The noteworthy finding here, however, is that within the context of civic networks, all the benefits are "packaged together" and are potentially attainable by all citizens regardless of income, education, race, or other traditionally access-limiting characteristics.

- Network access provides individuals and groups with opportunities for new and more effective ways of communicating. E-mail enables virtually instantaneous (but also asynchronous) one-to-one, one-to-many, and many-to-many interactions, regardless of geographical distance. Civic networks, therefore, have the ability to support interpersonal relationships, local community-building, and social integration.

- Civic networks serve an important information resource function. Via electronically accessible databases and direct on-line connections to service providers, individuals and groups can access, use, and distribute information relatively cheaply and effectively. The social and other benefits associated with such capabilities are clearly recognized by civic network organizers. For instance, increasing citizen access to important information on education and employment opportunities, health and community resources, and other related services were goals common to a greater or lesser degree at all five sites.

- Civic networks can facilitate the formation and restructuring of organizations by combining both communication and information functions of networked technology. The primary goal of two of the networks (LatinoNet and Playing to Win) is to connect nonprofit and community-based organizations. Such organizations are typically resource-constrained, so having the ability to communicate rapidly and reliably with key stakeholders, e.g., potential collaborators, regulators, and clients, as well as being able to gain access to and advertise information, is of substantial benefit to them.

- Civic networks may offer some services aimed at promoting greater efficiency and increased responsiveness of government institutions. An electronic network can change the status quo by restructuring delivery of government services, raising citizen awareness of local and national political issues, and encouraging participation in the political process.

In the following sections, we organize the findings according to the categories of benefits just described. In each case, we give examples of how the different civic networks are realizing these benefits for their members.

Improved Communication: Community Building and Social Integration. The following are the two clearest findings across all five sites: (1) E-mail is the most commonly used feature in the civic network environment and (2) it is the catalyst that stimulates user participation in other aspects of network life. E-mail not only makes it possible to communicate with individuals and groups regardless of sender/recipient time and location, it also gives users access to other exchange forums such as "chat rooms" (e.g., the "double trouble" chat room at the Community Access Center of the Playing to Win Network), electronic conferences (e.g., on homelessness), "listservs" (e.g., the "Seniors' Mailing List" on the Blacksburg Electronic Village), and electronic bulletin boards (e.g., listings of community events). According to many interviewees, such communication-enabling features are popular among civic network subscribers because they are typically easy to use and provide immediate social benefits.

Concerns that boundary-spanning networks might facilitate a reduction in community affiliation, or disinterest in local affairs, did not surface in our interviews. Posting defamatory or otherwise inappropriate message content appeared to raise little concern among administrators or users. In most cases, self- or peer-monitoring proves to be a sufficiently effective screening mechanism. We heard of only one instance in which administrators had to remove a user from the network. He was discovered downloading vast quantities of pornographic materials at a community-access site. On a different network, administrators intervened to prevent an organization from violating their policy about selling products over the network. One concern shared by administrators from at least two sites was the potential for electronic networks to help individuals and groups with extreme agendas (e.g., political, racist) to influence wider audiences. However, the consensus among interviewees was that new electronic technologies, similar to others in the past, can be used for positive and negative purposes, and that ultimately, increased interaction should not be feared.

Recognizing the power of e-mail to stimulate user participation in civic networks, all the sites in our study make e-mail accounts available to users—most at a cost well below the market price. For instance, they cover the cost of network connection at public access points and charge only a nominal registration fee to set up service.[4]

At Santa Monica's Public Electronic Network, city residents can register for an e-mail account free of charge. The Seattle Community Network asks for a small donation, typically $10, which it waives in the case of financial hardship to ensure that access is not limited to

---

[4]Users who connect to a network via a modem from home usually have to pay their own connection charges.

wealthier residents. Blacksburg citizens pay a $6 fee for an e-mail account on the Electronic Village. Many of the nonprofit organizations on the Playing to Win Network make e-mail accounts available to their staff and clients free of charge.

LatinoNet is the only network in the study that charges a sizable annual registration fee—$75 for organizational users and $60 for individuals. Since LatinoNet employs several full-time staff members but has no outside source of financial support, registration fees are necessary to cover staff salaries and operating costs. The other networks are supported by a combination of local government and foundation grants and volunteer time.

The general commitment of the civic networks to keep the price of registration low suggests that network organizers understand the role of e-mail as the catalyst for more advanced participation in civic networking. Many interviewees believed that encouraging the use of e-mail to support social and recreational interactions also increases its potential to raise awareness about community issues and activities, promote a community dialog, and improve social cohesiveness. In fact, electronic conferences organized around important social and political topics formed an important part of all but one of the networks (Playing to Win).

Organizers of the Seattle Community Network and the Public Electronic Network in Santa Monica are particularly focused on promoting the community-building capability of the civic networks in their cities. Since its conception, for instance, PEN has hosted hundreds of electronic conferences for its members, several of which elicited over a thousand responses from participants. In fact, three topics—religion, abortion, and homelessness—each generated over 2,000 responses (Moran, 1990). Examples of other conference topics aimed at increasing community awareness and participation include crime, environmental pollution, and city taxes.

Bulletin boards on locally relevant issues are a second tool that civic networks use to support community-building. Examples of topics posted on PEN's bulletin board include recreation and park schedules, bus schedules, earthquake safety tips, and information on pets for adoption. On SCN's community bulletin board, a large number of organizations post information about themselves and their meeting times and locations. These organizations include the League of Women Voters, the American Civil Liberties Union, and Sustainable Seattle—a group concerned with environmental, educational, and health issues affecting the long-term well-being of the Seattle community. SCN also allows several neighborhood subdivisions within the city to set up their own bulletin boards. Network users living in Wallingford, for example, can post or retrieve information about community events and programs specific to their neighborhood.

On the Blacksburg Electronic Village, the community bulletin board has two distinct focuses. One accessible area is called "About Blacksburg," on which is posted information about the city's history, weather, and restaurants. The other is labeled "Community Activities," where information about local organizations (e.g., reading groups, athletic clubs, the YMCA) and community events (e.g., block parties, "open house" events) is posted.

LatinoNet's community bulletin board is called the "Master Calendar of Events." Users access this feature to find detailed listings of Latino activities and events by region of the country. Network organizers say that the "Master Calendar" is one of the most commonly used features. Churches, social service organizations, and event organizers can post information to advertise activities to the broader community. According to network officials, its use is particularly high on key Latino holidays, when it is used to locate events at nearby community centers.

As a subset of their activities aimed at community-building, many of the sites in our study actively promote the use of the civic networks to facilitate the social integration of traditionally "disadvantaged" groups, e.g., older adults, and individuals with mental and physical handicaps and serious illnesses. The findings from research in other settings about the particular benefits of network access to members of otherwise peripheral groups—such as weakening status-based hierarchies and increasing integration of marginalized groups—are described in more detail in Chapter Two (e.g., Sproull and Kiesler, 1991b). These findings were corroborated by participants in the networks we studied here.

Many participants we interviewed agreed that membership in an electronic civic network can improve the quality of life in many ways for members of disadvantaged or marginalized groups (see, for example, Abramsohn, 1995). First, most interviewees agreed that electronic networks support the social integration of disadvantaged groups through increased access to informal peer support. For instance, social isolation often experienced by older adults or disabled individuals lessens when they are able to communicate easily with others who are experiencing common challenges, interviewees reported.

One network in the study, the New York-based Community Access Center—a social service organization in the Playing to Win Network—outreaches to a mentally ill and developmentally disabled population. Administrators at the center have organized a "double trouble" chat room on the network that gives individuals who are afflicted by a mental illness or are recovering drug users a forum to share problems, offer peer support, and simply "blow off steam."

Another advantage of communicating via on-line networks reported by interviewees in our study is the "equalizing" effect of the electronic medium. Discrimination and stereotyping are reduced when people interact electronically. According to an official from the Playing to Win Network, homeless people who communicate on-line do not experience the kind of disrespect often accorded to them in face-to-face interactions.

One organizer of the Seattle Community Network, discussing the benefits of network communication for people suffering from physical handicaps, described how such individuals often are the victims of negative stereotyping and false assumptions about their competency. He went on to say, however, that in the context of electronic interactions, "the only basis for discrimination is your typing speed."

Participants from the civic networks described another way in which electronic networks can be particularly beneficial to disadvantaged groups—they make access to relevant information and resources easier. As an example, Blacksburg has a large population of senior citizens. Organizers of the Blacksburg Electronic Village serve this group by devoting space on the network to seniors' issues and events. They have created a "Seniors' Page," which describes community events and resources targeted specifically for the elderly. In Seattle, the Washington Coalition of Citizens with Disabilities is expected to go on-line in mid-1995. The coalition representatives expect that the network will make it easier for handicapped individuals to gather information about particularly relevant social services.

Table 5.2 summarizes some of each network's most commonly offered and used services related to supporting community-building among their users and to increasing social integration of traditionally marginalized groups.

Improved Access to Information. Electronic networks also serve an important information resource function. In the same way that networked technology enables new and more effective point-to-point communication, it can facilitate effective access to, use of, and distribution of information. Via electronic networks, individuals and groups can tap directly into vast amounts and types of information

Table 5.2

Community Building and Social Integration

Civic Network	Community Information Services
Public Electronic Network, Santa Monica, CA	Electronic conferences (e.g., religion, home-lessness) Community bulletin board (e.g., earthquake safety tips)
Seattle Community Network, Seattle, WA	Electronic conferences (e.g., environmental pollution) Community bulletin boards (e.g., League of Women Voters, American Civil Liberties Union) Neighborhood forums (e.g., Wallingford on-line) Outreach programs (e.g., Coalition of Citizens with Disabilities)
Playing to Win Network, New York, NY	Outreach programs (e.g., "double trouble" chat room)
LatinoNet, San Francisco, CA	Electronic conferences Community bulletin boards (e.g., "Master Calendar of Events")
Blacksburg Electronic Village, Blacksburg, VA	Electronic conferences Community bulletin boards (e.g., "About Blacksburg") Outreach programs (e.g., "Seniors' Page")

from on-line databases and from organizations that advertise or offer their products and services on-line. The growing sophistication of network search applications, which makes it easier to find and retrieve on-line information, has supported the increased use of network technology as an information resource.[5] Current World Wide Web home pages or entry screens for the five networks are printed in Appendix B.

Universities and research organizations are among the best represented information providers on the Internet. However, nongovernmental organizations and government agencies at both the federal and local levels are starting to use the Internet more extensively to make their own databases and other information resources more widely available. At present, only a small percentage of corporations use the Internet for anything other than internal and external communications. However, they are trying increasingly to take advantage of the Internet as a medium for providing and for accessing information resources (e.g., Eng, 1995).

Organizers of all five civic networks talked about efforts to bring the benefits of on-line information resources to their users. All networks allow users to conduct on-line searches and to download information and files. Each of the networks except PEN is connected into the World Wide Web, allowing their users to access information from all over the globe. LatinoNet users also have access to and can download any of the information resources available via America Online. The Playing to Win Network and the Blacksburg Electronic Village both give their users full access to telnet and FTP applications. The telnet function allows users to move from one network site to the next; the FTP function gives users the ability to download information and files from on-line databases, e.g., university and government databases. SCN gives its users more limited access to the telnet function.

---

[5]Text-based interfaces to the Internet (e.g., gopher) are giving way to the graphics-based World Wide Web interfaces (e.g., Netscape, Mosaic). The Graphic, Visualization and Usability Center's Second World Wide Web survey at Georgia Institute of Technology writes that "the Web is one of the fastest growing of Internet resources, both in terms of the number of users and servers." (For more information see, http://www.cc.gatech.edu/gvu/user_surveys/.)

Although the amount and range of information available to users of on-line networks can be extremely useful, participants in this study reported that much information on the Internet is of only passing interest to most people. As one organizer of the Playing to Win Network said,

> jumping from New York to Paris and Washington and then back to New York is cool, but it's something most users only do once. If they don't find anything of direct relevance to their lives then they tend to stop using [the system].

Aware that users are most interested in having access to specific, individually relevant types of information, organizers of the Blacksburg Electronic Village and LatinoNet go beyond offering access to broad information resources on the Internet. Both networks work to make locally relevant information available on-line. For example, Blacksburg's organizers encourage local businesses, universities, and social service organizations to post information on the network that is directly relevant to the community.

The network, for example, has one area called the Village Mall. Here, users can access information on a large number of businesses in and near Blacksburg. Some firms post their location and business hours, some advertise products and services, and others accept on-line delivery orders. Another example of Blacksburg Electronic Village organizers' attempts to post locally relevant information is their on-line "Health Care Center." Here, users can access information from medical databases and local hospitals, health services, and support groups. They can also leave e-mail messages with questions about prescription drugs for a local doctor. Also, a section of the network called the "Village Schoolhouse" contains information on colleges and universities throughout Virginia.

Organizers of LatinoNet also emphasize making information available on-line that can be immediately used by their constituency—organizations and individuals in the Hispanic community. Important institutions—including research organizations, cultural centers, political action groups, youth leadership groups, charitable organizations, and a large number of university-based Latino research centers—use LatinoNet to reach their audience. LatinoNet users also can access information on employment, scholarships, and educational opportunities targeted to Latinos. According to the network organizers, students who work at the various nonprofit members of LatinoNet make frequent use of the on-line scholarship information. Professionals who belong to the network also post information about job openings.

Table 5.3 summarizes examples of the five network's on-line services that give citizens increased access to broad-based and locally relevant sources of information.

Table 5.3

Access to Information and Information Resources

Civic Network	Information Sources/Services
Public Electronic Network, Santa Monica, CA	Public library catalog on-line
Seattle Community Network, Seattle, WA	Public library catalog on-line Access to World Wide Web Limited telnet capabilities
Playing to Win, New York, NY	FTP and telnet functions Access to World Wide Web
LatinoNet, San Francisco, CA	Access to America Online Access to World Wide Web FTP and telnet functions Postings of employment, training, scholarship opportunities "Nonprofit Resources" "News and Events"
Blacksburg Electronic Village, Blacksburg, VA	Access to World Wide Web FTP and telnet functions "The Village Mall" "Education Center" "Health Care Center" "Other Virginia Resources"

Restructuring of Nonprofit and Community-Based Organizations.
Network technology's potential to facilitate intra-organizational communication and restructuring is the third area in which our and others' research suggests that electronic network access brings benefits (e.g., Bikson and Law, 1993; Eng 1995; Gross, 1995; Malone, Yates, and Benjamin, 1987).

Many of our study's interviewees discussed benefits associated with network access and the restructuring and formation of organizations. Two networks in particular—Playing to Win Network and LatinoNet—focus heavily on encouraging nonprofit organizations to use the network to help them organize and function more effectively. Officials at both networks described three significant benefits associated with nonprofits' use of electronic networks.

- On-line access facilitates collaborative idea generation and problem-solving. Since administrators of nonprofit organizations typically face similar challenges—often associated with resource constraints—the ability to learn from others' experiences and practices can save valuable time and money.

- Network technology streamlines internal communications and decisionmaking, particularly in large nonprofit organizations. For instance, at the Community Access Center of the Playing to Win Network, organizers can monitor their clients more effectively. When a client is moved from a hospital to a residential facility, he or she can contact the large number of social workers and social service agencies attached to the case via one network message.

- On-line access facilitates collaborative grant and report writing. Relevant background information can be collected and distributed on-line with greater speed and less cost, and drafts can be shared electronically among relevant colleagues.

Table 5.4 summarizes the services Playing to Win and LatinoNet offer clients to facilitate intra- and interorganizational processes.

Delivery of Government Services and Political Participation. The fourth category of emerging benefits associated with access to electronic networks involves more efficient delivery of local and federal government services and increased public awareness of and

Table 5.4

Organizational Formation and Restructuring

Civic Network	Organizational Resources
Playing to Win, New York, NY	Support for nonprofit administrators Communication with affiliates
LatinoNet, San Francisco, CA	Support for nonprofit administrators Communication with affiliates Grant and report writing

participation in government processes. Currently, opinions vary on how electronic networks will affect political participation (e.g., van de Donk, Snellen, and Tops, 1995). Some claim that network technology will enable a richer form of "semi-direct democracy," others fear it will give well-organized interest groups increased power and influence (e.g., "E-electioneering" 1995).

In the recently published book edited by van de Donk, Snellen, and Tops (1995), several authors discuss the potential dangers to democracy caused by increased "informatization" of local and federal governments. Condensing their various concerns to a core theme, they argue that unless citizens have access to "information management" tools, their participation in the democratic process will be constrained as a result of new information and communication technologies. As an example of how access to government officials currently is controlled, they cite the rule-based system that filters messages from citizens to the U.S. House of Representatives based on sender, subject line, etc. They also claim that new technologies now make it easier for representatives to delete official records and thus protect themselves from citizen scrutiny.

While the jury obviously is still out on the long-term effects of networked technology on the democratic process in the United States, in the meantime, local and federal government agencies are making increased use of technology to streamline the delivery of many services (U.S. Congress, Office of Technology Assessment, 1993). For example, state governments in Washington State and New York post employment and distance-learning opportunities on-line. At the federal level, two noteworthy examples of government agencies that have gone on-line recently are the Small Business Administration (SBA) and the Internal Revenue Service (IRS). The SBA allows small businesses to register on-line and to obtain information on raising finances, and, since 1993, the IRS has allowed citizens the option of filing tax returns electronically. Both organizations also respond to citizen queries on-line.

Our study found that the Blacksburg Electronic Village and Santa Monica PEN focus strongly on the potential of the network to restructure and deliver local government services. At present, Blacksburg government agencies post information on park and recreation schedules, recycling routes, and refuse pick-up schedules. They also post information on how to set up and register a small business on-line. By January 1996, all local water and refuse bills will be payable electronically and citizens will be able to renew simple licenses and register block parties on-line. To increase use of the electronic network, organizers of BEV aim to get as many local government services as possible on-line.

On Santa Monica's Public Electronic Network, on-line inquiries or complaints can be registered with the traffic, police, or fire departments. Simple licenses can be renewed on-line, and all local bills can be paid electronically. PEN members can obtain minutes of City Council meetings on-line as well as correspond with their representatives. The city plans to allow residents to pay parking tickets electronically. Echoing the thoughts of BEV organizers, one senior official at Santa Monica's PEN suggested:

> People have to perceive a value to using the network . . . [and] one of the best ways to convince them there is a value is by reducing the amount of time they must spend interacting with government agencies.

Although only the Blacksburg Electronic Village and PEN focus strongly on the potential of the system to deliver government services, all five networks try in some way to exploit the technology to increase citizen political involvement. For the most part, the three other networks have limited their activities to encouraging communication between legislative representatives and constituents. However this, in itself, is valuable: Officials and citizens engage in a two-way dialog, which is very different from simply posting government information.

For example, the Seattle Community Network organizes question-and-answer forums between local politicians and citizens. In the most recent forum called "Ask the Governor," members of the Seattle community were able to e-mail real-time messages to him and receive responses. Organizers of the Playing to Win Network and the Blacksburg Electronic Village encourage their members to e-mail senators, representatives, and the president.

Officials at Playing to Win's Harlem Computing Center registered it as a public access point for a series of "electronic town hall" meetings held nationwide during the summer of 1995. The National Telecommunications and Information Agency (NTIA) organized the meetings, which included subjects such as proposed cuts in welfare spending and the effect of electronic government. Organizers of Santa Monica's Public Electronic Network ask public officials to take part in electronic conferences and encourage citizens to contact the city representatives via e-mail.

LatinoNet has gone a step further. A primary objective of this network is to facilitate more effective political organization. As one senior official at LatinoNet put it,

> Other communication media have been used to define and stereotype Latinos. It is important that this medium be used to the benefit of the [Latino] community.

According to LatinoNet organizers, networking nonprofits, research centers, and political organizations together into one electronic community helps members of the Latino community organize and meet shared goals. They view electronic communication as a powerful tool to encourage political dialog and awareness on issues of concern to Latinos. The network hosts on-line question-and-answer conferences with important Latino politicians and conducts user polls on major political events to gauge members' opinions. There is also space on the network called "Policy Matters," which carries news on breaking political and legislative developments of particular interest to the Latino community.

LatinoNet illuminates another fundamental characteristic of on-line communities, namely, that they are defined not merely by geographic or political boundaries but also by unifying interests and goals. For instance, concerns such as immigration and foreign trade policies are likely to be common to many members of the LatinoNet community. As such, the potential for the network to expand its utility and influence beyond the current San Francisco/Bay area focus, and perhaps beyond the southern border of the United States, is high—particularly in light of increased trade and communication after the passing of the North American Free Trade Agreement (NAFTA). (See Chapter Six for more discussion of the international implications of electronic communities.)

LatinoNet's and the other networks' services are summarized in Table 5.5.

Implementation Implications of Universal Service

We now turn our attention to the second issue of interest in this report, namely, what are the major implementation implications of providing access to and encouraging use of electronic networks? As noted above, a distinguishing feature of civic networks, compared with commercial on-line services such as CompuServe, is that they

Table 5.5

Government Services, Public Awareness, and Participation

Civic Network	Government Interaction/Services
Public Electronic Network, Santa Monica, CA	Electronic communication with city officials and departments Information on city government services On-line bill paying and license renewal[a]
Seattle Community Network, Seattle, WA	Electronic "town hall meetings" "Ask the Governor" on-line question-and-answer forum
Playing to Win, New York, NY	NTIA electronic "town hall meetings" E-mail a senator/congress member
LatinoNet, San Francisco, CA	Electronic "town hall meetings" "Policy Matters"
Blacksburg Electronic Village, Blacksburg, VA	E-mail a senator/congress member Information on city government services On-line bill paying and license renewal[a]

[a]These services will become available in January 1996.

attempt to ensure equity of access to their services—particularly among traditionally underserved populations. In this study, we learned lessons about delivery of on-line services that could help policymakers think about the feasibility of providing ubiquitous access to electronic mail.

The findings in this study related to how implementation strategies affect subsequent use of on-line technology mirror those of prior research on introducing technologies in many other settings (e.g., Bikson and Eveland, 1986; Bikson and Law, 1993; Law, Bikson, and Frinking, 1995; Rogers, 1983). For instance, the availability of adequate resources, e.g., money, people, hardware, and software, was felt to be crucial to network setup and long-term viability. Also, we found that the successful delivery of civic networks depends on the presence of a committed individual, or "champion," of the network. In fact, the retirement of the founder of one network in our study who had been instrumental in promotion and fundraising had severe consequences for that network. The network's growth slowed significantly and over a year later still had not fully recovered.

The importance of the implementation issues just described should not be minimized. But two other issues emerged from our study as particularly critical in the context of providing universal access to on-line services, namely, location of computer access points and training.

Access to Computers. Calculations based on 1993 CPS data show that around 40 percent of the total U.S. population had access to a computer at home, work, or school. Far fewer had modems or access to network services. Clearly, then, for the goal of universal use of e-mail and other on-line services to be realized—at least in the near to mid term—access for the majority of citizens needs to be addressed (the costs of various universal access options are discussed in detail in Chapter Four).

Among the networks in this study, the percentage of users with access to a computer (and modem) at home or work varied widely. Organizers of the Playing to Win Network estimated that less than 10 percent of their members log on to the network from home. Interviewees at two of their affiliates, the Community Access Center and the Harlem Center, reported that very few of their users have access to a computer at home. However, about three-quarters of the Blacksburg Electronic Village and Santa Monica PEN users dial in via a modem from home. The rest of the networks fall somewhere in between.[6]

Administrators at the Seattle Community Network do not keep statistics on how many users access the network from home versus from public access terminals at the library. However, they believe that most users belong to the latter group. The nonprofit member organizations of LatinoNet all access the system from computers in their home offices. The few individual users of the network dial in from their home or work via a modem.

Although the proportion of users at each network without home access to a computer differs widely, in each case, a significant proportion needs access to the network from some publicly available terminal. With the exception of LatinoNet, whose members are mainly nonprofit organizations, all networks have made computers available in a number of public locations. Again, the amount and location of public terminals differed across the networks in the study.

Computer terminals are most commonly located in public libraries. In the case of the Seattle Community Network, libraries in Seattle and in King County present virtually the only public access option. However, currently 50 libraries have at least one computer with dial-up access to SCN. The only other public access terminal is located at a school in a low-income neighborhood participating in a project specifically aimed at bringing computers and network technology to poor communities. However, organizers plan to increase the number of public access sites to include additional schools, churches, community centers, and senior centers. Organizers are also raising funds to increase the number of phone lines available for dial-in access from private homes. At present, only one phone line is available for dial-in access during the day and six at night.

---

[6]Even the low end of this household-network-access range is higher than the national average, and the 75 percent home access figure is beyond the high-income quartile average (see Chapter Two). Therefore, civic nets may be a good strategy for providing access to universal e-mail. These figures may also imply, however, that the clientele of these particular civic networks are not representative of U.S. society as a whole.

Users of the Santa Monica PEN and Blacksburg Electronic Village have the greatest diversity of public access options. Both networks have placed terminals in libraries. In Santa Monica, there are public access terminals at the city library, as well as libraries at the local college and in all of the K–12 schools in the local school district. In Blacksburg, the public library has five dedicated computer terminals, all with World Wide Web software, that are linked to the network via a high-speed modem.

Members of the Santa Monica and Blacksburg networks also have other access options. Users of the Blacksburg Electronic Village can log into the network from public terminals at a number of locations. For instance, 17 public schools in Blacksburg and the outlying area have access terminals. Citizens can also use terminals located at City Hall, in buildings at the Virginia Polytechnic Institute and State University campus, and in a number of apartment complexes around town. Public access sites for Santa Monica's PEN, similarly, go beyond the public library to include terminals at senior centers and City Hall. Santa Monica's PEN also placed public access terminals in a youth center, the American Red Cross office, and at least one public park. However, all of these terminals have since been removed because of lack of use.

On the Playing to Win Network, questions of access are determined by the individual nonprofit organizations. All the nonprofits locate terminals in their administrative offices for use by staff members. Many also make terminals available for public use in residential care facilities, hospitals, day treatment centers, and community computing labs.

These efforts to ensure publicly available computer access attest to the important role this issue will play in efforts to bring about universal e-mail access. Even though increasing numbers of the population have access to computers at home or work, we know that education- and income-based gaps are widening between the technology haves and have-nots (see Chapter Two). For universal access to on-line networks to be feasible, at least in the short- to medium-term, providing publicly available access points is clearly important.

Training and Support. Initial training and ongoing technical and social support for providers and consumers of on-line information constitute the other essential components of implementation success stressed by organizers and participants at each civic network. Again, this mirrors previous research findings about implementing new technologies in complex user settings (e.g., Eveland et al., 1992; Gattiker, 1992; Nelson, Whitener, and Philcox, 1995).

Without exception, interviewees in this study viewed training as a critical first step to getting individuals on-line. Many of the network organizers maintained that real learning occurs only when users have enough knowledge and confidence to begin to explore the potential of network technology on their own. But in the absence of initial training, users often cannot reach this threshold.

Networks offer training in a number of ways. The Seattle Community Network and Blacksburg Electronic Village both provide short introductory training courses at the libraries where public terminals are located. SCN training is conducted by volunteer staff, who visit a different public library in King County and Seattle every two weeks. In Blacksburg, training is conducted centrally twice a week at the public library by an electronic reference librarian. In both cases, the introductory training session lasts two hours. Users are taught how to log on to the network, how to use e-mail, how to access the various communication forums, and how to search for information from different on-line sources. After an initial training session, ongoing user support is provided upon request by the electronic reference librarians as well as through on-line and telephone hotlines monitored by network support staff.

Santa Monica PEN offers users a short introductory training session at City Hall. However, according to project organizers, few users take this course—most learn the system at home, perhaps with the help of the on-line tutorial. Ongoing user support is provided by PEN technical staff who respond to user questions by phone and e-mail.

LatinoNet provides initial on-site training for administrators and staff of the nonprofit member organizations on how to use the network. A LatinoNet trainer visits the nonprofit headquarters and gives instruction on basic network applications and features. After the initial training session, user support is provided both on-line and over the telephone. LatinoNet has no training program for the individual users of its services.

Playing to Win Network organizers also provide on-site training to nonprofit administrators. For nonprofits that do not have an existing telecommunications program or staff with no telecommunications experience, Playing to Win administrators conduct an on-site training session on the basics of network usage. Training for individual users of the Playing to Win networks depends on the level of commitment of administrators at each nonprofit site to integrate network technology fully into their social service programs. Many of the nonprofits offer lectures and formal training seminars to their clients, but this is not true in all cases. Ongoing user support on the Playing to Win Network tends to take place informally. Staff members and individual users at each nonprofit site are encouraged to rely on one another as they continue to learn about the network.

Most civic networks also offer training to on-line providers of information—both individuals and organizations. Many administrators talked about the importance of enabling various community, political, and research organizations to post and update information on their own. This makes the information more timely and accurate, and it conserves already scarce network resources.

LatinoNet and the Seattle Community Network provide particularly extensive training to information providers. SCN has established a mentoring system whereby a technically competent volunteer is linked to each information provider. The "mentor" typically goes to an information provider's office to teach staff members there how to enter and update information on-line. Once an information provider begins to supply information to the network, the mentor continues to lend support and troubleshoot problems as they arise.

At LatinoNet, an experienced trainer visits each nonprofit member organization. During the site visit to provide initial training on network use, the LatinoNet representative will also teach staff members how to supply information directly on-line. Follow-up site visits may be scheduled also depending on the technical competence of the staff members at each site. LatinoNet administrators try to resolve as many technical problems as possible from a distance but will conduct additional site visits where there is a need for additional help on database management and information formatting.

Because the goals of the Santa Monica Public Electronic Network are less focused on making information available from social- and community-based organizations, it does not offer special training to information providers. Rather, system administrators load postings as appropriate. Administrators of the Blacksburg Electronic Village hold training classes for information providers periodically at the local Chamber of Commerce. Whenever possible they try to teach a volunteer at each social, community, or business organization how to submit on-line information to the network.

Our study suggests that two implementation issues need to be resolved in any attempt to offer access to, and encourage participation in, electronic networks:

- Availability and location of publicly accessible computers, and

- Training and learning support.

We summarize how each network approaches these issues in Table 5.6.

CONCLUSIONS

These conclusions are based on our in-depth study of five civic networks. We do not claim that these networks are representative of all examples in the country, especially since the number of networks of this type is rapidly growing. However, we are confident that the findings we presented in the previous sections yield useful answers to the questions: What are the benefits, if any, to participation in electronic communities? And, what are the important implementation issues that affect the delivery of on-line access to target populations? In the following sections, we present our conclusions about these issues.

Access to Electronic Networks Leads to Benefits

Individuals, groups, organizations, and the broader U.S. society can benefit from access to electronic networks. Networks provide opportunities for new and reliable informal and formal communication. They can support interpersonal relationships and facilitate the social integration of otherwise marginalized groups. Concerns that

Table 5.6

Terminal Access and User Training and Support

Civic Network	Public Access Terminals	Initial Training	Ongoing Support
Public Electronic Network, Santa Monica, CA	City Hall Libraries (e.g., city, high school) Senior centers	Self-guided tutorial 45-minute session at City Hall	On-line/phone On-site at City Hall and library
Seattle Community Network, Seattle, WA	50 public libraries	Two-hour session at library Mentoring for information providers	Reference librarians SCN voice mail hotline On-line
Playing to Win, New York, NY	Residential care facilities, hospitals, community computing centers	Site visits to nonprofits Classes for individual users	Peer mentoring and informal support at nonprofits
LatinoNet, San Francisco, CA	None (all terminals at nonprofits)	Site visits to nonprofits No training for individuals	On-line/phone Site visits for difficult problems
Blacksburg Electronic Village, Blacksburg, VA	Public library 135 buildings on university campus 17 public schools 27 apartment buildings Town Hall	Two-hour sessions at university Two-hour sessions at public library Three-hour sessions at Chamber of Commerce for information providers	Public library Telephone hotline On-line

boundary-spanning networks might facilitate a breakdown of community affiliation, or disinterest in local affairs, appear unfounded. Although individuals benefit from access to wider national (and international) resources, ties to their local communities remain strong (and, arguably, are strengthened). Also the fear that individuals will be overwhelmed by a deluge of "junk mail," or subjected to defamatory or otherwise inappropriate message content, appears to be, although not a trivial issue, at least not one requiring too much attention at this point.

Networks also make access to vast amounts of information quick and easy. Facilitating access to information on, for example, education and employment opportunities should benefit traditionally disadvantaged groups relatively more than their socioeconomically advantaged counterparts. It should have the effect of "leveling the playing field." In addition, network access promises to facilitate organizational formation and restructuring. This is a particular benefit for nonprofit and community-based organizations that typically operate under severe human, financial, and technical resource constraints. Such organizations are starting to use electronic networks to share ideas, solve problems, conserve resources, and ultimately sustain viability.

Moreover, electronic networks can facilitate citizen participation in the political process. Some individuals now use e-mail to contact government representatives, for instance. However, at this point we can only speculate about whether or not this trend will grow. As the PEN experience makes clear, the answer depends, in part, on how willing government agencies and representatives at varied administrative levels are to respond interactively in civic dialogs.

E-Mail Is the Catalyst to Network Use

Electronic mail is the critical first entry point to participation in electronic communities for the majority of individuals. E-mail and other communication tools, such as electronic chat rooms and conferencing, are the most commonly used network features. They are typically user friendly and provide the most immediate and obvious benefits to users.

Also, because e-mail is immediately popular with network users, it plays a crucial role in stimulating them to experiment with other features of an electronic environment. The value of e-mail's role as a catalyst to other, more advanced network use is significant in two ways. First, many of the benefits to individuals and groups outlined above depend on the exploitation of other, perhaps more intimidating, features of networks, including those with international links far beyond the immediate vicinity (e.g., search/retrieval applications and file transfer/download protocols). Second, return on investments made by commercial businesses and other enterprises in network services also are likely to rely on use of more advanced, value-added features.

Successful Implementation of Electronic Networks Combines Access, Training, and Ongoing Support

Our research leads us to conclude that two implementation issues are particularly critical in this context: ensuring access to computers and providing adequate training and ongoing technical support. In addition to home access, options for network access in public places (e.g., libraries, schools, public buildings, hotel lobbies, business centers) should be established. Offering training and support services at such locations also should be considered.

These issues take on even more importance in light of the question of making electronic networks universally accessible. If a U.S. goal is to exploit the potential of electronic networks to equalize opportunities between haves and have-nots, making computers and training available will be essential. Also, access and training in combination is important—making computers available with no training or technical support is unlikely to lead to effective use—in the same way that introducing computers into classrooms positively influences outcomes only when teachers and students are trained to use them and have opportunities to do so regularly as a part of their routine educational activities.

Increased Access Supports Network Viability

Extending the use of network resources to individuals without computers at home or at work creates two positive outcomes. First, on-line services would be made available to traditionally underserved groups who can be expected to gain higher marginal benefits from access. Second, a larger target population is created for a range of services, which increases the network's own future viability.

Suppliers of network services can sustain their operations only if they can generate a sufficiently high level of demand. For instance, local businesses in Blacksburg are willing to invest in the Electronic Village because they assume they will benefit economically by doing so. By extending access to groups that otherwise are not able to make use of the technology, networks raise demands for a wide range of services and therefore encourage support from a broad constituency.

Content of Information and Services Is Important to Determining Usage

Information content influences access and use. We noted that each network focused efforts on ensuring access to information and services relevant to its target audience. The benefits of on-line access to information directly relate to the quality and accessibility of that information. If the information and services that users need are not available, or are hard to find, it is likely that attrition will result, and potential new audiences will be lost.

In sum, we conclude that there are important national benefits associated with access to e-mail and other network services and that these benefits could help level the playing field for traditionally disadvantaged populations. However, this will not happen unless we follow the example of the civic networks that we described in this report. These and other networks have expended much effort to reach underserved populations—an effort that relies on ongoing commitment and resources to ensure that access is available and outreach is supported.

Chapter Six

INTERNATIONAL IMPLICATIONS FOR GLOBAL DEMOCRATIZATION

Christopher Kedzie

We have argued that electronic mail networks create social capital by strengthening the mission-oriented and interpersonal ties within on-line communities. The social benefits in the domestic setting are addressed in Chapter Five. We now turn to the international arena into which the democratizing influences of e-mail extend. Since the technology, unconstrained by geographic borders and political barriers, shrinks the globe, the effect of interconnectivity on democracy worldwide is only one of myriad international implications warranting particular attention.

Increasingly, formal and informal e-mail assist relationships in transcending national frontiers. Universal e-mail in the United States with abundant international connections can help to spread the seeds of democracy even to nondemocratic lands. Global democratization is critically important to the future of democracy in America. According to scholars such as Samuel P. Huntington (1984) and Charles S. Maier (1994), the prospects for democracy here are inexorably linked to the state of democracy worldwide and our national commitment to global democratization.

COINCIDENT REVOLUTIONS

Coincident revolutions at the end of the 1980s—breakthroughs in democracy, communication, and information technologies around the globe—have suggested to pundits and politicians that democratic freedom worldwide and electronic interconnectivity might be positively correlated. Prominently on Russian television in 1994, President Clinton made the association, "Revolutions [in] information and communication and technology and production, all these things make democracy more likely" (1994). Analysts too have postulated this relationship, but to date, all evidence has been anecdotal.[1] Most common are stories of fax messages rallying prodemocracy demonstrators outside the Chinese "Forbidden City" in 1989 and of the e-mail messages emanating from the besieged Russian "White House" during the failed coup of 1991.

This chapter begins substantive examination, both empirical and theoretical, into the relationship between new information and communications technologies and democracy. First, our investigations reject the "null hypothesis" that interconnectivity and democracy are not correlated. Then, we empirically examine the relationship through a variety of statistical lenses, followed by some comments on causality and some policy conclusions.

Visual evidence of this relationship is provocative. Figure 6.1 shows Freedom House democracy ratings for all countries of the world. Darker shading indicate higher levels of democracy.

Figure 6.2 is a comparable world projection denoting prevalence of major worldwide e-mail exchanging computer networks.

The metric used in the second chart is termed "interconnectivity."[2] Darker shading indicates a greater level of interconnectivity. Corresponding regions of dark and light on every continent reveal striking similarities between the two charts. The pattern similarity suggests a correlation and inspires more rigorous examination.

The two variables, democracy and interconnectivity, underlie this chapter's statistical analyses. Freedom House publishes quantitative measures of democracy in the *Comparative Survey of Freedom* for 1993–1994. This survey ranks every country in terms of "political

---

[1]See, for example, Builder and Bankes (1991) and Ganley (1991).

[2]"Interconnectivity" is a term popularized by Larry Landweber for his measures of the proliferation of global e-mail networks.

rights," the extent to which people freely participate in selecting pol- icymakers and formulating policy and "civil liberties," the extent to which people are able to develop and express ideas independent of the state's. Since the correlation between these two measures is high, the independent "democracy" variable used here is the normal- ized average.[3]

This use of Freedom House data conforms with academic practice for evaluating correlates to democracy.[4] There are inherent difficulties in quantifying a subjective multidimensional democratic quality across widely varying governments with a single scalar.[5] Despite these problems, a practical consensus for relative rankings prevails quite broadly. Conformity in ordinal rankings suggests that, although the concept of democracy may be difficult to describe ex- plicitly, it is well understood intuitively (at least by Western analysts). Alex Inkeles noted this agreement between various metrics for democracy:

> [D]emocracy is a distinctive and highly coherent syndrome of char- acteristics such that anyone measuring only a few of the salient characteristics will classify nations in much the same way as will another analyst who also measured only a few qualities but uses a different set of characteristics, so long as both have selected their indicators from the same larger pool of valid measures. Far from being like the elephant confronting the blind sages, democracy is more like a ball of wax. (Inkeles et al., 1990, p. 5.)

The prevalence of information revolution technologies may seem easier to quantify because it involves keeping track of tangible equipment. Yet, this variable is problematic, too. Some difficulties

---

[3]Freedom House rates countries on a decreasing basis from 7 to 1 in both categories, civil liberties and political rights. A ranking of "1" indicates the highest relative accor- dance with the principles of democracy, and a ranking of "7," the lowest. The normal- ized average used here and elsewhere (see Rowen, 1995, or Muller and Seligson, 1994, for other examples) converts the scale to one that increases from 0 to 100, such that maximum democracy has the highest rating.

[4]For several examples see, the World Bank (1991), Starr (1991), Helliwell (1992), Lipset, Seong, and Torres (1993), Muller and Seligson (1994), Boone (1994), and Rowen (1995).

[5]Many of the measurement and statistical difficulties are addressed in considerable depth by Inkeles et al. (1990) and Dahl (1971).

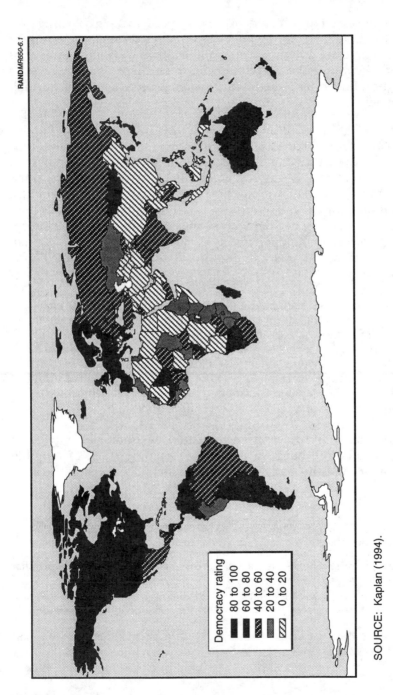

Figure 6.1—Democracy Rating

SOURCE: Kaplan (1994).

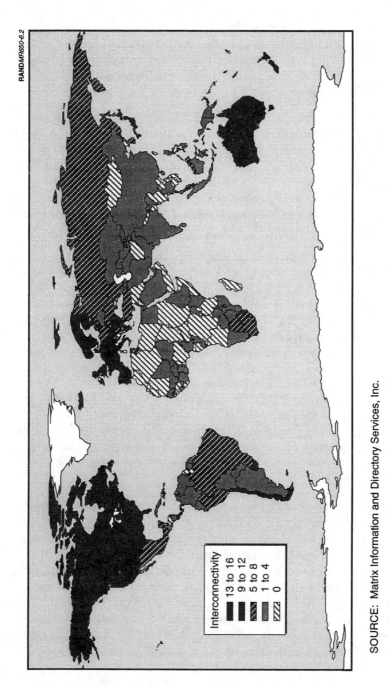

SOURCE: Matrix Information and Directory Services, Inc.

Figure 6.2—Interconnectivity Scores

are definitional.   As communication technologies increasingly overlap, recalling Ithiel de Sola Pool's "convergence of modes" (1983, p. 23), what to include becomes a difficult question to answer. Computers can send faxes; radio waves and television cables can carry e-mail messages.

Electronic mail is the specific focus of this study because it enables people to discourse across borders in ways that have never been possible. Of the numerous e-mail networks, four are globally dominant: Internet, BITNET, UUCP and FidoNet. Record keeping has not been consistent, regular, or accurate across the networks. The best available and most comprehensive data are for the numbers of nodes, which therefore constitute the basic unit of measure for interconnectivity in this report.

Nodes themselves, however, are not equal, even within the same network. A node may consist of a single computer and user or an entire organization with many of both.   The Matrix Information Directory Service (MIDS) tracks and maintains historic data on the size of these networks aggregated by country.   The "interconnectivity" metric used here is a combined measure of MIDS data on nodes per capita per country for each of the four major computer systems that can exchange electronic mail. Within each network, countries are ranked and scored with a number from 0 to 4. The 0 is assigned to all countries with no nodes in a particular network. The numbers 1 through 4 are assigned by quartile. The lowest quartile of countries with one or more nodes for a network receives a score of 1. The highest quartile of countries receives a score of 4. The sum of the four scores determines the level of interconnectivity on a scale from 0 to 16.

The combined scores weight each of the four networks equally because the ability to exchange e-mail is a relatively generic capability. Nevertheless, the equal weightings introduce some theoretic difficulties. Although each network supports e-mail, they are not necessarily comparable in other respects. For instance, the Internet, with specialized services such as the World Wide Web and remote log on, has much more functional capacity than the others. Therefore, it is arithmetically possible that a country with a low interconnectivity score and Internet actually may have more communications capability than a country with a higher score but no Internet. In practice, this is not likely to occur, and our analysis shows none of the potential degradation of this variable.

For several reasons, this theoretic possibility is not a practical problem. First, e-mail, but not necessarily the other services, offers the specific capability that is hypothesized to have dynamic implications for democratization: multidirectional discourse across borders in a timely and inexpensive manner, unbounded by geographic and institutional constraints.[6] Second, interconnectivity evolves. Less-capable systems are similarly less expensive and easier to implement, so initially they are more prevalent. Improvements to these systems ultimately incorporate Internet capabilities. Thus, a general progression emerges in the enhancement of interconnectivity that this scale approximates. Furthermore, to the extent that interconnectivity as a predictor for democracy is measured imprecisely, the effect is reduced statistical significance of the predictor. Thus, the conclusions would still be valid, a fortiori, from this analysis.

EMPIRICAL ANALYSIS

Univariate Correlation

Figures 6.1 and 6.2 suggest a specific conjecture that univariate analyses support. A strong correlation between democracy and interconnectivity does, indeed, exist.

The scatterplot and accompanying regression line in Figure 6.3 display this relationship graphically, and the following correlation matrix in Table 6.1 displays this relationship numerically. The correlation matrix includes a set of social indicators that are often

---

[6]The essence of multidirectional communication is that all people who receive information via a certain information channel can participate equally within the complete and identical context of the discussion. Another term commonly used to describe multidirectional communication has been "many-to-many." However, this term can be misleading. The connotation of "many" in one-to-many can be the billion or so people around the globe who watch soccer's World Cup, which would of course be impossibly unwieldy for many-to-many. More important, quantifying the number of participants misses the most critical aspect of multidirectional communication. Independent of how many people are involved—even if there are only three—e-mail technology creates a different dynamic from unidirectional broadcast or bidirectional intercourse and thus might be expected to have differing social and political outcomes.

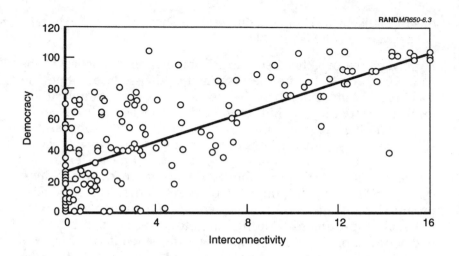

Figure 6.3—Democracy and Interconnectivity Regression and Scatterplot

Table 6.1

Matrix Showing First-Order Correlations

	Democracy	Intercon- nectivity	Schooling	GDP	Life Ex- pectancy	Ethnicity	Log (Pop)
Democracy	1.00						
Interconnectivity	0.73	1.00					
Schooling	0.67	0.82	1.00				
Per-capita GDP	0.57	0.84	0.79	1.00			
Life expectancy	0.53	0.71	0.87	0.71	1.00		
Ethnicity	0.27	0.26	0.35	0.23	0.42	1.00	
Log (Pop)	−0.09	0.07	0.10	0.05	0.07	0.11	1.00

hypothesized as democracy's causal correlates. Descriptions and explanations of the variables follow these graphics.

The question of causality will be addressed in detail below, but as the matrix attests, the correlation coefficient for interconnectivity is not only large, it is substantially larger than that of any other traditional predictors of democracy. The coefficient on per-capita gross domestic product (GDP) is smaller by 0.16.

Economic development, reported here as a per-capita GDP (and abbreviated simply as GDP), is quantified in terms of purchasing power parity, as is traditional. Education is commonly paired with economic development as a predictor of democracy.[7] Direct causality is easy to imagine. An educated public is likely to be both more aware of political events and more capable of intervening to influence them. Indirectly, education conceivably enhances democracy by contributing to economic growth. The average number of years of schooling across the entire population is considered to be the best measure of education for analyses such as these (Rowen, 1995, p. 57).

Human development and health indicators also are often correlated with democracy. Most prevalent in the literature are infant mortality rates and life expectancies.[8] A causal argument could be posed that as citizens become more assured of their own well-being they have more incentive and wherewithal to demand civil rights and political liberties. Although these two measures, infant mortality and life expectancy, are highly correlated, forward causality seems more plausible in terms of the latter.[9]

Cultural and ethnic factors also may have certain roles in democratization. "Homogeneous national entities may be more likely to evolve into peaceable democracies than states rent by harsh linguistic and cultural antagonisms" (Gottlieb, 1994, p. 101). A measure of ethnic homogeneity is the percentage of the population that constitutes the largest ethnic group in a nation.[10]

In multivariate analyses, cultural differences across countries are potentially more important than the internal mix. Debates continue as to whether certain cultures or civilizations are favorably disposed or

---

[7]For examples see Lipset (1959), Helliwell (1992), Lipset, Seong, and Torres (1993), and Rowen (1995).

[8]For examples, see the World Bank (1991) and Boone (1994).

[9]United Nations Development Programme (1993) provided all the economic, education, and health data used in these analyses.

[10]These data are published in the CIA *World Fact Book* (1993). In a few cases, mostly in Northern Europe and Africa, these data were not available. Where applicable, the percentage of largest religious affiliation substituted for the missing data.

fundamentally disinclined to embrace democratic principles.[11] In either case, it is not difficult to believe that cultural aspects influence the characterization of the political regimes and the appreciation of personal liberties. To account for these effects, the dataset includes binary variables that indicate the culture with which each country most closely identifies. Demarcation between cultures can never be exact. Inexorably, the classification of some countries into any of the regional categories is susceptible to quibbling. Six regional categories were defined that incorporated elements of geography, history, and religion.

These six—Africa, Asia, Eurasia, Latin America, the Middle East, and Western Europe—map reasonably well onto the eight civilizations identified by Samuel Huntington (1993). Western Europe also includes countries that are not on the continent but that have a dominant Western European heritage: the United States, Canada, Australia, and New Zealand. Israel also is included in the West European category. The Middle East category is predominantly Muslim, includes the Islamic North African states, and extends from Egypt to Pakistan. Africa is defined in fairly obvious geographic terms including South Africa, minus the northern states grouped into the Middle East. Asia includes the Confucian countries and the Pacific Islands, plus India and Japan, minus North Korea. Latin America stretches from Mexico through Argentina including all the Caribbean except Cuba. Cuba and North Korea, plus Albania and the splinter states of Yugoslavia, in addition to the members of the former Warsaw Pact countries, are all grouped in the Eurasian category.

Cultural influences may also shape the ways various people use communication technologies. Therefore, some of the regression models that follow include interaction terms that are the products of the binary regional variables and the interconnectivity scores.

Population completes this list of independent variables. Presumably, the size of a country could influence the type and effectiveness of governance. Small countries may be anomalous. Therefore, only countries whose populations exceeded 1,000,000 (and for which data

---

[11]For characteristic arguments from both sides of the debate, see Huntington (1993) and Schifter (1994).

are available) in 1993 are included in this study.[12]   Above this threshold minimum, country populations have a skewed distribution that spans more than three orders of magnitude. Population, therefore, is best included here as an independent variable in a log form.

Multivariate Dominance

Like the maps presented above, the correlation matrix exhibits a surprisingly powerful correlation between interconnectivity and democracy. In large complex systems such international politics, simple relationships can rarely tell the whole story. Multiple linear regression can be a powerful technique to provide insight into convoluted interactions. As with other techniques, the answers are often influenced by the way the questions are asked. In other words, regression results can be model-specific. Therefore, several versions of the model offer various perspectives that can be integrated to form a comprehensive understanding of the interactions. Ultimately, the multiple linear regressions in this research provide further evidence that we cannot dismiss this correlation as spurious. Regression results of six representative and most informative models are shown in Table 6.2. Models I and II show the resulting statistical output of ordinary least squares (OLS) regressions. Model I is an inclusive model involving six predictors.

Immediately apparent is that, again, interconnectivity emerges as the dominant predictor. With greater than 99.9 percent certainty, higher than that for any other predictor, one can reject the null hypothesis that there is no relationship between democracy and interconnectivity. Furthermore, the coefficient on interconnectivity is large. A single point increase on the interconnectivity scale corresponds to an increase of 5 points in democracy rating.

The correlation of GDP with democracy in this model, which is also statistically significant, is interesting in that the sign is negative. This result supports arguments of some scholars, as well as apologists for

[12]Data were either missing or relative to inconsistent entities for many of the new countries resulting from the recent breakups of Czechoslovakia and Yugoslavia. Therefore, the Czech and Slovak Republics, Bosnia-Herzegovina, Croatia, Serbia, and Slovenia were excluded from this study. Additionally, critical missing data precluded the inclusion of Taiwan.

Table 6.2

Regression Models

	Model								
	I	II	III	IV	V		VI		
LHS Variable	DEM	DEM	DEM	DEM	DEM	INT	DEM	INT	GDP
N	136	141	136	141	136		136		
Adj. R-square	0.583	0.536	0.643	0.588	0.583	0.832	0.472	0.833	0.597
Constant	61.7**	36.1***	35.59	85.40*	31.5**	−1.14*	35.9*	−1.30	1407
Democracy						−0.0102		0.0126	−30.5
Intercon.	4.43***	5.57***			4.72**		8.82***		1478.00***
GDP	−0.0014*	−0.0008	−0.00057	0.00030	−0.0015		−0.0034*	0.00009	
Log (Pop)	−4.21**	−3.48**	−3.73**	−2.98*	−4.21**		−4.09**		
Av School Yrs	4.81**		4.81**		4.61**				−288
Life Expect.	−0.076*		−0.35		−0.75*		−0.129		
Ethnicity	0.13		0.18*		0.13		0.12		
Literacy						0.034**		0.033**	
Telephones						0.22***		0.19**	
Africa			0.11	−53.06					
Asia			dropped	−44.98					
Eurasia			−19.22**	−59.82					
Latin America			−15.10	−29.92					
Middle East			−17.00*	−62.83					
West Europe			30.98	dropped					
INT*Africa			7.02**	7.15***					
INT*Asia			1.93	2.22					
INT*Eurasia			3.87**	4.93***					
INT*Latin Am.			1.98	3.24*					
INT*M. East			3.87	2.63					
INT*W. Europe			0.72	0.98					

NOTE: "INT*" indicates an interaction term as the product of the interconnectivity variable and the categorical region variable.

t-statistics are in parentheses.

***=Significance at the 0.1 percent level.

**=Significance at the 1 percent level.

*=Significance at the 10 percent level.

the Pinochet and Lee Kuan Yu economic development theories, that democracy is not without cost.[13] All else being equal, such as interconnectivity and population, greater economic development might be available only at the expense of democratization.

Years of schooling and life expectancy also show statistical significance. In the case of the latter, the negative sign is more difficult to explain, although this is the weakest of the significant predictors. The coefficient on population is also significant, but the size of a country's population, largely inaccessible to foreign intervention, offers scarcely few policy recommendations (except perhaps to shine a glimmer of hope on the fractious states of Yugoslavia and the former Soviet Union, which potentially may have a more democratic future than their larger predecessors.)

Model II contains a more parsimonious model retaining only GDP, the log of population, and the interconnectivity variable. These fewer variables continue to explain more than 50 percent of the variation in democracy for 141 countries. After excluding three predictors, the small drop in Adjusted R^2 (0.047) underlines the relative importance of interconnectivity. Alternatively, when retaining those three variables and excluding interconnectivity, the goodness of fit measure decreases by more than twice as much. In other words, interconnectivity alone may be more important for predicting the level of democracy than these three independent variables combined.

The effects of multicollinearity also deserve some attention. The correlation matrix in Table 6.1 indicates high correlations between many of the independent variables, particularly those of specific interest to this investigation: GDP, interconnectivity, and schooling. Collinearities between independent variables will tend to reduce the efficiency of predictors, but without bias. This means that the reported statistical significance may be less than the actual because the standard errors will be excessively large but the estimated coefficients will be neither higher nor lower than they ought to be. Relative to the result-specific tests, inferences regarding interconnectivity would not change because they appear with the highest reported level of statistical significance anyway. However, we may be

---

[13]For more discussion on the potentially negative economic consequences of democratization, see Shin (1994) or Rothstein (1991).

slightly understating the effect of GDP (or the other predictors), since they may lose some statistical significance to the interconnectivity variable with which they are collinear. The magnitude of the coefficient on GDP is, nevertheless, quite small, and it is reported without bias in Model I. Furthermore, the coefficients themselves to not vary much with the consecutive inclusion or exclusion of the other independent variables. This indication, too, downplays the likelihood that multicollinearities could be adversely influencing these results.

Models III and IV, with the addition of the regional interaction terms, are analogous to I and II, respectively. These next two models show that the positive correlation of interconnectivity with democracy is consistent across and within regional boundaries. In all the regions, the coefficient is positive. In half of the regions, the coefficient is substantial and statistically significant. The correlation is most pronounced in those regions undergoing dramatic political transformation. This fact is important when considering causality. If the correlation were positive only where democracy preceded the information revolution, one might be able to argue that the latter strengthened the former but certainly not that the latter caused the former. The evidence, however, is that the relationship is weakest in regions characterized by established democracies and strongest in regions that are cultivating nascent democracies.

In Africa, the coefficient on the interaction term is the highest, and the t-statistics correspond to a 1 percent level of significance or better. In Eurasia, the results are similar with the t-statistic also indicating 1 percent as the lowest significance level. The coefficient is also substantial for Latin America with a 10 percent significance level on Model IV. The regression lines that accompany the six scatterplots in Figure 6.4 approximate these multivariate regression results for visual comparison. Western Europe shows the most paltry correlation. In this region, the high interconnectivity levels do not vary much and the high democracy ratings move even less.

QUESTIONS OF CAUSALITY

It may be tempting to infer causality from these strong correlations and conclude that interconnectivity influences democratization. However, to do so might be premature. Causality could, in fact, flow

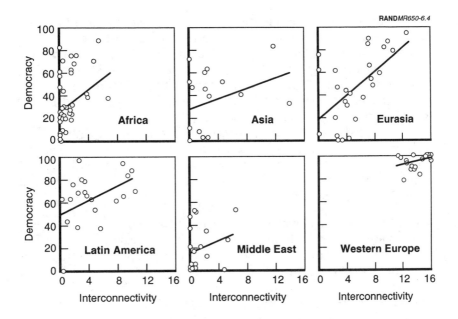

RAND*MR650-6.4*

Figure 6.4—Regional Regressions and Scatterplots

in the opposite direction. Democracies rely on an informed public and uninhibited communication and may therefore seek interconnectivity. One way to test this possibility analytically is via a system of simultaneous equations and two-stage least squares (2SLS) estimation. Simply, this two-equation model assumes that interconnectivity can influence democracy and also that democracy can influence interconnectivity. Then we can compare the relative statistical significance and sizes of the coefficients on these variables in each of the two equations. To perform these tests, both democracy and interconnectivity are both dependent variables in Model V. And to obtain a unique solution, at least one additional variable called an "instrumental variable" must be included in the interconnectivity equation. Since electronic mail is text-based and travels over telephones lines, appropriate instruments are percentage literacy and the number of telephone lines per capita. Independent variables in the democracy equation are, as before, related to economic growth, human development, and ethnicity.

The resulting regression coefficients are also listed above in Table 6.2. Interconnectivity remains a powerful predictor of democracy as before. The magnitude of the coefficient for interconnectivity on democracy is even greater than in the comparable OLS model. The level of significance remains exceptionally high. Democracy, however, does not prove to have any significant effect on interconnectivity. Thus, the suggestion that democracy leads to interconnectivity is not supported while the hypothesis that there is no positive effect cannot be rejected. The coefficient on population is still negative and significant. The coefficient on GDP is also still negatively and nearly significant at the 10 percent level. The other outputs also closely parallel those of Model I.

The other alternative explanation for the strong correlation between interconnectivity and democracy is that a third variable may influence both simultaneously. The obvious candidate is economic development, which many contend is an important prerequisite for democracy.[14] The correlation between interconnectivity and GDP, at 0.84, is also high, suggesting that the third variable hypothesis deserves further examination. In practical terms, equipment necessary to communicate electronically is expensive, especially for citizens of the Third World regions that Western democratization policy would be most eager to influence. The same economic resources that can finance participation in the communications revolution could conceivably fuel demands for personal rights and freedoms.

Again, a system of simultaneous equations can help unravel complex reciprocal effects. Model VI includes all three dependent variables: GDP, democracy, and interconnectivity. The following are the set of assumptions that underlie this three-equation model: Economic development and interconnectivity predict democracy; democracy and economic development predict interconnectivity; and interconnectivity and democracy predict economic development. We can compare the relative effects of the predictors as before in Model V. The interconnectivity equation uses the same two instrumental variables. The independent variables in the democracy equation are the same

---

[14]The seminal work on this topic is Lipset (1959) but the literature is large. Also see, for example, Helliwell (1992), Lipset, Seong, and Torres (1993), and Rowen (1995).

as before except that schooling is used to serve as an instrument for economic growth in accordance with prevailing theory. Scholars surmise that education can influence democracy by increasing personal and national wealth, as discussed above. The 2SLS estimation results, shown in Table 6.2, are consistent with all those that preceded and do not support the hypothesis of economic development as the confounding third variable. Strongly to the contrary, the regression coefficients for interconnectivity on democracy and GDP are both substantial and statistically significant, again above the 0.1 percent level. Neither democracy nor GDP proves to influence interconnectivity strongly. GDP again shows a negative correlation with democracy at a 10 percent significance level.

In each model presented here, without exception, interconnectivity positively correlates with democracy at high levels of significance. In each model, at lower but still high significance, the correlation with population on democracy is negative. Stories to explain both the country size and the interconnectivity phenomena may share a common plot. Smaller size and greater interconnectivity may similarly be conducive to democracy by facilitating coordinated civic action. Although perhaps cliché, the often repeated analogy that information revolution technologies are shrinking the world offers appropriate insight. Interestingly, the most populous country that Freedom House labels as completely "free" became a democracy in 1776 when its population was only a fraction of its current size. At that time and at that size, available communication technologies, such as pamphleteering, were sufficient to gel public support into popular action.

It is the globe as a whole, however, that is "shrinking" in the wash of information flows. The worldwide expansion of democracy may have less to do with how these technologies favor domestic democratic processes than with how they spread democratic ideals internationally. Information revolution technologies enable citizens of prospective democracies to learn more about how other societies operate. If they discover that others living elsewhere live better thanks to democratic governance, they are likely to seek democratization. At the same time, information revolution technologies empower citizens anywhere to broadcast charges that their own governments have violated inalienable human rights. Thus, world pressure can be brought to bear against repressive regimes unable to hide their misdeeds as successfully as before. That demonstrators in Tiananmen Square displayed signs written in English was not a co-incidence. Cross-border communication in the defense of democracy and human rights is the activity on which citizen diplomacy groups such as Amnesty International stake their success. The new technologies enhance these capabilities.

Governments that try to squelch the new information technologies to protect their monopoly on power do so essentially at the peril of economic growth. This is the inference from Model VI and is precisely what leading analysts have been predicting: "For nations to be economically competitive, they must allow individual citizens access to information networks and computer technology. In doing so, they cede significant control over economic, cultural, and eventually political events in their countries" (Builder, 1993, p. 160).

CONCLUSIONS AND RECOMMENDATIONS

Despite inherent limitations of statistical analyses, every analytic perspective of this study coherently and repeatedly emphasizes that interconnectivity is a powerful predictor of democracy, more so than any of democracy's traditional correlates.

Measurable effects of this technology on global democratization resonate with arguments to justify a national universal e-mail system: E-mail can help vitalize or reinvigorate democratic governance. Thus, the analysis from this chapter leads to two important conclusions. First, the United States should support increased interconnectivity abroad, as this may aid the spread of democracy. Second and more broadly, the development of a national e-mail system must consider the international implications. Worldwide democratization is both a critical and demonstrable implication, but there are others. Previous chapters have alluded to standardization and security, for example. "National" in the context of e-mail is at best a misnomer; at worst, it could mislead policy. Policies that derive specifically from a commitment to universalize e-mail within this country will interact with and affect events far beyond the domestic milieu.

Chapter Seven

CONCLUSIONS AND RECOMMENDATIONS

Robert H. Anderson, Tora K. Bikson, Sally Ann Law,
Bridger M. Mitchell

This report presents our considerations of the notion of universal access to electronic mail from demographic, technical, economic, social, and international perspectives. Various conclusions and recommendations may be found throughout the previous six chapters at points where they seemed salient and could be considered in context. Here we consolidate what we feel to be our most important conclusions and recommendations.

POLICY CONCLUSIONS AND RECOMMENDATIONS

We find that use of electronic mail is valuable for individuals, for communities, for the practice and spread of democracy, and for the general development of a viable national information infrastructure. Consequently, the nation should support universal access to e-mail through appropriate public and private policies.

The goal of achieving universal access has two main subgoals: (1) achieving interconnectivity among separate e-mail systems and (2) widespread accessibility of individuals to some e-mail system.

Universal connectivity among systems appears to be occurring through market forces, although the portability of e-mail addresses and current regulations that distort the prices among potentially competitive communication offerings are likely to remain an issue.

Individuals' accessibility to e-mail is hampered by increasing in-come, education, and racial gaps in the availability of computers and access to network services. Some policy remedies appear to be re-quired. These include creative ways to make terminals cheaper; to have them recycled; to provide access in libraries, community cen-ters, and other public venues; and to provide e-mail "vouchers" or support other forms of cross-subsidies.

The literature reviewed plus information gathered and analyzed in Chapters Two and Five make clear the central role of e-mail as the activity that promotes use of electronic networks; the role of these networks as social technologies is salient. Interpersonal communi-cation, bulletin boards, conferences, and chat rooms, of course, also provide information and help individuals find or filter information from other sources.

Much study and discussion, both within our government and else-where, focuses on the content, design, and policies related to a "national information infrastructure." If this report demonstrates anything, it is the importance of person-to-person, and many-to-many communication within such an infrastructure. Therefore,

> It is critical that electronic mail be a basic service in a na-tional information infrastructure.

To the extent that public policy guides the evolution of an NII, it should consider universal access to e-mail as a cornerstone of that policy. Specifically, one-way information-providing technologies—whether broadcasting systems or technologies that provide only search and retrieval—are inadequate. Two-way technologies sup-porting interactive use and sending or dissemination by all users are key. And everyone should be able to participate:

> It is important to reduce the increasing gaps in access to basic electronic information system services, specifically, access to electronic mail services.

Implementation of such policies should begin as soon as possible since it will undoubtedly take as much as a decade before full im-plementation is accomplished, no matter what strategy is envi-sioned. We recommend that the gaps that are greatest now and that are still widening be addressed first. Specifically these are deficits in access to computers and electronic networks found in the low-income and low-education segments of the population.

Directory services and addressing mechanisms must be considered core components. Additionally, any obstacles to full connectivity and interoperability must be minimized.

Virtually every study of electronic mail establishes that immediate convenient access is the single most powerful predictor of use. To the extent that national or other policies attempt to redress imbalances caused by the market for electronic access, we conclude that

Policy interventions should give priority to widespread home access.

In addition, and not as a substitute, multiple options for network access located in convenient places (including, for instance, libraries, schools, public buildings, hotel lobbies, business centers, and the like) are important auxiliary access sites. Such common facilities could be considered good locations for help or training centers as well.

Prior studies as well as information presented in Chapters Two and Five show little reason to be concerned that citizens will abandon the needs of their local (physical) communities in favor of virtual communities in cyberspace. Rather, communications are typically addressed to a community of concerned individuals, and either for reasons of subject matter or prior acquaintance, these concerns are often (although not necessarily) geographically bounded. Thus, network access can be expected to enhance rather than detract from community involvement.

Provision of community services and activities on-line should be actively supported.

Local nonprofit providers experience many of the same resource constraints—costs, technical expertise, and so on—that households and individuals face. Engaging people in participatory democracy is not just a matter of giving citizens access but also a matter of enabling the service and information providers. Specific policies might be designed to facilitate and support the development of on-line civic activities offered by government agencies and nonprofit organizations.

Our study of the technical considerations in providing universal access to e-mail concluded that

> *There are no fundamental technical barriers to providing universal access to electronic mail services.*

We concluded that current and evolving Internet standards for e-mail (SMTP and MIME, in particular), although perhaps not the definitive standards for electronic mail, provide a good basis for further evolution of a universal system. To the extent possible, gateways among dissimilar e-mail systems should be avoided, or be regarded as only temporary measures, because information is lost at least one way, and possibly both ways, in such transactions. Therefore, migration of Internet standards down into organization-level systems appears preferable.

We find that access to, and the location of, physical devices for e-mail use significantly affect universal access. With only about half of U.S. households containing personal computers by the year 2000, a robust set of alternative devices and locations is needed, including keyboard attachments to TV set-top boxes and video game machines, and extended telephones providing e-mail (and likely integrated voice mail) access. Public access is vital, with libraries, post offices, kiosks, and government buildings each playing a role. There might well be a market for "pay" terminals analogous to the ubiquitous pay telephones.

The state of software for "user agents," "knowbots," and similar filtering programs appears capable of handling, sorting, prioritizing, and presenting the large volumes of e-mail that may result from universal access. Similar technologies can give the user sufficient control over content (at least initially using the address or site that is the physical source of the material as an indicator of content; later "filters" may use other cues), so that avoiding objectionable materials should pose no greater problem than it does in other aspects of contemporary life.

We have concluded that e-mail white pages or yellow pages directories will be developed by market forces, and therefore conclude that

There appears to be no need for governmental or regulatory involvement in the development, or centralization, of directories for universal e-mail addresses (both white and yellow pages).

In considering the architecture of a universal e-mail system, we were strongly influenced by the recommendations developed by the CSTB (1994):

The design of a universal e-mail system should follow "open data network" guidelines, with a small number of transport services and representation standards (e.g., for fax, video, audio, text).

Upon this base, a larger but still quite bounded set of "middleware" services such as file systems, security and privacy services, and name servers may be built. An evolving, growing set of applications can then thrive without requiring redesign of the underlying "bearer" and "transport" portions of the network. This model closely resembles that developed over the last several decades within the Internet development community.

Until more is known about appropriate user-computer interfaces for all segments of our society (see our "Recommendations for Further Research," below), we believe that—to the extent inexpensive computing devices can support it—the "Web browsing" model for user interactions, including access to e-mail services, is an important, highly usable, interface model. Within the forseeable future, it is an important means of access to a burgeoning amount of on-line information and services. Because the cost of computing power continues to drop, we cautiously recommend

The "Web browser" model of user-computer interaction should at least be considered a candidate for the minimum level of user interface for e-mail access as well as other hypertext-style access to information.

This report has considered the need for a simple e-mail address system that gives every U.S. resident a "default" e-mail address by which they can be reached. Such a development would "jump start" a universal access system, because governmental and other organizations could then assume that "everyone" was reachable by this means and design procedures and systems accordingly. The advantages of this approach lead to our recommendation that

> *A simple e-mail address provision scheme should be developed giving every U.S. resident an e-mail address, perhaps based on a person's physical address or telephone number.*

If such a universal addressing scheme were developed, services would then be required, at least in transition, to "migrate" electronic materials received into paper form for persons not capable of, or desiring to, access them electronically. Such services could be provided by third-party entrepreneurs or established agencies and companies such as the U.S. Postal Service or one's local telephone service provider.

The economic analysis presented in Chapter Four suggests that economies of scope and scale on the supply side, together with the easy substitutability among messaging and communications services on the demand side, may result in both vertical and horizontal integration—and the formation of strategic alliances—of suppliers in related markets. The growing use of bundled offerings and term and volume discount pricing are consistent with that analysis. The convergence of previously distinct messaging and communications services, and the emergence of a unified communications/messaging environment, raise a number of significant public policy issues. The following are two major areas in which policy may need to be reformed:

1. Uniform regulatory treatment. It is virtually impossible to distinguish among video, voice, and data services in a modern digital environment. As the discussion of MIME made clear, an e-mail message may contain audio and video clips, and might substitute for video-on-demand offered by a cable television provider. However, video services can support data communication. Real-time interactive voice conversations can be carried by the Internet using a variety of commercially available software products, and many consumers access the Internet using modems and ordinary telephone lines.

Nevertheless, given their very different histories, voice, data, and video communications services have been treated very differently by regulators. With the convergence of the communications/messaging market, regulatory distinctions are creating artificial distortions in the marketplace and may be creating incentives for customers to use economically inefficient messaging options. The discussion in Chapter Four of access charges and the "enhanced service provider" exemption is one example of artificial cost differences that arise from regulations designed for one application (standard telephony) that must now compete with other applications. We conclude that

> *Policies developed separately for telephony, computer communications, broadcasting, and publishing that create artificial distinctions in the emerging information infrastructure should be reviewed, and a consistent framework should be developed that spans all the industries in the unified communications/messaging industry.*

Address portability provides an example of the need for a consistent regulatory framework. Portability reduces the switching costs of consumers and increases market competitiveness. It was shown in Chapter Four that with the use of bundling, the portability of telephone numbers could be negated through the use of nonportable e-mail addresses.

> *Policymakers should develop a comprehensive approach to address, number, and name portability.*

Efforts at implementing the above recommendation should be compatible with, and cognizant of, our earlier recommendation that "default" electronic addresses be provided for all U.S. residents. Although there may be some important tradeoffs between address portability and simplicity of routing, policymakers should attempt to make this tradeoff consistently across all competitors.

2. Open network architectures. As technologies converge, each business and residence will have the choice of several access technologies and providers who will offer circuit- and packet-based services. In addition, multiple long distance and international service providers will offer a comparable range of services.

Given the large sunk costs and nominal marginal usage costs of facilities-based providers, competition in raw transport is likely to be unstable. Providers are likely to integrate vertically or form alliances that allow them to differentiate their products. Regulations requiring the nondiscriminatory sale of unbundled transport may not be consistent with emerging vertical relationships and competition.

In the near term, regulation should adopt a light-handed approach that specifies minimum capabilities that can be transferred across networks to allow providers sufficient flexibility to develop enhanced features that differentiate their products. In the longer term, when technologies have more fully converged, subscription to multiple networks by each customer may be inexpensive and widespread, and regulations governing interconnections may not be necessary. Providers may then be free to differentiate their offerings based on market demand.

Our study of the economics of e-mail provision concluded that subsidization for current household access could require approximately $1 billion per year, but we have mentioned (in Chapter Four) interesting commercial experiments providing "free" e-mail to those willing to accept advertising; similarly, "near-free" computers might be provided to those willing to subject themselves to additional advertising (e.g., on a built-in "screensaver" display). So the $1 billion amount may possibly be a mid-level estimate, not a minimum required.

Although e-mail penetration is expanding rapidly, some program of economic assistance to marginal consumers may be necessary to achieve universal levels of services. Obligating service providers to offer subscriptions to large classes of customers at low rates that are financed by contributions from other services is unlikely to succeed in the competitive messaging industry. Instead,

Any e-mail assistance will require public funding from an industrywide tax or from general revenues. Subsidies will need to be narrowly targeted to reach consumers who would not otherwise subscribe.

There are international dimensions to "universal" e-mail within the United States. Policies to influence the development of a national e-mail system should recognize the borderless nature of this technology. Perhaps more than other national systems, an e-mail system will affect and be affected by worldwide standards, policies, and events.

The analysis in Chapter Six leads to the conclusion that democracy in the nations of the world is positively correlated with interconnectivity. In nations emerging into democracy, or attempting to, connectivity is likely to have a positive influence on democratization. We conclude that

> *The United States should support increased interconnectivity abroad, since this may aid the spread of democracy.*

The results of this study support the conclusion that important results and benefits accrue to those becoming internetted, and that the problem to be addressed is the growing disparity among some society segments in access to that internetting. Universal access to electronic mail within the United States is an important solution strategy; achieving universal access will require dedication, focus, and cooperation by individual citizens, commercial companies, nongovernmental organizations, and government at all levels.

RECOMMENDATIONS FOR FURTHER RESEARCH

Our research has uncovered inadequacies in the statistical data describing the phenomena we studied. We encountered other shortfalls in the existing literature or in current field experiments. We therefore recommend that the following research initiatives be undertaken to permit a better understanding of problems and issues related to universal access to e-mail and related interactive information systems.

- Cost-benefit analysis should be initiated to answer the question: What mass of the U.S. population, if it were network-accessible, is necessary to support electronic delivery of major government services (e.g., filing Medicare claims or income tax forms, delivering at least some of the postal mail, or distributing Social Security benefits or disability benefits) in a cost-effective manner? It is possible that the benefits to many government agencies and other organizations could outweigh costs of subsidization, so that a straightforward business case could be made for universal access.

- A sizable and diverse number of "grass roots" civic networks (i.e., those not designed, like HomeNet, and supported as field research) should be selected and followed from conception through efforts to raise start-up funding, and so on until they have been operating for some years. Getting comparable information across such activities about what works and what does not through early to later stages in the introduction of these networks (including what proportion of them do not make it), plus the kinds of civic, social, and economic roles they play, would vastly enhance what we have been able to learn from cross-sectional studies and site visits at a single point in time.

- CPS data should be collected on a panel basis to monitor access to and uses and effects of computer networks. In particular, the success of policies and markets to close the identified gaps should be tracked and social benefits assessed. This may require revision or extension of CPS questions and administration schedules.

- Most e-mail systems have been designed for use in academic or business settings. Better understanding of the capabilities and limitations of current user-computer interfaces is needed, especially related to electronic-mail handling. Existing interfaces rely on metaphors and analogies common to current users: multilevel "filing cabinets," commands to be issued, "Rolodex"-type address files, and forms to be filled out. How should these interfaces (including perhaps modest extensions of Web point-and-click browsers) evolve so that they can serve the entire range of users, including those in bottom-quartile income and education households? Field experiments concentrating on interface design for these prospective user groups are needed.

ADDITIONAL INFORMATION ON COMPUTERS AND CONNECTIVITY

Constantijn W. A. Panis, Tora K. Bikson

INTRODUCTION

This appendix contains additional information related to Chapter Two, "Computers and Connectivity: Current Trends." It consists of two parts, the first somewhat technical and the second nontechnical in nature. The first part explains in detail the methodology used to compute "net" percentages of individuals who have a computer in the household and who use network services. It also reports the estimated coefficients of the regressions used to explain disparities across socioeconomic groups and contains tables with gross and net differences. The second part contains a number of tables illustrating occupational regional differences, as well as differences in the type of use that various socioeconomic groups make of their computers.

THE COMPUTATION OF NET DISPARITIES ACROSS SOCIOECONOMIC GROUPS

One focus of Chapter Two is on disparities across socioeconomic groups in their access to a computer in the household and their use of network services. As briefly outlined in the main text, tabulations based on raw data may generate misleading insights. For example, to assess the effect of income on the diffusion of computers, it would be misleading to look only at disparities across income groups. Part of the gap between low- and high-income families may be due to other socioeconomic characteristics, such as educational attainment. To account for the effects of all other predictor variables of interest, we employ a multivariate regression technique. The characteristics we examine here are household income, educational attainment, race and ethnicity, age, sex, and location of residence (urban or rural).[1]

Both outcome variables—presence of a computer in the individual's household and use of network services anywhere—are binary (yes/no) variables. The use of linear regression techniques, such as OLS or analysis of variance (ANOVA), would be inappropriate, since these do not guarantee that predicted fractions are between 0 and 1. The most commonly used statistical models to estimate binary outcomes are the logistical regression (logit) and probit models. The choice between them is largely arbitrary; we opted for the probit model (Maddala, 1983).

The procedure is as follows. First, we estimated multivariate probit models to explain, say, presence of a computer in the household using the six categorical predictor variables listed above. Second, to determine net disparities by, say, sex, for each individual in the sample, we predict the probability that he or she has a computer in the household under the counterfactual assumption that everyone is female. That is, if everyone were female, but otherwise with the same characteristics that he or she actually has, what would be the probability that each person would have a computer? Third, we average these predicted probabilities over all individuals in the sample to obtain the predicted fraction of the population that would have a computer if everyone were female. This prediction is repeated under the counterfactual assumption that everyone is male, and averaged over all individuals in the sample to obtain an estimate of the fraction having a computer among males. The resulting

---

[1]In addition, household size was found to be a powerful predictor of having access to a computer in the household. However, given our objective to provide net differences that may be under the influence of public policymakers, we decided not to control for household size in the multivariate analysis. It is relatively simple for a government to manipulate people's incomes; changing household size is more difficult. The effect of household size probably operates through income effects: Bigger households are more likely to have computers (net of income) because of economies of scale—it thus remains a matter of purchasing power.

fractions are termed "net" fractions, since they represent differences that are due only to sex, controlling for all other socioeconomic characteristics of interest. This procedure is repeated for the other five socioeconomic predictor variables. The same procedure is used to compute net percentages of network users.

The multivariate probit estimates are of interest in their own right. They allow us to test whether net differences across socioeconomic groups are statistically significant. Given the fact that our samples are very large (146,850 individuals in 1989 and 143,129 in 1993), virtually all estimated differences are indeed statistically significant.

We also needed to test whether the disparities have grown or narrowed between 1989 and 1993. To achieve this, we pool all individuals and estimate two sets of coefficients. The first set applies to all individuals; the second applies only to individuals in 1989. This second set is thus a full interaction of the year 1989 with all characteristics of interest. (The result is that the first set provides estimates for the 1993 sample, whereas estimates for the 1989 sample are given by the sum of the first and second sets.) The sign and significance of the interaction terms determine whether differences across groups have significantly narrowed or grown.

Table A.1 presents the probit estimates to explain the presence of a computer in the household. The omitted category is a non-Hispanic white male who lives in a rural area, is between the ages of 20 and 39, is a high school graduate, and lives in a household with a total income that is in the bottom quartile. Most coefficients are significant at the 5 percent confidence level. The exceptions are, first, the main and interaction effects for female, i.e., there is no significant net difference in access to a computer in the household between males and females in 1993 or 1989. Second, the 1989 interaction effects for race and ethnicity are neither individually nor jointly significantly different from zero. This implies that there has been no significant narrowing or widening of the disparities across racial and ethnic groups.

Similarly, Table A.2 presents probit estimates to explain the use of network services. Again, most coefficients are significantly different from zero. The chief exceptions are, first, the main and interaction effects for female, i.e., there is no significant net difference in use of network services between males and females in 1993 or 1989.

Table A.1

Probit Estimates of Presence of a Computer in the Household

				Number of obs	=	289,979
				chi2(37)	=	50,942.12
				Prob>chi2	=	0.0000
Log Likelihood =−128,757.53				Pseudo R2	=	0.1652

Predictor	Coef.	Std.Err.	z	P>|z|	[95% Conf. Interval]	
Main (1993) Effects						
constant	−1.40768	.0151655	−92.821	0.000	−1.437404	−1.377956
female	−.0056483	.0076325	−0.740	0.459	−.0206077	.0093112
urban	.1884759	.0101801	18.514	0.000	.1685232	.2084286
urban missing	.1777551	.0127749	13.914	0.000	.1527168	.2027934
age ≤ 19	.5618734	.0178238	31.524	0.000	.5269393	.5968075
40 ≤ age ≤ 59	.0223262	.0101142	2.207	0.027	.0025027	.0421497
age ≥ 60	−.5169305	.0141962	−36.413	0.000	−.5447546	−.4891064
dropout	−.320794	.0146202	−21.942	0.000	−.3494489	−.292139
college	.4437498	.0106616	41.621	0.000	.4228534	.4646461
child	−.3914426	.0188003	−20.821	0.000	−.4282905	−.3545947
income Q2	.3837589	.0135796	28.260	0.000	.3571435	.4103743
income Q3	.7164771	.0130568	54.874	0.000	.6908862	.7420679
income Q4	1.23902	.01325	93.511	0.000	1.21305	1.264989
inc missing	.5581935	.0177545	31.439	0.000	.5233953	.5929918
Hispanic	−.446318	.0160255	−27.850	0.000	−.4777275	−.4149086
black	−.4009989	.0136128	−29.457	0.000	−.4276795	−.3743182
native	−.36061	.0586441	−6.149	0.000	−.4755503	−.2456696
asian	.0842046	.0213779	3.939	0.000	.0423046	.1261045
other	.0411175	.0900561	0.457	0.648	−.1353892	.2176241
1989 Interaction Effects						
constant	−.1518498	.0230642	−6.584	0.000	−.1970548	−.1066448
female	−.0280799	.0113564	−2.473	0.013	−.0503381	−.0058217
urban	−.0719295	.015203	−4.731	0.000	−.1017269	−.0421321
urban missing	−.0453937	.0190238	−2.386	0.017	−.0826796	−.0081077
age ≤ 19	−.0247632	.024765	−1.000	0.317	−.0733017	.0237753
40 ≤ age ≤ 59	.0814371	.0150917	5.396	0.000	.051858	.1110163
age ≥ 60	.0388747	.0220309	1.765	0.078	−.004305	.0820544
dropout	.0653409	.0212214	3.079	0.002	.0237477	.106934
college	−.0377222	.0156432	−2.411	0.016	−.0683822	−.0070621
child	.1016498	.0260059	3.909	0.000	.0506792	.1526204
income Q2	−.1944075	.0210918	−9.217	0.000	−.2357467	−.1530684
income Q3	−.2222411	.0199182	−11.158	0.000	−.2612802	−.1832021
income Q4	−.3267594	.0197295	−16.562	0.000	−.3654285	−.2880903
inc missing	−.16462	.026801	−6.304	0.000	−.2214753	−.1164171
Hispanic	.0148037	.0249261	0.594	0.553	−.0340505	.0636579
black	.027525	.0208093	1.323	0.186	−.0132605	.0683106
native	−.0575121	.0882743	−0.652	0.515	−.2305267	.1155024
asian	−.0361922	.0323962	−1.117	0.264	−.0996875	.0273032
other	−.133135	.1476562	−0.902	0.367	−.4225359	.1562659

Table A.2

Probit Estimates of Use of Network Services

				Number of obs	=	289,979
				chi2(37)	=	40,744.48
				Prob>chi2	=	0.0000
Log Likelihood=−65,393.606				Pseudo R2	=	0.2375

Predictor	Coef.	Std.Err.	z	P>|z|	[95% Conf. Interval]	
Main (1993) Effects						
constant	−1.571832	.0210189	−74.782	0.000	−1.613028	−1.530636
female	−.0053962	.0100413	−0.537	0.591	−.0250769	.0142845
urban	.1587448	.0138119	11.493	0.000	.131674	.1858156
urban missing	.1508773	.0171523	8.796	0.000	.1172594	.1844953
age ≤ 19	−.507376	.0305335	−16.617	0.000	−.5672206	−.4475315
40 ≤ age ≤ 59	−.0254984	.011045	−2.309	0.021	−.0471462	−.0038507
age ≥ 60	−.8241301	.0195688	−42.115	0.000	−.8624842	−.785776
dropout	−.783959	.0247028	−31.736	0.000	−.8323755	−.7355425
college	.5282557	.0114802	46.015	0.000	.505755	.5507565
child	−1.176104	.0417958	−28.139	0.000	−1.258022	−1.094185
income Q2	.3980891	.0198657	20.039	0.000	.359153	.4370252
income Q3	.5810355	.0190995	30.422	0.000	.5436012	.6184698
income Q4	.8352291	.0191383	43.642	0.000	.7977187	.8727395
inc missing	.2084536	.0267462	7.794	0.000	.1560319	.2608752
Hispanic	−.2583873	.023208	−11.134	0.000	−.3038741	−.2129005
black	−.1802587	.0184221	−9.785	0.000	−.2163654	−.144152
native	−.0260504	.0747693	−0.348	0.728	−.1725955	.1204947
asian	−.348791	.0316593	−11.017	0.000	−.4108421	−.2867399
other	−.2651235	.1454948	−1.822	0.068	−.5502881	.0200411
1989 Interaction Effects						
constant	−.1626417	.0336713	−4.830	0.000	−.2286362	−.0966472
female	−.01391	.015826	−0.879	0.379	−.0449284	.0171085
urban	−.0311699	.0220242	−1.415	0.157	−.0743366	.0119968
urban missing	−.0004659	.0271554	−0.017	0.986	−.0536895	.0527577
age ≤ 19	−.0618868	.0466009	−1.328	0.184	−.1532229	.0294492
40 ≤ age ≤ 59	−.0498573	.0174102	−2.864	0.004	−.0839806	−.015734
age ≥ 60	−.1673704	.0363032	−4.610	0.000	−.2385232	−.0962175
dropout	−.0074475	.0418955	−0.178	0.859	−.0895612	.0746662
college	−.0746875	.0177005	−4.220	0.000	−.10938	−.0399951
child	.290189	.0653084	4.443	0.000	.1621869	.4181911
income Q2	−.2367647	.0324797	−7.290	0.000	−.3004238	−.1731057
income Q3	−.2240777	.0305314	−7.339	0.000	−.2839182	−.1642372
income Q4	−.2816908	.0300223	−9.383	0.000	−.3405335	−.2228482
inc missing	−.0127442	.0415234	−0.307	0.759	−.0941285	.0686402
Hispanic	.0190499	.038103	0.500	0.617	−.0556306	.0937304
black	−.0471272	.0300801	−1.567	0.117	−.1060831	.0118288
native	−.1355706	.1240715	−1.093	0.275	−.3787462	.107605
asian	.0716735	.0510456	1.404	0.160	−.0283741	.1717211
other	.0328307	.2347375	0.140	0.889	−.4272463	.4929077

Second, in 1993, Native Americans are not significantly more or less likely to use network services than non-Hispanic whites (the omitted category). Third, the 1989 interaction effects for race and ethnicity are neither individually nor jointly significantly different from zero. This again implies that there has been no significant narrowing or widening of the disparities across racial and ethnic groups.

Table A.3 presents gross and net percentages of individuals with access to a computer in the household and of individuals using

Table A.3

Gross and Net Disparities in Access to a Household Computer and Use of Network Services Anywhere

| | Household Computer | | | | Network Services | | | |
| | 1989 | | 1993 | | 1989 | | 1993 | |
	Gross	Net	Gross	Net	Gross	Net	Gross	Net
Household income								
Bottom quartile	5.7	7.8	7.4	10.4	1.7	3.1	2.7	4.8
Second quartile	9.3	10.8	16.6	18.5	3.4	4.2	7.8	9.2
Third quartile	18.0	17.1	30.2	28.0	6.4	5.9	13.3	12.0
Top quartile	35.0	28.9	54.8	46.3	11.5	8.2	23.0	16.6
Educational attainment								
Less than high school	7.9	10.7	13.4	16.9	0.5	1.2	1.3	3.1
High school graduate	15.6	15.5	23.7	24.6	6.7	6.4	13.2	12.7
College graduate	31.9	25.6	48.7	37.8	18.3	13.5	33.8	25.4
Race and ethnicity								
Hispanic	7.7	10.4	12.4	17.5	2.4	4.2	4.8	8.4
Non–Hispanic white	20.2	19.1	30.6	28.8	6.9	6.3	13.1	12.0
Non–Hispanic black	8.2	11.4	13.3	18.5	2.9	4.3	6.3	9.4
Native American	7.5	10.7	12.9	19.4	2.8	4.8	7.5	11.6
Asian	24.1	20.3	37.4	31.3	5.2	3.9	9.7	7.3
Age category								
0–19 years	21.5	28.3	30.7	40.4	0.6	2.7	1.0	6.4
20–39 years	17.5	14.8	27.6	24.0	10.7	7.6	18.6	13.5
40–59 years	22.1	17.0	32.7	24.6	9.8	6.7	20.1	13.1
60+ years	5.5	7.2	10.1	12.8	0.9	1.1	3.2	3.7
Sex								
Male	18.9	18.1	27.9	26.9	6.4	6.0	11.8	11.4
Female	16.6	17.3	25.9	26.8	5.5	5.9	10.9	11.3
Location of residence								
Rural	13.2	15.5	19.3	22.9	3.9	4.9	7.6	9.5
Urban	19.0	18.1	29.2	27.8	6.5	6.1	12.5	11.8

network services. The gross percentages were also graphically shown in the bar charts of Chapter Two. The net percentages control for all other socioeconomic characteristics, as explained above.

REGIONAL AND OTHER VARIATION IN COMPUTER ACCESS AND NETWORK USE

Table A.4

Types of Computer Use at Home (Percentage of Respondents by Age Category; Conditional on Using a Computer at Home)

	0–14[a]	15–39	40–59	60+	Total 15+
Analysis	na	12.06	15.35	14.85	13.44
Bookkeeping	na	21.97	30.55	30.51	25.58
Bulletin boards	1.95	8.22	8.25	8.05	8.23
Calendar/scheduling	na	13.98	17.18	15.86	15.28
Communications	na	17.84	24.00	23.79	20.41
Connect to work computer	na	7.66	8.67	4.27	7.85
Computer assisted design	na	5.39	5.70	3.67	5.42
Databases	na	17.82	24.74	21.31	20.58
Desktop publishing	na	19.27	21.13	16.32	19.80
Educational programs	39.22	12.67	17.97	13.83	14.71
Electronic mail	0.90	25.55	34.52	38.11	29.50
Games	85.23	19.87	18.93	19.07	19.50
Graphics	14.68	13.98	14.01	10.	13.87
Home-based business	na	4.08	6.40	6.39	5.06
Household records/finance	na	14.79	19.84	17.01	16.80
Learning computer use	24.96	21.06	20.35	15.17	20.51
Programming	2.56	8.33	9.53	6.69	8.68
Sales	na	41.71	30.57	23.93	36.68
School assignments	40.44	32.85	13.56	2.12	24.20
Spreadsheets	1.14	17.96	24.10	19.85	20.31
Telemarketing	na	0.95	1.03	1.33	1.00
Word processing	26.13	58.14	63.99	57.44	60.26
Work at home	na	22.25	33.26	21.47	26.22
Other	4.06	6.43	8.03	15.	7.51

[a]na = not available; question not asked in child questionnaire.

Table A.5

Household Computers and Use of Network Services, by Metropolitan Area

	Computer	Network
Albuquerque, NM	32.3	18.7
Ann Arbor, MI	65.9	26.6
Atlanta, GA	32.6	13.8
Baltimore, MD	29.2	15.2
Battle Creek, MI	5.6	5.2
Boston, MA	36.3	14.1
Buffalo, NY	25.2	9.1
Champaign, IL	29.7	5.1
Chicago, IL	28.2	11.6
Cincinnati, OH	36.0	12.5
Cleveland, OH	25.9	11.3
Dallas, TX	30.6	16.9
Dayton, OH	24.2	12.0
Denver, CO	43.7	20.5
Detroit, MI	28.5	12.2
Flint, MI	16.2	5.4
Hartford, CT	38.8	21.3
Honolulu, HI	31.1	10.6
Houston, TX	33.9	13.3
Kansas City, KS	32.1	16.5
Las Vegas, NV	25.7	11.6
Los Angeles, CA	27.4	10.7
Madison, WI	50.4	25.9
Memphis, TN	17.4	7.7
Miami, FL	17.0	7.3
Minneapolis, MN	33.7	20.2
New Haven, CT	38.6	11.7
New Orleans, LA	19.1	7.9
New York, NY	18.9	7.7
Oklahoma City, OK	27.1	10.8
Peoria, IL	22.8	6.9
Philadelphia, PA	31.5	11.8
Pittsburgh, PA	23.4	9.0
Providence, RI	22.0	8.9
Sacramento, CA	35.7	14.8
Salt Lake City, UT	45.2	15.7
San Diego, CA	36.1	11.7
San Francisco, CA	39.0	15.8
Santa Cruz, CA	37.4	18.4
Seattle, WA	41.8	22.0
Sioux City, IA	21.9	18.3
Springfield, MO	18.0	1.0
Stamford, CT	41.4	27.5
Tucson, AZ	34.1	12.5
Youngstown, OH	23.8	7.2
Washington, D.C.	42.6	19.4

Table A.6

Household Computers and Use of Network Services, by Region

	Computer	Network
New England	33.9	13.2
Middle Atlantic	25.4	9.7
East North Central	26.3	11.0
West North Central	27.4	13.0
South Atlantic	25.1	11.6
East South Central	16.3	7.1
West South Central	23.5	10.4
Mountain	32.8	14.2
Pacific	32.5	13.0
United States Total	26.9	11.4

Table A.7

Frequency of Computer Use at Home
(Conditional on Having a Computer in the Household)

	Male	Female	Total
0–2 days per week	45.2	57.8	51.1
3+ days per week	54.8	42.2	48.9
Total	100.0	100.0	100.0

Table A.8

Household Computers and Use of Network Services, by Employment Status

	Computer	Network
Student	31.9	1.6
Employed	29.4	23.0
Self-employed	36.8	16.7
Unemployed	20.7	6.2
Other	15.1	3.9
Total	26.9	11.4

Table A.9

Household Computers and Use of Network Services, by Type of Employment

	Computer	Network
White collar—knowledge work[a]	47.9	36.9
White collar—other	33.5	22.9
Pink collar[b]	30.2	28.7
Blue collar	19.0	6.7
Total	30.8	20.7

[a]Occupations that fall into Reich's "symbolic analyst" category.
[b]Secretarial and clerical positions.

Table A.10

Household Computers and Use of Network Services, by Disability Status

	Computer	Network
Not disabled	26.7	14.8
Disabled	12.3	6.9

Table A.11

Household Computers and Use of Network Services, by Employment Sector

	Computer	Network
Private	28.8	20.2
Public	36.5	30.1
Total employed	30.0	21.7

INTERVIEW NOTES FROM CIVIC NETWORKS

Brent Keltner

This appendix contains the protocol used to structure interviews with key participants at five civic network sites, followed by notes integrated for each site from the resulting interviews. The analysis resulting from these interviews is presented in Chapter Five.

INTERVIEW PROTOCOL

[Start by describing the goals of the project. Explain why the site was selected and assure confidentiality of responses.]

Objectives and Network Development

1. Please describe how the network started. What was the main impetus behind its conception?

   [Probe: perceived need, key players.]

2. What are the main goals of the network? Who are you mainly trying to reach? What are you hoping to achieve?

   [Probe: short- vs. long-range goals, homogeneity/heterogeneity of target population.]

3. Please describe any obstacles you first encountered when you began to develop the network. What other ongoing challenges do
you face? How (did) do you deal with them?

4. Were there any fortuitous events that contributed to a smoother
beginning or has anything unexpected happened during the
course of operations that has made running the network easier?

Organization and Finance

5. Please describe the governance structure of this network. Who is
in charge and how are decisions made?

> *[Probe: decisionmaking process, degree of centralization,
> formalization.]*

6. Do you have any formal or informal collaborative arrangements
with other organizations?

> *[If yes, please describe.]*

> *[If no, are there any plans to develop such arrangements?]*

7. How is the network funded? Does the funding come from a single
or multiple sources? Have there been any funding changes since
the network's inception?

> *[If yes, how, if at all, have the changes affected the operation of
> the network?]*

> *[Probe: cost-sharing arrangements, funding crunches.]*

On-Line Services

8. Please describe the major services available to users of this network.

> *[Probe: e-mail, Internet access (types of) on-line databases,
> local/federal government.]*

9. What are the most frequently used services? Which appear to have sustaining appeal? Which are least popular?

    [Probe: reasons for (un)popularity.]

10. Can users access local and/or federal government on-line?

    [If yes, how and for what purposes?]

11. Does the network provide any special services targeted to traditionally disadvantaged groups (e.g., special training, recycling used personal computers)?

    [If yes, what services and how are they offered?]

    [Probe: Does it impose extra burdens on network provider?]

12. How are users trained to access and use the network? What, if any, ongoing technical support is provided to users?

    [Probe: formal vs. informal training and mentoring, (hidden) costs to training?]

13. Do you see a relationship between training provision and user behavior?

    [Probe: more advanced use, greater user satisfaction?]

User Characteristics

14. Please describe the growth rate of the network. About how many user accounts do you currently have?

    [Probe: initial vs. current demand, any indication of drop-off, any population differences.]

15. Please describe the characteristics of your target users.

    [Probe: individual or group focus, age, sex, race, education, income.]

16. How do potential new users learn about the network? How, if at all, do you advertise it in the community and to wider potential audiences?

Physical Access to Network and Technical Characteristics

17. How do users typically access the network? Are there public access terminals?

    [If yes, where are public terminals located, how is use there supported?]

18. What hardware and software does the network rely on? What is the user interface like?

19. How, if at all, can users access other networks?

    [If access permitted, how popular is this feature?]

Benefits of Civic Networks/Universal Access Issues

20. What do you see are the major benefits to users of this network?

21. Is there an economic argument for supporting civic networks and encouraging their use among traditionally underserved populations?

22. Do you see any drawbacks to civic network use?

    [Probe: problems with privacy, security, objectionable materials (other).]

23. Do you plan to expand this network? What are the technical, social, and financial implications for gearing up to reach an even wider audience?

    [Probe: thoughts on universal access.]

Recommendations

24. Do you have any recommendations for others thinking about starting a civic network or for peers facing the same sorts of challenges as you in running this network?

    [Probe: reaching underserved target populations, dealing with resource constraints.]

25. Do you have any recommendations to local, state, or federal policymakers who may be considering whether and how to increase citizen access to electronic mail, on-line resources, government documents and services, etc.?

26. Do you have any last comments or recommendations you'd like to make?

    Thank you so much for participating in our study.

PUBLIC ELECTRONIC NETWORK, SANTA MONICA, CA

Goals and Development

Objectives and Network Development. The impetus to set up the Public Electronic Network came out of the Santa Monica City Hall. Impressed with how using e-mail had improved communication and responsiveness within City Hall, city officials wanted to expand the concept to include the community. It was hoped that establishing the Public Electronic Network would improve communications between the residents of Santa Monica and their government, and among the residents themselves.

The main goal of the network is to provide an alternative means of communication between residents and city officials. The network also offers another mechanism to support a dialog on social and political issues between individuals living in Santa Monica.

The opening screen of the PEN system is shown in Figure B.1.

Figure B.1—Opening Screen of Santa Monica PEN System

Obstacles to Establishing. The most difficult challenges faced in setting up the network were deciding on the best usage, etiquette, and appropriate-use guidelines.

A major obstacle to setting up the network was getting city officials to participate in on-line conferences. Some city officials and workers felt overburdened by the network. To get real-time feedback from city residents required reading through a large number of e-mail messages.

Fortuitous Events. PEN organizers have benefited from private sector interest in helping to set up its network. Hewlett-Packard donated the hardware that supports the system and Metasystems Design Group donated the software. Both companies hoped that a successful demonstration of a Public Electronic Network in Santa Monica would lead to demand for their products from other communities.

Organization and Finance

Organization and Governance Structure. PEN is run by the Information Systems group at the Santa Monica City Hall. Two staff members—one working full time, the other part time—are responsible for administering the network. They develop new ideas for services, gather information to be put on-line, monitor on-line content, and provide user and technical support.

Involvement with Other Organizations. The Annenberg School of Communications at USC, Hewlett-Packard, and the PEN Action Group (a local user group) all played a role in setting up the network. They provide ideas for services, network design, and technical support. The Information Sciences Institute at USC is presently providing technical assistance.

The public library and the library at Santa Monica College have made their catalogs available to on-line users. PEN organizers have encouraged use by public elementary and secondary schools by organizing on-line conferences with students in other parts of the country and world. PEN also works with senior centers, youth centers, and several libraries—including the public library and the libraries at Santa Monica College and Santa Monica high school—to increase the number of public access terminals in the community.

Budget and Funding. At the time they were donated, the hardware and software together cost approximately $350,000. The annual operating budget is approximately $120,000, most of which goes to paying the salaries and benefits of PEN administrators. One of the part-time employees works exclusively on development projects and does not participate in the day-to-day operations of PEN. The operating budget is covered by the city government.

On-Line Services

Major Services. The services offered by PEN include e-mail, an electronic bulletin board, electronic conferences, and various on-line catalogs and databases.

E-Mail. PEN users can make use of their e-mail accounts to send messages directly to City Hall with questions, comments, or complaints; to send messages to friends; or to participate in on-line conferences.

Electronic Bulletin Board. Users can scan the electronic bulletin for information on a broad range of topics. Examples of things posted on the bulletin board include recreation and park schedules, bus schedules, job openings, earthquake safety tips, and information on pets for adoption. City residents can also use the bulletin board to find out how to apply for licenses and permits.

Citizens can also use the bulletin board to access a number of electronic databases (see below).

Electronic Conferences. There have been several hundred electronic conferences on the network since it began operation. Fourteen conference topics have registered over 1,000 responses. Three—on religion, abortion, and homelessness—registered over 2,000.

On-Line Catalogs. Both Santa Monica College and the Santa Monica public library have their catalogs on-line.

On-Line Databases. Databases that are available for use include (1) the City's Municipal Code, (2) the Maximum Allowable Rents Ordinance, (3) the City Service Guide, (4) the City Council Archive—with agendas, meetings, and staff reports from the City Council (from 1989), and (5) the Planning Commission Archive—with agendas, meetings, and staff reports from the Planning Commission (from 1994).

Governmental Items On-Line. Users can e-mail different city departments (e.g., the City Attorney, the City Maintenance Department) to ask for services or to register complaints. Users can also e-mail city council members to volunteer their input and opinions about political topics.

Services to Underserved Groups and Targeted Outreach. There are no services specifically directed at underserved groups, but PEN organizers have tried to ensure access for all by putting terminals in easily accessible places.

User Support/Training/Mentoring. An introduction to the system is available with the help of either an on-line tutorial or a 45-minute training session at City Hall. Few people actually come to the City

Hall to take advantage of training. According to project organizers, those who call up to schedule an appointment often call back and cancel after having time to experiment at home on their own.

User support is provided by an on-line help line as well as by reference librarians at the different library sites. The ability of reference librarians to provide help depends on their technical competence—they receive no formal training. Technical support and troubleshooting is done by PEN administrators at City Hall.

User Characteristics

Number and Growth/Decline. The system has 6,700 registered users and about 50–100 new users are added each month.

Demographics of Users. PEN keeps no demographic statistics about their user population. However, officials report that users appear to represent a broad cross-section of the population. This includes wealthy, middle-income, low-income, homeless, and disabled individuals. Network organizers estimate that about 60 percent of users have computers and modems at home, 25 percent log-in from public access sites, and the rest access PEN from work.

New User Procedures/Advertising. New users first fill out an account application form. PEN administrators then send the subscriber a package of information about the system and how to use it, an invitation to come to City Hall for training and instructions on how to get into the newcomers' conference that offers on-line help to new users.

The main outreach activities are through *Seascape*—the city's quarterly newsletter—and by word of mouth.

Physical Access and Technical Characteristics

Location of Terminals. Public access terminals are to be found in the Santa Monica public library—the main library and all three branch offices—the Santa Monica College library, all of the schools in the Santa Monica-Malibu Unified School District, City Hall, and the Ken Edwards (Senior Citizens) Center.

There used to be public access terminals at the Police intervention league's main office, the American Red Cross, and in one of the city's public parks. These terminals were removed because they were not being used.

Hardware/Interface. The PEN has recently converted to World Wide Web software to make its user interface graphical and easier to use. All servers to support the network are located at City Hall.

Network Connections/Access. Users can connect to PEN in one of two ways: They can use one of the many public access terminals in one of the public libraries or they can dial-in via modem from home.

For individuals outside Santa Monica, the PEN has a Web site that can be accessed via the World Wide Web.

Benefits of Civic Networks/Universal Access Issues

Benefits of Network. The major benefits of the network are the improved availability of information and improved communications.

Availability of Information. For people who work all day or who have little time to visit City Hall, the ability to log on for information at home and around the clock is a valuable tool.

Improved Communication. Some city council members see the electronic Network as an "ongoing town-hall style forum." Correspondence via the network is more convenient for city council members. It allows them to take and respond to questions on their own time. The electronic network also encourages a dialog among citizens on important political and social topics. An electronic dialog removes many traditional barriers to interaction between different groups. Young people and homeless people participate in confer- ences on the same footing as others.

Drawbacks of Network. The major drawback of the network is that it contributes to information overload for public officials. Having raised the expectations of community members about increased ac- cess, city officials now feel they need to meet this expectation by an- swering mail and participating in conferences. Additional resources have not been put at their disposal to help them fulfill these obliga- tions.

Privacy/Security Issues. There have only been one or two incidents of people using obscene or offensive language during an electronic conference. One conference was stopped because the dialog became pornographic, but usually self-monitoring among users is sufficient to minimize objectionable content. Users will write things like "better watch it, they'll pull the plug" to other users.

Ideas for Expansion. PEN organizers would like users to be able to pay their city water bills electronically.

As a separate project, there are also plans to set up kiosks in public places to allow Santa Monica residents to pay traffic tickets and parking citations as well as to file claims for small claims court electronically.

Another idea for expansion is to begin to cooperate more with nearby city governments and communities. Organizers would like to encourage users in other communities to visit Santa Monica "electronically" to get information about pets for adoption, on restaurants, etc.

Technical/Financial Problems in Gearing Up. There are no anticipated problems in gearing up.

Recommendations

For Other FreeNets. PEN organizers believe that people need to perceive a value to the services on-line or they will not use them. They recommend adding information and on-line services that will save people time. Furthermore, they believe that the key problems and issues are social not technical. They involve setting appropriate usage policies, deciding whether and how to moderate messaging, and figuring out how to be responsive to the volume of messages that will be generated.

To Government. There is no real role for the federal government in increasing the number of public networks; rather, it is the work of local and city governments. The best model for a national network is one that connects multiple, geographically close networks.

SEATTLE COMMUNITY NETWORK, SEATTLE, WA

Goals and Development

Objectives and Network Development. The impetus to begin the Seattle Community Network was the success of FreeNets in other parts of the country—namely, Berkeley, Cleveland, and Big Sky in Montana. Organizers wanted to set up a similar resource in Seattle to promote communication and awareness within the community. Planning for the network began in June 1992. The network first opened for public use on May 16, 1994. Since May, members of the Seattle community have been able to access SCN at public library terminals, by telneting, or by dialing in.

The network is viewed primarily as a mechanism for fostering community building—to provide Seattle with a virtual community to promote a sharing of ideas. Dozens of organizations within the Seattle community have been able to increase awareness of their activities by putting themselves on SCN. Ideals of the network include free and universal access, noncensorship, and privacy. The network's services and technology are structured around the principle of catering to the "lowest common denominator." No one should be shut out from access because they do not have a sophisticated enough computer or do not have a computer at all.

The opening screen of SCN is shown in Figure B.2.

Obstacles to Establishing. The biggest obstacle to establishing the network has been sustaining an organization that is completely dependent on private donations and a volunteer staff. All of the equipment used by SCN—including its server, terminals, and phone lines—has been donated or purchased from donated funds. All of the members of the organization volunteer their time.

Fortuitous Events. In setting up the network, the organizers have benefited from the large amount of interest and support within the Seattle community. There are at present 100 unpaid volunteers supporting different parts of the network's operations. New individuals continue to turn up at each of the network's monthly meetings.

Welcome to the Seattle Community Network's Web Server!

Seattle Community Network is a free, public computer network run by volunteers. Founded by the Seattle chapter of Computer Professionals for Social Responsibility, SCN went online serving the Greater Seattle area in the Spring of 1994.

SCN is committed to providing equal access to information for all users, and thanks to the support of the Seattle Public Library, and a number of other generous benefactors, we are able to offer accounts to everyone. Please feel free to browse, and request registration materials.

SCN uses the Freeport Menu Software, you can only browse it with your web browser. If you want to contribute to the forums, the bulletin boards within the SCN system, you will need to telnet to scn.org, and be a registered user.

SCN Menus

SCN Information Providers' Homepages

SCN Links to Other Freenets and Community Resources

Comments? Volunteers? If your browser has 'mailto' capability, you can click here - or send mail to webadm@scn.org.

FAQ | Registration | SCN Policy | Telnet to SCN

Figure B.2—Opening Screen of Seattle Community Network Web Page

The organizers also benefited from the mutual interest of the Seattle public library in setting up a FreeNet. The Seattle public library was seeking ways to go beyond their existing on-line services at the time that the founders of SCN first began to organize. The public libraries in Seattle and King County have become the main conduit for delivery of SCN's services. There is at least one on-line terminal in each of 50 different libraries throughout these two counties.

Organization and Finance

Organization and Governance Structure. SCN is sponsored by the Seattle chapter of Computer Professionals for Social Responsibility (CPSR). SCN is not a nonprofit organization in its own right—at least not yet—and so derives its nonprofit status from being affiliated with CPSR. All donations, monetary or otherwise, are made through CPSR, Seattle.

Organizational responsibilities for the SCN are divided between a coordinating council and five working committees. The coordinating council acts as a steering committee for the project and is responsible for approving any large expenditures. It has eight members, including the head of each of the five working committees, a representative of the Seattle public library, and two members at-large. The five working committees are in the areas of hardware/software, policy, services, outreach, and fundraising.

The hardware/software representatives deal with all technical issues. The policy committee sets high-level policy related to the goals and values of the network. It addresses such issues as the appropriateness of censorship, fees for services, allowing exclusive areas on SCN, etc. The services committee is responsible for dealing with information providers and putting content on the system. They obtain and maintain information services on SCN. As part of this job, they train IPs.

Members of the outreach committee are responsible for promoting SCN. They organize talks and interface with local media interested in writing stories about the network. They also collect equipment to be recycled and used in their operations. Fundraising has recently been separated from outreach. To support their efforts to gear up operations, SCN needs a group of individuals dedicated solely to raising money

Involvement with Other Organizations. SCN has strategic alliances with several organizations in the Seattle community:

Public Library. SCN signed a two-year agreement with the Seattle public library in the Spring of 1994, which has allowed them use of a limited number of telephone lines. The libraries and librarian have been integral to the success of SCN in the community. They have been very supportive of users.

Neighborhood Organizations. SCN also has strategic alliances with several neighborhood organizations, allowing these organizations to put information on-line and to use the network as an organizing tool.

Public Television. The network signed an agreement at the beginning of 1995 with KCTS—the public television station—to work together to promote dialog within the Seattle community on political and social issues. The first event that will be sponsored jointly is a program called "Ask the Governor." The KCTS representative responsible for organizing this program hopes it will be the first in a series of "town meeting" events supported by the on-line network. The network is one way people will be able to ask questions. As part of the agreement with KCTS, $10,000 has been set aside for a member of SCN to act as a liaison between the two organizations.

Another outgrowth of the KCTS agreement is a working arrangement with the Powerful Schools Project—a project designed to bring information technology to inner-city schools. Organizers of SCN view this working arrangement as one way to support its commitment to universal access.

Budget/Funding. At present, SCN has no operating budget. The network has spent an estimated $800–$1,000 in its first year of operation on administrative costs such as copying and mailing. Ninety percent of these funds have been raised through donations mailed in with registration forms. To guarantee universal access, registration is free, but donations are welcomed. The average donation is $10. Small amounts of money also come occasionally from the local chapter of CPSR to help cover operating costs. The one paid staff member is funded by a grant from KCTS. All hardware costs have been covered through donations. This includes the cost of a $5,000 Sun server, telephone lines, and access to the Internet provider. Access to the Internet is free by piggybacking onto the Seattle public library.

Efforts at fundraising are presently gearing up. The expanding member base will necessitate more phone lines into the library, more servers, and a standardized package of training. As part of the library's own expansion of its phone lines, SCN will, within a few months, have access to 16 phone lines. SCN members want to raise $50,000 to pay for the installation and continued operation of these lines. They also hope to raise $15,000 to design a customized training package. Supporting the increasing volume of users will mean acquiring at least one and possibly two more servers for the library. They hope to raise these funds through grants and fundraising within the local community.

On-Line Services

Major Services. The major services provided by the network include e-mail, user forums, community bulletins, and question-and-answer forums.

E-Mail. SCN views e-mail as the most important service: 30 percent of all log-ins are for the purpose of using e-mail.

User Forums. User forums are on a wide range of subjects from local politics to environmental issues and the meaning of economic development. A recent forum was on children and violence. User forums are sometimes put on by members of SCN but also can evolve spontaneously from dialogs on the Internet.

Community Bulletins. A broad range of groups publish information about themselves on the network. These include the League of Women Voters, King County Democrats, the American Civil Liberties Union, and Sustainable Seattle—a group concerned with all environmental, educational, and health issues that effect the long-term well-being of the Seattle community. There are also a number of neighborhoods with space on the network. Neighborhoods use the network to promote a community dialog and organize crime-prevention programs.

SCN itself has always posted its meeting times and events on the network but has recently begun to put the minutes and agenda of its meeting on-line as well to keep the organization open and accessible.

Question-and-Answer Forums. Among the question and answer forums, there are regular and on-going forums as well as those held on a one-time basis. The regular forums include one called "Mr. Science," one on consumer law, and one for restaurant recommendations. Examples of one-time question-and-answer forums include one with one of Washington's U.S. Senators as well as an upcoming one called "Ask the Governor." E-mail and the telephone will be mechanisms interested citizens can use to ask questions of the sitting governor.

Governmental Items On-Line. The organizers of SCN have steered away from using the network for political purposes, though there is the occasional forum, and political groups post information on the network. Ideas for how they might expand the number of political services on-line without becoming partisan include posting government documents and posting draft proposals of legislation on-line. The Seattle public library already puts many government documents on-line, including the entire Civil Code for the state of Washington.

Services to Underserved Groups and Targeted Outreach. Information related to distance learning or job opportunities is not posted on the SCN network. Again, these are informational resources that the library does have on-line.

However, SCN does have other services related to the needs of underserved groups: The Washington Coalition of Citizens with Disabilities will soon post bulletins on-line; one SCN volunteer has organized a user group of low-income women who meet once a month for hands-on training and to discuss potential uses of the Internet; and individual members of SCN are also working with the Powerful Schools Project, which is an attempt to bring schools in low-income areas onto the network. On-line projects at these schools include information searches, cooperative learning with schools around the country and world—typically on themes related to geography and the environment—and a pen-pals program.

User Support/Training/Mentoring. Support services offered by the SCN come in three forms. The first type of support service—called a "road show"—is directed at users of the network. Twice a month members of the network visit the public libraries in Seattle and King County and give hands-on training to members of the community. People interested in using the network come to these meetings to be walked through the process of getting on-line, to have questions answered, and to learn about new and upcoming services. Other than the road shows, no formal measures are taken to help network users gain access. There is no user's manual. Librarians at each site are usually available to lend assistance, when they have time.

The other type of support service offered by SCN is directed by IPs— those who put information on the network. Through a system of mentoring, with one network member assigned to each IP, SCN's goal is to make all IPs self-sufficient in getting information on-line. Rather than SCN volunteers taking information from the IPs and structuring it to make it suitable to be on-line, the IPs learn to do this for themselves.

A final type of support service is the SCN hotline. Users, IPs, or others can use SCN's voice mail to ask questions and to make suggestions.

User Characteristics

Number and Growth/Decline. After 10 months of operations, the SCN has over 3,500 individual account holders and registers over 20,000 log-ins each month.   SCN receives 250 requests for registration forms every 10 days, and about 50 percent of these individuals actually sign up for accounts. The network projects having 10,000–12,000 members by the end of the year.

Demographics of Users. SCN has no demographic breakdown of their users, but officials say they include the homeless, low-income groups, and disabled individuals.

New User Procedures/Advertising. Becoming a new user is as easy as submitting a registration form to get a user ID and password. New members can register at the monthly meeting, at one of the road shows, or by requesting a registration form by mail. Once or twice a year, SCN volunteers also go to computer user conferences in Seattle to register new members.   At the last conference held at the University of Washington, 1,800 registration forms were handed out, but it is not known how many of these individuals actually registered. The road shows and conference visits along with press releases in local newspapers are the main means of getting the word out on SCN.

Physical Access and Technical Characteristics

Location of Terminals. Public access terminals are all located in libraries in Seattle and King County.

Hardware/Interface. A text-based interface allows the network to cater to the lowest common technical denominator. Even individuals with old or low-end computers can access SCN services.

In March of 1995, the network organizers set up a Web server to allow people from outside SCN to access the network through any graphical Web browser.

SCN has one Sun server housed in the main Seattle public library. This supports the operation of the entire network.

Network Connections/Access. Users can connect to the SCN in one of three ways: (1) They can use a public access terminal in one of the public libraries; (2) they can telnet in through another Internet account; or (3) they can dial-in via modem from home.

At present, users of SCN are not able to telnet to other networks nor are they able to run an FTP. Telnet and file transfer would overload the local server; the capacity of telephone lines is not sufficient to allow users to do this regularly.

Benefits of Civic Networks/Universal Access Issues

Benefits of Network. Network organizers feel there are several important benefits that the community derives from their services.

Community Building. Internet communication can encourage community building by creating a dialog between people living in close proximity to one another. This type of communication helps people learn what those around them are doing, while at the same time giving people different perspectives.

Freedom of Communication. There is a "freeing" aspect to Internet communication. People can get together anytime, anywhere. Also, there is no basis for discrimination on the Internet. As one official put it, "The only basis for discrimination is your typing speed."

Work Skills. Use of the Internet can potentially increase the skill level of the workforce by increasing technical literacy. Students using computers often motivate parents to do the same. Having computers in the classroom is a great leveler because all children, not just those with wealthy parents, have access.

Political. One advantage of using the Internet for political purposes is that it makes lobbying efforts quicker and cheaper.

Drawbacks of Network. SCN organizers see one drawback to electronic networks in the potential to promote physical isolation. If everyone just accesses the Internet from home, then it may actually act to break down community. In addition, the higher price of entrance into the Internet world necessitates more money and education, which may act to reinforce a two-tiered society.

The Internet is very vulnerable to those with an extreme view. Because of low barriers to entrance for those with an ax to grind, it may actually increase social tensions. In other words, bad apples have easy access. There is also the potential for "Balkanization," with the loss of cultural literacy and common points for discussion as everybody retreats into their own small community of like-minded users.

Ideas for Expansion. Network organizers have several good ideas for expanding their operations.

Neighborhoods. One major idea for expansion is to get more neighborhoods on-line and allow them to organize their own forums and do their own marketing. One SCN member would like to create a template that would allow each neighborhood to store information on its history, geography, demographics, and community resources.

Increase Scope. Another idea for expansion is to increase the number of terminals and diversify their locations to include more schools, religious organizations, senior centers, and community centers.

Increase Access. Increased ability of network members to access and use other on-line resources around the country would aid in expansion. Up to the present, the network has focused only on community-building within Seattle; now it may want to expand contact to other networks.

Governmental. A final idea for expansion is to get more government documents and draft legislation on-line.

Technical/Financial Problems in Gearing Up. The number of phone lines and the number of servers must both be increased before expansion can take place. The major recurring costs are the phone lines. Increasing memory and central processing unit on the servers is relatively cheap, and most new computer terminals are donated.

Recommendations

For Other FreeNets. It is important not to neglect the business aspect of setting up a network, and to plan and forecast for longer-range needs. It is helpful if there are people involved in the process with business acumen, particularly marketing and strategic planning skills. As those involved try to raise money, they need to be able to convey how their service adds value.

As many local groups as possible should be part of any effort to set up a network. This not only increases resources available but also contributes to the legitimacy and credibility of the organization (e.g., it does not appear to be leftist or rightist). Similarly, "techno-arrogance" should be avoided.

To Government. SCN officials' primary recommendation to government is to think of the Internet as a utility: A certain percentage of it should be available for public access. If necessary, changing tax structures and incentives to ensure universal access should be considered. At present, a huge amount of money is being spent to control the unfolding telecommunications regime. The consumer must not get "squashed" in the process. The costs of getting on the network and of obtaining equipment need to be regulated, as do issues of how and where people are able to get on. Finally, regulations on content should favor free speech as opposed to censorship.

PLAYING TO WIN, INC., NEW YORK, NY

Goals and Development

Objectives and Network Development. Playing to Win, Inc., is a 15-year-old organization based in New York. Its mission is to bring computer and information technology to inner-city communities. The organization's founder, Antonia Stone, recognized the powerful effect that the desktop computer would have on society, employment, and educational opportunities. She also understood the potential for the disparities in access to computer technology to further marginalize disadvantage groups. She began Playing to Win to bring computing resources to the Harlem community to counteract what she expected to be a growing gap between information and technology haves and have-nots.

The opening screen of Playing to Win's Community Computing Center Network is shown in Figure B.3.

Harlem Center. Playing to Win started as a single technology center in Harlem. The technology center was equipped with computers, printers, and limited multimedia equipment and was made available to members of the Harlem community who were interested in improving their computer literacy. Over time, the Harlem Center became a recognized technology resource in the community not only in its capacity to provide access but also in its ability to advise other inner-city organizations how to set up and operate technology programs. Since its founding in 1981, Playing to Win, Inc., has advised over 100 different organizations in the greater Harlem community on how to use technology for both administrative and educational purposes.

```
\\\\\\\\\\\\\\\\\\\\\\V///////////////////////
              Welcome to the
              PLAYING TO WIN
         Community Computing Center
             Electronic Network

///////////////////////////\\\\\\\\\\\\\\\\\\\\\\\
You have new conf entries in pn.announcements pn.alerts headlines ...

PeaceNet: (c)onf (m)ail (i)nternet (d)ata (u)sers (n)ews (e)xtras (bye):
```

**Figure B.3—Playing to Win's Community Computing Center Network
Opening Screen**

Network Project. As an outgrowth of its technology consulting activities, Playing to Win, Inc., with the support of a grant from the National Science Foundation, set up a Playing to Win Network in 1993 as a way to support the introduction of technology into educational and social service organizations serving low-income communities throughout New England and the rest of the country. The goal of the network project is to organize institutions with similar goals, which are confronting similar challenges, into a mutually supportive community. There are 56 organizations connected to the network. Many of these organizations are in New York, Boston, and Washington, D.C. These organizations include shelters for youth and women, counseling centers, resource centers for immigrants, cable access centers, and a number of computer user organizations.

Through seminars and site visits, Playing to Win staff help these organizations meet the challenge of running a community computing center on a limited budget. Telecommunications is meant to facilitate the exchange of information between administrators at each of the affiliates on subjects ranging from grant-writing and recruiting volunteers to community outreach and ideas for new projects.

Community Access Center. The Community Access Center (CAC) in New York is a social service organization participating in the Playing to Win Network. The center serves a mentally ill and developmentally disabled population. It has a long-standing, independent telecommunications/network service program. CAC joined the Playing to Win Network with the hope of taking advantage of increased contact with other nonprofit administrators.

Obstacles to Establishing/Fortuitous Events. To keep PTW Network operating, organizers have had to grapple with a number of obstacles, none of which have proved unsurmountable.

Harlem Center/Community Access Center. Like other social service organizations, both centers are constantly trying to raise money through grant-writing and soliciting donations. Their computer and telecommunications programs depend on a continual infusion of new resources to pay for both equipment and personnel. Thus far, both organizations have been able to maintain and in some cases expand their technology programs, but the funding environment remains insecure.

Network Project. The largest obstacle to running the network is the difficulty in coordinating individuals at the 56 different social service organizations participating in the project. Large geographical distances between the centers and busy schedules of the social service organizations' administrators mean that it is not always easy to get together to discuss common goals and strategies.

A potential boon in setting up the network is the attention that the information superhighway is getting at present. One interviewee felt that there is a window of opportunity to highlight what it will take to truly get universal access. In his opinion, people must start thinking in terms of a community access model—getting terminals to libraries, religious organizations, etc.—where they can be used by individuals who do not have computers.

Organization and Finance

Organization and Governance Structure. The administrative offices for Playing to Win, Inc., are at the Harlem Center. The administrative office for the network project has recently been relocated to Massachusetts. Its new home is with the Educational Development Center in Newton, Massachusetts.

In each of the three urban areas with the highest density of affiliates—New York, Washington, D.C., and Boston—a regional network coordinator organizes seminars and site visits.

Involvement with Other Organizations. The Harlem Center works with a broad range of social service providers in New York to improve these groups' access to computer technology. Social service providers use the Harlem Center to conduct computer training for their staff or clients. Participating organizations include the Morningside Daycare Center, the Trinity House (a halfway house), Central Harlem Montessori School, and the Metropolitan Hospital.

The Community Access Center works with a number of organizations to increase the usefulness of its network operations and breadth of coverage of its telecommunications activities. These organizations include residential care facilities, hospitals, and a day program center.

The Playing to Win Network project involves a broad range of social service organizations in several large urban areas.

Budget/Funding. The operational budget for the Harlem Center is $350,000. Ninety percent of this funding comes from private foundations and grants, about 10 percent comes from user fees. For the first three years of its operation, funding for the network project came from an NSF grant in the amount of $950,000. In November 1995, the network project will receive an additional NSF grant in the amount of $2 million to be spent over five years.

On-Line Services

Major Services. Service offerings on the PTW Network include e-mail, access to a wide array of electronic bulletin boards, and access to a number of social service providers.

Institute for Global Communications (IGC)/Playing to Win Network. The Playing to Win Network is on the IGC's Network. All of the Playing to Win affiliates can access and use all the services on the IGC Network. The IGC services include the following:

- *E-Mail/Internet Conferences.* E-mail and discussion room features are used frequently by administrators of the affiliated social service organizations as an information resource. Both are used to support a dialog between the different social service and community groups on the network about common problems. Directors or administrators at the different organizations can post problems and questions about a range of topics—e.g., how to integrate equipment and software into their programs, how to get volunteers, or how to raise funds—and can expect to get answers from people who have confronted similar challenges.

- *Information.* The network allows users to telnet and download materials. Users can also access an on-line news service.

- *Government.* The network is used to send messages to politicians and members of Congress.

Harlem Center. The most important services at the Harlem Center are basic computer services, not telecommunications services. Just under 10 percent of the members of the Harlem Center use the Internet. Most members of the Harlem Center come to take classes and receive informal tutoring in a broad range of basic computer and software applications or to work on computer projects (e.g., to write papers, resumes, and letters).

The Harlem Center's main Internet provider is IGC. They have also held Internet accounts on New York Kids Network and America Online (AOL). The main services used are the e-mail and chat features, although occasionally a user will conduct an information search.

Community Access Center. Unlike the Harlem Center, the Community Access Center does not depend on IGC to connect to the Internet. The center has its own direct Internet connection.

There are four main network features used by clients and administrators at the CAC.

- *Progress Reports.* Clients can access progress and status reports written by their doctors and counselors, which are stored on line. The open access policy is designed to empower clients; if they do not like, or are uncomfortable with, what they read they can take issue with whomever wrote the reports.

- *E-Mail.* Staff and clients use e-mail to facilitate communication within the organization; they post meetings, up-coming events, etc.

- *List Serve.* A list serve called "madness," which is posted by St. John's hospital in New York and forwarded over the CAC's server to its staff and clients, makes it possible to keep track of all patient movements. Lists about who is in or out of the hospital are updated constantly—when someone goes into the hospital all appropriate parties are notified instantly. Lists of residence changes and vacancies are also kept up to date.

- *Chat Room.* Clients afflicted by mental illness or recovering from a drug addiction can participate in an e-mail mailing list/chat room called "double-trouble." The chat room functions like an anonymous recovery group, allowing those facing similar challenges to provide one another with peer support.

Governmental Items On-Line. One political feature on the IGC is the ability to e-mail one's congress member/representative or the president. Harlem Center Staff try to use this program as a hook to get more people using the e-mail feature.

The Harlem Center registered as a public access point for a series of electronic town hall meetings held in May 1995. The project was organized out of Washington by the National Telecommunications and Interaction Agency and National Public Radio. Over a two-week period, a set of topics related to recent public policy was covered (e.g., proposed welfare cuts and the effect of electronic government). Citizens used public access points around the country to pose questions directly to policymakers.

Many public agencies, including the IRS and the Small Business Administration, are on-line. They offer question and answer services to facilitate paying taxes or getting information about how to raise finance for their firm.

Services to Underserved Groups and Targeted Outreach. PTW offers a number of services targeted at disadvantaged groups.

Chat. A number of community computing centers offer underserved groups conference/chat room features outside of the IGC. These features allow individuals facing common challenges to offer peer support to one another. The Playing to Win Network has no chat room feature of its own.

Clients at the CAC often log into the "double-trouble" chat room.

Some gay users at the Harlem Center have made use of chat rooms targeted to a homosexual audience.

Job Listings/Distance Learning. At both sites, users can telnet into the databanks of governments and local educational institutions to gather information about job listings or distance learning. These features are rarely used because the information is poorly organized and often not current.

Software Training. At the Harlem Center, training in basic software applications (e.g., Microsoft Word or Lotus) is considered very important in helping individuals improve their employment possibilities.

Computer Recycling. Up until 1994, the Harlem Center worked with an organization called the National Christina Foundation based out of Connecticut to acquire recycled computer equipment. The foundation acts as broker of used computer equipment, gathering it from corporations that are upgrading and distributing it to nonprofit organizations that serve a disabled or underserved clientele.

Most Popular Services. E-Mail, chat rooms, and information searches are the most popular services offered by the network.

E-Mail/Chat. Individuals at the Harlem Center, CAC, and PTW Network Office universally agreed that the e-mail and chat features were the most commonly used and most useful of the network features. Once people figure out the e-mail technology, they are usually hooked, and their frequency of usage increases. The chat room feature shows a bi-modal pattern of usage. After an initial exposure, some users return to using the chat rooms over and over again, others stop using the chat feature altogether.

Information Searches. Information searches are the feature that has the greatest difficulty in sustaining appeal. Excited by the hype, many people may use Netscape or another search software package once and then stop using it altogether. Users tend to be frustrated by the disorganization of information on the Internet. To sustain interest, people must be able to get information that is relevant to them quickly. It is not normally clear how they can get relevant information from the Internet—even if the information is there, it is not always obvious how to access it.

User Support/Training/Mentoring. The Harlem Center presents lectures and formal seminars—lecture style—and interactive seminars on using the Internet on an ongoing basis. Many of the seminars are given by volunteers; others are given by paid instructors. Though seminars are offered regularly, most user support still takes place informally. If a user has a question, he or she can ask one of the center staff or a peer for help.

The Community Access Center has four individuals involved in providing formal and informal user support. Two of the residential facilities working with the CAC along with the day program center have technology coordinators on staff. At the residential centers, user support is offered informally. The technology coordinator at the day program center offers informal support as needed but also puts on between two and four formal training classes per week. At the CAC's administrative center, the Management Information System (MIS) director is available to offer informal support. Clients and administrative users of the network system are also encouraged to turn to their peers for support.

User Characteristics

Number and Growth/Decline. The lack of formal training has contributed to low participation rates at both sites. Typically, only those with an interest in technology and with the self-motivation to persevere beyond the frustrations of using the network become regular users.

At the CAC, both administrators and clients make use of the system. Up until the present, the number of administrators using the system has been much greater than the number of clients. To date, only 75 of the organization's 350 clients make use of the telecommunications services. Twenty-five of these clients are regular, active users; the other 50 clients have accounts and make occasional use of the network services.

However, the number of client users is growing rapidly. CAC registers a 10 percent increase in log-ins each month, with most of the growth in use coming from the client side. As the number of client users increases, the character of the system is changing from one that is primarily oriented toward completely administrative functions to one that is more user-driven and spontaneous.

Dropout Rates of Users/Role of Training in Minimizing Dropout. There was universal agreement from all interviewees that increased training and support would increase usage. Individuals in the inner city typically have no access to computer technology. They find it intimidating and are not sure how it can be useful to them. Before getting on the Internet or using e-mail, they have to become comfortable with computers. Training is also key to getting people to use other than the basic e-mail and chat features. According to one interviewee, there are many useful informational resources on the Internet. They include financial information, news, and other information from different government agencies. Getting people to use these means showing them how to conduct searches effectively.

All of the individuals interviewed at Playing to Win also suggested that use of network resources by people living in the inner city will increase as the information on-line becomes (a) easily accessed through good search programs and (b) relevant to the needs of inner-city users. Training is important, but only to the extent that people actually believe that there is something useful on the Internet, and that they are being trained to find easily.

Demographics of Users. Community Access Center users include both administrators and individuals with developmental disabilities or mental illnesses.

Harlem Center users are 80 percent African American. Children are more likely than adults to use network resources.

Frequency of Use. At both organizations, users fall into one of three categories for frequency of use. The first category includes those who tend to integrate the network into their daily or weekly communications. They feel comfortable with the e-mail and chat technologies and use them often. This may lead them to do other things, such as information searches. A second category of user includes those who participate in the occasional project and may read some mail from the network. These users are not "hooked" and tend to use the network only when it is the obvious choice. A third category of account holders are those who seldom or never use the network.

New User Procedures/Advertising. All of the organizations participating in the PTW Network have full Internet access, including access to e-mail accounts for their administrators. Most have made some arrangements to make e-mail available to individual users.

Community Access Center. At the CAC, the MIS director assigns a log-in user ID and password to any client who wants one. They do not advertise beyond their client base.

Harlem Center. Anyone who is a member of the Harlem Center can use one of the center's e-mail accounts free of charge to test out the Internet. If they decide to become a regular user, then they have to set up and pay the monthly fees on their own e-mail account.

Playing to Win. To get onto the IGC/PTW Network, an individual must belong to one of the PTW affiliates. The Playing to Win Network will assign each affiliate one free Internet account, which includes access to e-mail; the affiliates handle how these are used in their respective offices and technology labs. Additional accounts are available at a cost. The network administrators help the computing centers find accounts with other Internet providers.

Physical Access and Technical Characteristics

Location of Terminals. The Community Access Center has terminals at its main business office, its main intake facility, at six residential sites, and at the day program center. The Harlem Center has terminals only in its technology lab.

Hardware/Interface. The CAC has its own server in its main office. The organization has sites that are far enough apart and enough users to make it cost-effective to be their own Internet host. CAC has its own Web page but with a graphics-based interface, which the MIS coordinator has attempted to make very user-friendly. The system was set up originally for administrative purposes, and it has not been difficult to expand to serve client users as the demand has arisen.

The Harlem Center has no server on site, but it has 10 telephone lines and six modems, which allow its users to access the Internet. They have been given free accounts from various Internet providers at different times. Their stable provider is now IGC.

Benefits of Civic Networks/Universal Access Issues

Benefits of Network. PTW organizers stress a variety of benefits to the services they offer.

Information Searches. If Internet resources were better organized and people received some training, the network could become a very important resource in facilitating information searches.

Organizing. The network provides a valuable resource for like-minded individuals who are trying to organize from the ground up (e.g., environmentalists, gay rights groups, affiliates of the Playing to Win Network). The network allows groups to get information to a large number of individuals more quickly and cost-effectively—it enables more than just one-to-one communication. Also, there is no need for printing and addressing and posting envelopes.

Administrative Functions. The network allows many administrative functions to be completed collaboratively. Grant- and report-writing can be done by individuals working together even if they are in different geographic locations. All can work at their own pace on the project to give input. The costs of administrative communication can also be lowered by using the network, because it reduces the time and money that go into mailing. The network can also make directed information searches cheaper and more efficient.

Programmatic Uses. The Internet allows social service organizations to enhance the educational component of their programs. Projects can be made interactive with groups around the country or can be conducted on a real-time basis within ongoing science research or exploration.

Therapeutics. For inner-city children, Internet access can increase access to the outside world. For individuals belonging to disenfranchised groups, e.g., the mentally ill or handicapped, it can serve as a good resource for peer support. Communicating over the Internet, these individuals do not face the same level of prejudice and impatience.

Drawbacks of Network. Despite the generally positive view of the network as a resource, some interviewed individuals expressed the opinion that it also has a number of potential drawbacks. The network can create an additional burden, becoming yet another media that individuals must monitor and respond to. It may be dehumanizing and discourage interaction between people. The network may encourage fragmentation, as different groups retreat into their chat room of like-minded individuals.

Privacy/Security Issues. The Harlem Center lost an e-mail account on N.Y. Kids Network after children at the center repeatedly used the network to pull down pornographic materials. They also had problems with an intern who used the Center's AOL account as a chat room on homosexual erotica and to send and receive pictures. All members of the staff had access to the account, and many found its usage for this purpose unacceptable.

Harlem Center staff feel that it is normal and useful for people—children in particular—to want to explore and push the limits on how to use this new technology. Rather than try to stop exploration, staff members prefer to monitor and structure usage to make the exploration as creative as possible.

Ideas for Expansion. Both the CAC and Harlem Center want to encourage more people to use e-mail. They feel this is the hook to getting people to use other network services

Technical/Financial Problems in Gearing Up. Gearing up definitely requires purchasing more technical equipment, resources, and human support. A large financial constraint in gearing up, however, is the lack of resources to pay for trainers and training. Among inner-city and disadvantaged groups, network usage will increase only if these individuals have technical support.

Recommendations

For Other FreeNets. If FreeNets really want to create universal access, then they must think about a community center model. They have to get networked computers to community centers—e.g., libraries and religious organizations—where people can make use of them.

The Internet must be demystified by creating a user-friendly interface. This is the most important thing in increasing use—it makes it less necessary to invest heavily in training.

To Government. Policymakers interested in creating universal access need to take training and support just as seriously as getting the wiring out there. People need to have access to the hardware but they also must have the capacity to use it. There are plenty of examples of schools that have invested in computer equipment but never successfully integrated it into their instruction because of the lack of support for users. The same thing could happen with the Internet.

Two recommended measures to assist in creating universal access on the technical side are giving everyone an Internet account at the post office and having some of the large Internet providers allocate a part of their excess capacity, say 5 percent, to nonprofit organizations.

LATINONET, SAN FRANCISCO, CA

Goals and Development

Objectives and Network Development. LatinoNet grew out of a research project funded by the Hispanic Community Fund Office (HCFO) in San Francisco. The project was designed to determine the needs of Latino nonprofit organizations. One of its major findings concerned the need for better channels of communication between nonprofits serving the Latino community. It was hoped that improved communication about common goals and challenges would allow each organization to better serve its clientele. Efforts to get LatinoNet going began at the outset of 1992, and the network first began operation in November of 1994.

The principal goal of LatinoNet is to use telecommunications as a vehicle to improve the flow of information between organizations concerned with addressing political, social, economic, and community issues within the Latino community. There are at present 80 nonprofit organizations working within the network. The nonprofits are of two types—either Key Information Providers (KIPs) or simply members of the network. The KIPs, all national in their scope and activities, provide information about their activities on the network. The other members of the network, most of whom are local or regional in scope, are information consumers.

The network is seen as a tool that will help each nonprofit organization better fulfill its mission through mutual support and dialog. It is also hoped that the network will evolve into a powerful tool for political organization and community awareness, allowing individuals and important agencies in the Latino community to stay abreast of politically sensitive issues and to organize responses.

Providing access to individual users is a less important goal of the networks. Individuals who want to join are welcome to, but they must already have computer access, a modem, and the ability to pay for on-line services.

LatinoNet's opening screen is shown in Figure B.4.

Obstacles to Establishing. The main obstacle to getting the network running smoothly is the conservatism of the KIPs. It is the organizers of LatinoNet who see the network as a major opportunity for many of the national nonprofit groups. The nonprofit groups are, as with any new technology, a little resistant to change. They are not sure they want to spend the time and resources necessary to get up to speed on how to use the network. The organizers of the network find themselves needing to emphasize repeatedly the potential benefits of network access, including (a) another way for the nonprofits to market themselves, (b) a way to reach a broader audience, and (c) the ability to communicate more effectively with their regional and local affiliates.

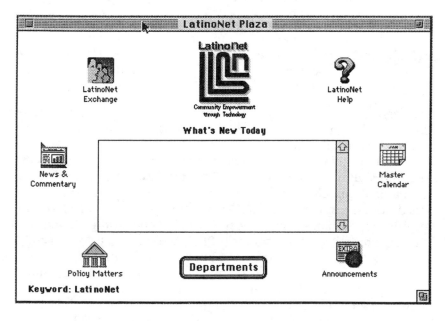

Figure B.4—LatinoNet's Opening Screen

Fortuitous Events. LatinoNet's ability to persuade AOL to enter into a strategic alliance has been a major boon to their operations. It means that they do not have to maintain the hardware of a network system but can concentrate on acting as an information broker. They have also benefited from corporate sponsorships and donations. While AOL charges most organizations between $50,000 and $85,000 a year for space on their network, they have given LatinoNet space for $5,000 a year. LatinoNet has also received equipment and monetary donations from PacBell, GTE, Ameritech, NYNEX, and South West Bell. A third source of support for LatinoNet's activities has come from other networks that are already up and running. Organizers of the LatinoNet drew heavily on the technical expertise of these already established networks, i.e., IGC, PeaceNet, and SeniorNet.

Organization and Finance

Organization and Governance Structure. At present, LatinoNet has a staff of four in their main San Francisco office. All administration, training, and support is done out of this office. They also have a national board of directors consisting of nine individuals—the president and eight representatives of the KIPs sit on the board.

Involvement with Other Organizations. There are 35 key information providers for LatinoNet. The organizations are all over the country but are concentrated in Los Angeles, New York, Chicago, and Texas. They include cultural centers (National Association of Latino Arts and Culture, Galeria La Raza Posada), research organizations (Hispanic Research Center, Southwest Voters Research Center), political action groups (National Association of Latino Elected and Appointed Officials, Southwest Voter Registration Education Project), youth leadership groups (APIRA Association, Congressional Hispanic Caucus Institute, Hispanic Leadership Opportunity Program), news organizations (Latino U.S.A., Hispanic Link), charitable organizations (Fiesta Educativa, United Latino Fund), and a large number of university-based Latino research centers (University of Texas, El Paso and Austin; University of Arizona; Hunter College of CUNY; Stanford University; De Paul University; University of New Mexico; Florida National University).

LatinoNet has an agreement with each of the KIPs to outfit them with the necessary modems and software and give them the training needed to get on the network free of charge in return for two years of their participation. The KIPs are asked to contribute information to the various network services provided by LatinoNet on an ongoing basis.

GTE, PacBell, and other regional operating Bells around the country have been very helpful in supporting LatinoNet's outreach to the KIPs. The phone companies have donated modems and contributed funds to support training. (The phone companies' interest is in being seen as technology leaders—i.e., paving the way to the information superhighway.) In addition, LatinoNet is in the process of negotiating an agreement with Apple to receive a number of donated computers.

Budget/Funding. The president said that they expect the operating budget for fiscal year 1994/1995 to be $300,000. Since most of the equipment and training costs have been covered by private donations and since their contract with AOL costs only $5,000 a year, most of this money goes to paying staff salaries. Some of the money also supports overhead at the San Francisco office. They expect the operating budget to double over the next year or two as the organization gears up its technical and training activities in different regional offices.

LatinoNet's operating costs are covered by charging membership and user fees, and by a grant from the NTIA. As an incentive to encourage their members to use the network, AOL gives LatinoNet 10 percent of the revenues earned on all activities on LatinoNet's accounts. Organizational memberships are $75 a year; individual memberships are $60 a year. Membership fees for the KIPs are waived because they provide a service.

On-Line Services

Major Services. Services on LatinoNet can be divided into four categories. A first category of services is all the features of the AOL network in general. Users of LatinoNet must first subscribe to AOL, at a charge of $10 a month. The other three categories of services are on the LatinoNet proper. They include the following:

User-Driven Services.   On an area of LatinoNet called the Inter-cambio, users can create their own topics and forums. They can post questions or participate in ongoing chats via e-mail. The AOL software makes the forums easy to follow. It includes features that allow users to go directly to the first or last posting and to see all entries after a certain date or since the last log-in.

KIPs-Driven Services.   Another area of the LatinoNet is devoted specifically to information posting by the 35 KIPs. This part of the network is organized into seven departments. The departments include nonprofit resources, arts and culture, education, professional organizations, policy and planning, news and information, and demographics and census data. Each KIP contributes information to one or more department. The departments are organized with a file explaining the basic types of information to be found and how to search by key-word function.

LatinoNet-Driven Services. A third category of service on LatinoNet includes those posted by the network's organizers. These services included a calendar—broken down by region of the country—of Latino activities and holiday events, a daily posting of news, weekly postings of important political occurrences, forums with prominent members of the Latino community, and polls.

Most/Least Popular Services. The most popular services include the master calendar of events, which many people use to find out about activities taking place on major Latino holidays; the self-driven chat area; and employment, education and training, and scholarship listings. Students working at the various nonprofit organizations use these last services most frequently. Professionals who belong to the network also post information about job openings. It is too early to say if interest in any of these services will decline over time. The network has been up and running for almost one year. Thus far, the use of all services has increased over time.

Governmental Items On-Line.   Political items on-line include listings by many of the political KIPs of their schedules and activities, user polls, and a political news service.

Services to Underserved Groups and Targeted Outreach.   There is information on-line about employment, scholarships, and educational opportunities. However, to access this information a user must either already have a computer and modem or must work for one of the nonprofit organizations on LatinoNet.

User Support/Training/Mentoring. All of the nonprofit groups that are members of LatinoNet are given training and technical support. At present, all training is done by one training coordinator out of the San Francisco office. In the future, training will be done out of regional offices. The training consists of three phases, as follows.

The first phase of training is for both the KIPs and the organizations that will be users of the LatinoNet services. It involves training on how to set up modems and software and help in learning to navigate the network. The essence of this phase of training is to make people comfortable with the new technology and to give them a basic understanding of what a modem does and what the information highway is.

For organizations that will become KIPs, a second phase of training follows. This second phase covers how to prepare and post information. The KIPs learn how to format information correctly to make it easier for employees at LatinoNet to integrate it into their various services. For the KIPs, there is also typically a third phase of follow-up training. LatinoNet's training coordinator often goes back to the site to give additional support on database management, word processing, and information formatting. Competency levels in these areas among personnel at the KIPs are often lower than originally indicated.

For the initial two phases of training, the training coordinator tries to get as many groups as possible into each training session but will also go to individual organizations as needed. The follow-up phase of training is typically done at single sites, which allows training to be tailored to specific needs. For about one-fifth of the KIPs, no site visit is required. Many of the universities and research organizations employ individuals who are sophisticated users of the Internet, so getting these organizations up to speed can be done over the phone. In addition to training, the San Francisco office provides as much technical support as they can from a distance.

User Characteristics

Number and Growth/Decline. The LatinoNet has three categories of users: the KIPs, other nonprofit organizations, and individual users. There are 35, 55, and 270, respectively, of each type of user, totaling 350 accounts. Growth to the present level has taken place within five months, and growth is expected to accelerate.

Dropout Rates of Users/Role of Training in Minimizing Dropout. Statistics on dropout rates are not well kept, but a training coordinator did say that at the first big group training session in Los Angeles, eight organizations participated and three have subsequently dropped out; at their next group training session in Washington, D.C., 12 groups participated and two are likely to leave. She attributed the decline in dropout rates from the first to the second session to getting a higher level of commitment from the nonprofits before enrolling them in training.

Training is considered to be extremely important in encouraging the nonprofits to use the system. Many do not have experience with the Internet, do not feel confident with it, and do not understand its usefulness. Group training is particularly helpful. Each group will ask slightly different questions and take a slightly different approach, allowing all participants to learn the system in greater detail. Group training also provides an opportunity for the nonprofits to network with other nonprofits in their community.

Demographics of Users/Frequency of Usage. The individual users are heavily professional. The KIPs use the network an average of 12 hours a month. That includes using it to communicate with LatinoNet, their affiliates, and other organizations, as well as the time employees spend doing information searches or responding to e-mail questions. There was no information on frequency of use among other types of users.

New User Procedures/Advertising. New users can subscribe through AOL and can get a registration form sent to them directly on-line. LatinoNet also contacts new users by sending out brochures to nonprofits as part of their outreach activities. Individuals who do not have AOL accounts can sign up for one at the same time that they sign up for LatinoNet. Because their main target audience is the nonprofits, LatinoNet does not advertise much to the general public. They reach potential nonprofit members through informal networking.

Physical Access and Technical Characteristics

Location of Terminals. The terminals are all located either at the nonprofits' sites or at the homes of individual users.

Hardware/Interface. LatinoNet officials have gone to great lengths to make the interface user-friendly. During an early phase of the organization's development, nonprofits were using both text-based and graphics-based interfaces. Officials found that groups with graphical access made more use of the network and required less training. This experience was one factor driving them to choose AOL as their network provider—AOL's services are easy to use, and its graphical interface is user-friendly. LatinoNet has also customized its user software to build a LatinoNet icon into the interface. Because of its alliance with AOL, LatinoNet does not have to maintain any network hardware.

Network Connections/Access. Users can connect to and access any networks that AOL is connected to.

Benefits of Civic Networks/Universal Access Issues

Benefits of Network. The benefits of the network to the Latino community are manifold.

Faster Communication. The network allows communications between a nonprofit and its affiliates to take place more quickly. It eliminates the need for faxes and overnight mail delivery. The estimated cost of using LatinoNet and AOL for a year for a single nonprofit is $350, which for many organizations will be less than their fax and mail delivery budget.

Access. The network also puts more information at the fingertips of the nonprofits. They can get statistical and demographic information and studies that would otherwise require resource-consuming research to track down.

Control of Information. The network acts as a mechanism to allow the Latino community to break down stereotypes.

Drawbacks of Network. People say a potential drawback of the network is that it can disrupt interpersonal contact. The network is seen as just another form of communication and cannot supplant a personal relationship. In the absence of an interpersonal rapport and trust, officials believe the network will be useless.

Privacy/Security Issues. AOL has very strict requirements about obscene materials and language, proprietary materials, and the use of the network for commercial advertising. LatinoNet has adopted all of these policies: They monitor mail bulletins and chat rooms to make sure there are no problems with obscene materials or proprietary information. They have only once had to ask a user to change his language to avoid the appearance of selling things on the network. If LatinoNet experiences problems in any of these areas, they can turn to AOL to suspend the user account.

Ideas for Expansion. LatinoNet is in the process of gearing up its operations to move from a San Francisco focus to having regional offices in Los Angeles, Texas, Chicago, and New York. The president expects there will be 10 regional offices within a couple of years. Each regional office will have responsibility for training, providing technical support, and electing members to the board of directors. The board of directors is to expand from 9 to 25 members.

Technical/Financial Problems in Gearing Up. No technical problems are expected in gearing up. There is enough space on the AOL account, and it is always possible to buy more. As long as LatinoNet continues to have successful strategic alliances with private sector firms and continues to get grant money, there should be no financial problem either.

Recommendations

For Other FreeNets. Recommendations for other FreeNets stressed the importance of recognizing that the Internet is just one means of communication and not a substitute for strong relationships between people. A network will only be as strong as the confidence and trust that has been built up between the organizations using it, so interpersonal dynamics are important to nurture.

Furthermore, it is critical to take the time to clearly define the goals of the network; i.e., they should not be technology-driven. The lack of a clear, focused idea of what the network is trying to accomplish can lead to failure. Officials believe this will certainly make it more difficult to solicit support from potential sponsors.

To Government. In building new schools, libraries, or local government facilities, policymakers need to think about how to integrate the network technology. Society cannot afford to leave any ethnic group or community behind.

BLACKSBURG ELECTRONIC VILLAGE, BLACKSBURG, VA

Goals and Development

Objectives and Network Development. The Blacksburg Electronic Village emerged out of a partnership between Virginia Tech (VT), Bell Atlantic of Virginia, and the town of Blacksburg. Virginia Tech wanted to expand its network access and high-capacity servers to faculty, students, and staff living off campus and convinced Bell Atlantic to lay the necessary fiber-optic backbone. The original idea of serving university-affiliated residents in the community was subsequently expanded into an "electronic village" encompassing the public schools, local businesses and other local organizations, the public library, and private homes. The Town of Blacksburg's main contribution to the project has been to contribute on-line information about local government and community services.

The overall goal of the project is to build a replicable model for community networking—including evaluation, training, user support, and documentation—for ubiquitous access to the Internet and local network resources. Planning for BEV began in early 1991, and the network was opened to users in October 1993.

The BEV Web home page is shown in Figure B.5.

University employees, professors, and administrators were the first to push for expanding VT's network presence into the Blacksburg community. For computer scientists and systems analysts at the

Figure B.5—Blacksburg Electronic Village Web Home Page

university, the electronic village was viewed as an opportunity to study the effects of network communication on social interaction and the effect of information technology in a community setting. For school administrators, it was a way to give students and faculty living in the community access to the university's computing resources. By encouraging students to move off campus, it also helped to relieve a housing crisis. Many students did not want to move off campus, owing to the lack of Internet connectivity in the apartment buildings in the community.

For Blacksburg town officials, the benefits of the electronic village were of two sorts. First, Internet access promised to improve the quality of lives of Blacksburg's citizens by facilitating a whole range of government interactions and by allowing underserved or housebound groups, e.g., senior citizens, greater access to social services. Senior citizens' access to their health care providers via network communication has been pitched subsequently to the American Association of Retired Persons as a feature of Blacksburg that makes it a more attractive community for retirees. The second type of foreseen benefit was the network's potential to improve the local economy. By encouraging students to move into apartment complexes in the community, it supports the local construction industry. Further, by putting Blacksburg on the cutting edge of technology, it was expected new industry would be attracted to the area.

For the telephone company, helping to set up the Internet was a good public relations move. The telephone company was portrayed as sensitive to the needs of rural communities. Of course, it also expects to reap future advantages over the long-term revenues from increased usage.

Configuration/Scope of the Network. Virginia Tech has a network facility that predated BEV. Many of the university buildings and offices are outfitted with ethernet connections to network servers. Students and staff off campus had limited access to the universities computer facilities via modem banks located at the university. Bell Atlantic was brought in to lay down T-1 lines to other sites in the community, expanding connection to the University's network servers. Bell Atlantic later installed T-1 lines at 27 apartment buildings, City Hall, the library, and 4 schools in the county. Other schools and community organizations have dial-up access to the electronic village.

Obstacles to Establishing. The major obstacle to establishing the network was convincing Bell Atlantic to put up the capital investment necessary to install the network hardware in the community. Short of laying fiber optic cable to allow interactive video on demand—which was not part of BEV's plan—officials at Bell Atlantic remained skeptical, for a long-time, of the likely economic returns to the investment.

Fortuitous Events. The fact that Blacksburg is a university town made getting the network up and running considerably easier. Also, VT's existing network capability reduced BEV personnel and technical costs. Therefore, while integrating the community into the existing network entailed some incremental cost, it was considerably lower than it otherwise might have been. Another factor contributing to the smooth start to BEV is the high level of computer penetration and high computer literacy in Blacksburg. VT's students, staff, and their families account for about two-thirds of the total population of Blacksburg. 82.4 percent of BEV users report being somewhat or very experienced with computers. Finally, the university's influence has also made Blacksburg a more progressive community than others in the area. As BEV organizers expand their services to the more socially conservative communities around Blacksburg, they are finding that residents of these communities are more likely to be concerned about the possible negative aspects of the network, e.g., pornography on the Internet.

Organization and Finance

Organization and Governance Structure. BEV has a board of directors consisting of ten individuals. One member represents each of the three key partners—VT, Bell Atlantic, and the town of Blacksburg—and the other seven are professionals in the Blacksburg community. The board of directors provides recommendations and counsel to the three key partners on strategic questions involving the network. All of the day-to-day operations of the electronic village are conducted by six BEV staffers. Such operations include registering new users, organizing the information on the network, providing technical support to users, maintaining the hardware—i.e., modem banks—for all dial-in users, and planning the network's expansion. The BEV staff members also conduct research related to use of services and the social, economic, and cultural effect of networking on the community. Bell Atlantic is responsible for maintaining the network hardware for all users connected via T-1 lines. The city government is responsible for posting information about the community and local government services on the network.

Involvement with Other Organizations. In addition to the three key partners, a number of other organizations are involved in BEV:

The Public Library. The library is the main point of public access and the primary source of Internet training for members of the BEV community who are not affiliated with the university. The library has a T-1 connection to the university's server. It has five public-access computers with Internet connectivity on-site.

A study by the National Commission on Libraries and Information Science (NCLIS) released in 1994 found that only 2.7 percent of public libraries were providing the public with direct access to the Internet. The study found that 20.9 percent of public libraries had Internet connectivity, and of these, 12 percent allowed their patrons to use the Internet as well.

The Business Community. Ninety businesses in the Blacksburg community, or one-third of the total number of businesses, currently provide information on-line via the network. Some of these businesses only post their opening hours and location, others take orders for delivery and advertise their products and services.

Educational Institutions. All 17 schools in the county are connected to the network. Some of the schools are more active than others in trying to get information about themselves and their activities on-line. A number of universities and community colleges in other parts of Virginia also put information onto the network.

Budget/Funding. BEV's operating budget is $30,000 per year. This budget covers operating overhead—printing and mailing costs—as well as the wages of two graduate students working part time. The salaries of four full-time university staff members working on the BEV project are paid directly by the university. Also paid directly by the university are the costs of operating the network hardware on campus and providing technical support via a telephone answer service to users. The costs of supporting the technical infrastructure in the community are paid for by Bell Atlantic. Much of this cost is recouped through user fees of $30 a month for ethernet connectivity in the apartments.

The library has supported its Internet operations through private donations and grants. Installation and the first year of usage of a T-1 line to the library were donated by Bell Atlantic. The library purchased its hardware and has supported its training operations with money from a federal LSCA grant. Total software, hardware, and supplies start-up costs were $50,000. The annual cost of salaries and benefits for two additional staff members hired to act as electronic reference librarians is $48,000. One electronic librarian has a part-time appointment of 30 hours a week, the other is a full-time employee. The grant supporting the two network librarians will run out in September 1995.

On-Line Services

Major Services The most important services are access to e-mail and discussion groups, to search engines, and to local information.

Search Engines. With payment of their monthly fees, members of BEV can make unlimited use of the World Wide Web, including the use of the Telnet and FTP functions.

E-Mail and Discussion Groups. There are over 20 electronic discussion groups on the network. The two most popular discussion groups are on home brewing and car repairs. Members share tips and ideas about both.

Local Information. "About Blacksburg" provides area history, weather, and information on places to stay and eat. "The Village Mall" provides a showcase of local businesses. "Village School-house" contains information on colleges and universities throughout Virginia, on day care and preschools in Blacksburg, and on primary and secondary schools throughout the county. There is also a "Local Government" site with information on the town of Blacksburg and various county resources.

Social Service Information. The "Seniors' Page" provides information on seniors' events and bulletins, local and regional resources for seniors, and financial information requested by seniors. "The Health Care Center" gives access to a medical database, hospitals, health resources, and support.

Governmental Items On-Line. A whole range of government and public service information exists on-line. These include parks and recreation schedules, information on recycling and refuse pickup, information on how to register and set up a small business, voting information, etc. By January 1996, all local water and refuse bills will be payable electronically. Renewing simple licenses, e.g., dog licenses, and registering to organize a block party or post leaflets will also be possible electronically. Via the World Wide Web, users of BEV can send e-mail messages to local officials as well as to President Clinton and Vice President Gore.

Services to Underserved Groups and Targeted Outreach. Seniors are the main "underserved" group served by BEV. Via the Internet, they can get information about, and stay in touch with, a range of health and social service providers. Also, an electronic mailing list keeps seniors abreast of events of interest to them.

Other targeted services include job search information and educational and medical resources. The local government, university, and school system post information about jobs on-line. The only other job search information is on the World Wide Web. There is on-line information about most of the major colleges and universities in Virginia. Also, a local doctor takes questions and gives advice on-line about prescription medicine.

BEV does not do computer recycling. Organizers have decided against getting involved in computer recycling for two reasons. First, most recycled computers do not have the computing power needed to support the network's sophisticated graphical interface. Second, the amount of support time needed to debug the recycled computers, install software, and get them connected to the Internet would overwhelm BEV's existing technical support capabilities.

Most/Least Popular Services

(1) For BEV as a whole

E-Mail. Fully 97 percent of BEV users report using the e-mail and chat features, with almost two-thirds using it at least daily. Eighty-five percent use e-mail for chit-chat with friends and family, 43 percent use it for professional or academic purposes, 39 percent for business uses, and 48 percent report recreational uses of e-mail.

Information Searches. 80 percent of BEV users use the network to access databases, library catalogs, and remote computers. Twenty-five percent of subscribers made use of these resources daily or every other day; another 23 percent use these resources about once a week. The most frequent use of the network for databases and other information sources was for recreational purposes (60 percent), such as hobbies or special interests. Thirty percent used electronic information sources for academic purposes and 20 percent for business purposes.

Community Information. Local news items are the most popular in this class of information resources. Seventy-nine percent of BEV users report some or much interest in local news postings. Examples of specific postings include the schedule of local events (83 percent), posting of business hours (74 percent), TV listings (54 percent), and bus schedules (50 percent).

Health Services. Sixty-eight percent of the general community membership, whether BEV users or not, report some or much interest in "ask a nurse or doctor" type of service, and 67 percent report some or much interest in on-line prescription drug information.

(2) Library Usage

At the library, reasons for using the BEV are somewhat different. Library patrons tend to use search and gopher programs the most heavily, and e-mail is the second most-used feature. A user survey in April 1994 found that 39.3 percent of respondents had made use of the gopher program to access information, read a newsgroup, or tel-net to a remote computer; 15.5 percent had received or sent e-mail; and 45.1 percent had done both. A second item on the survey confirmed the relative greater use of gopher and search functions. Only 7.1 percent of respondents said that the e-mail function was the only one they had ever used, whereas 34.2 percent said the gopher function was the only one they had ever used.

Although there are no statistics on services that lose their appeal, the project director suggested that use of the gopher and search functions were probably used intensively at first "as people checked out everything on the Web" and then used less intensively as people settled on a couple of items of particular interest.

User Support/Training/Mentoring. A number of training programs support the smooth operation of the network.

Training for End-Users. Nonuniversity affiliates can get Internet training through sessions offered every weekend at the public library by electronic reference librarians. These training sessions are two hours long and offer a comprehensive introduction to e-mail, to the Internet, and to information search vehicles. The goal of these training sessions is to make people comfortable with the Internet and to show them that it is a powerful communication and information tool. To date, the library has held over 80 public workshops, training approximately 800 people on the use of the Internet and Internet search engines.

Library patrons can get informal support from an electronic librarian at any time over the phone, with e-mail, or in person. The library considers helping its clients with information searches on the NII similar to helping a patron find books and other printed reference materials. It feels this service is an important part of being an information resource for the community.

Users at the university can get technical support from the university's computer support telephone service, which is partly monitored by BEV staff. BEV staff will also advise clients on how to obtain and set up their network software. The university offers introductory training on the Internet for its staff, faculty, and students on a regular basis.

Training for Librarians. In addition to the two electronic references librarians working at the library, 10 librarians provide normal library services. To make these librarians competent "Internet guides," each has received five hours of paid training. Training for the librarians was conducted by the electronic reference librarians and took place in four iterative sessions. The first session was an introduction. In the second session, librarians were exposed to a broad range of Internet commands and search techniques. The last two sessions were interactive. Librarians were asked to complete a set of "Internet exercises" while a trainer stood by to give assistance. When the grant supporting the electronic reference librarian position ran out in June 1995, the regular librarians were left to provide training and support functions for the community.

Training for Teachers. BEV staff have conducted several training sessions for primary and secondary teachers at Blacksburg schools.

To support ongoing training at the school sites, they handpicked six teachers who were the most interested in technology and who have been made responsible for holding Internet training sessions for their colleagues.

Training and Support for Information Providers. BEV staff have held four Internet training sessions of three hours each at the Blacksburg Chamber of Commerce for local business and community organizations. Eighty organizations took part in these training sessions. The sessions offered an introduction to the Internet and examples of how businesses or community organizations could use the network to improve their operations.

There is information on-line addressing how to put information on the BEV, including the name of several Internet service providers in the Blacksburg area that will help business and organizations set up a home page. BEV is committed to helping all interested organizations post information on-line but prefers to minimize the amount of time its staff spend working with the information providers. If an organization wants to post a short text, one-time, BEV staff will do this. But if a business, for instance, wants a posting with graphs, images, or order forms, it is sent to a local, private Internet service provider.

BEV also encourages volunteers to take on responsibility for keeping different parts of the information on the network up-to-date. One volunteer posts all the movie listings, a faculty member at VT supplies information listings for public schools in the county, and the information manager is trying to find a couple of seniors to take over the seniors' page.

Cost/Importance of Training and Support. At the library, the costs of training and informal support is equivalent to about three-quarters of the combined salaries of the two network librarians ($50,000). These two individuals spend the vast majority of their time training end-users and other librarians as well as offering informal support. After the grant for the network librarian positions ends, the level of resources devoted to training and informal support will probably fall.

BEV has consumed a total of 51 labor hours on formal training. Four BEV staff members worked at each of the three-hour sessions for the business community—of which there were four. One BEV staff member led the three-hour training session for the six elementary and secondary school teachers. In addition, one full-time BEV staff member is available to assist teachers at their school sites on an as-needed basis.

The costs of informal support of the network are hard to estimate. A full-time network coordinator and a part-time graduate-student systems analyst spend about one-quarter of their time on informal support.

Individuals at both the library and BEV said that the main role of training is to make people comfortable with the technology and to show them its usefulness. Training is used to get individuals excited about the possibilities of network use, but to learn the system they need to spend time on their own experimenting through trial and error. It was also noted that system BEV users have had prior exposure to computer technology, so they only have to be convinced of the usefulness of the Internet. In some of the outlying communities, however, the lack of computer literacy is an additional hurdle to overcome.

User Characteristics

Number and Growth/Decline. By January 1995, there were a total of 10,000 users of the electronic village. Of these, 8,500 are university students or affiliates who probably had Internet accounts with the university before BEV began operations. Through its first year and one-half of operations, BEV added about 1,500 users from the Blacksburg's community. In the first several months of operation, BEV joined 75 individuals per month. This figure jumped to 100 per month, then 125 per month, where it has stayed since the beginning of 1995.

Dropout Rates of Users/Role of Training in Minimizing Dropout. About 15 percent of those who sign up drop out. The main reason for dropping out is not the lack of training but the complexity of BEV's software. Some users have found it so difficult to set up that they have left BEV to go to another network provider.

Demographics of Users. All percentages are based on two user surveys conducted in mid-1994—one was conducted by BEV and the other was conducted by the library.

Computer Ownership. Of the BEV users, 75 percent report having their own computer. Of the users at the library, 67 percent report having their own computer. It is estimated that about 50 percent of Blacksburg residents own computers. All of these figures are high— probably because Blacksburg is a university town.

Sex. Of those using BEV for Internet access, 78 percent are male and 22 percent are female. At the library, 46 percent of users are female and 54 percent are male.

Age. The average age of BEV users is 38. Retirees account for 40 percent of the 1,500 community members who had joined BEV by January 1995.

Household Income. Of library users, 30 percent report an annual household income below $10,000; 18 percent of all BEV users reported incomes below this level. Conversely, whereas 58 percent of all BEV users reported a household income of about $30,000, only 41 percent of library users reported a similarly high income.

Education Level. Of users at the library, 26 percent have graduate degrees, compared with 37 percent of users at BEV. Of library users, 17 percent have not graduated from high school, compared with around 4 percent of other BEV users.

Public Access. Of respondents in the library's user survey, 54 percent reported that the library was their only form of Internet access. Around 70 percent of those surveyed said they were not regular library users before the Internet service was made available; however, they reported that they now visit the library more frequently because of the Internet access.

Frequency of Usage.

Library Usage. Between January and June of 1994, the library users averaged 2,603 Internet sessions per month. (See *Most/Least Popular Services* for information on particular services.)

New User Procedures/Advertising. To become a new user, individuals must sign up and present identification at the BEV office. There is a $6.00 registration fee for all new users. Those dialing into BEV via a modem bank pay a flat monthly fee of $8.60; those in one of the apartment buildings with an ethernet connection pay $30.00 a month.

Information about how to join BEV is posted at the libraries, city hall, and the Chamber of Commerce. BEV also advertises in the local media.

Physical Access and Technical Characteristics

Location of Terminals. Users can access BEV through 3,374 terminals; 3,187 of these are computers in individual homes or businesses. Other sites with access to BEV include 135 buildings on campus, 17 public schools, 27 apartment buildings, the public library, the town hall, and the Virginia Museum of Natural History. Many of these sites have tens or hundreds of computers with network access, e.g., the apartment complexes and buildings on campus.

Hardware/Interface. BEV uses 10 of the university servers for different functions. To support these operations, the capacity of three self-standing servers would be required. Students and faculty on campus can access BEV servers directly via ethernet connections. About one-third of BEV users dial in from the community via university-supported modem banks. Some 15 percent of users access BEV via T-1 lines at the library, apartment buildings, and six schools. BEV can be accessed using either the text-based gopher software or the graphics-based World Wide Web software

Network Connections/Access. BEV servers are connected to all networks that are on the World Wide Web and can also connect to universities and research institutions that are not on the Web.

Benefits of Civic Networks/Universal Access Issues

Benefits of Network. The network offers people living in Blacksburg a variety of benefits.

Community Building. The electronic network expands the channels of communication available to discuss political, social, and community issues. People who previously have been able to participate only by attending face-to-face meetings (e.g., for town council, community organizations, and special interest groups) can now expand discussions of important issues on-line.

Skill Development. Use of the network for information searches encourages users to think in a task-oriented research mode. Information searches via the Internet are often less time consuming than traditional library information searches, but they still require individuals to think through how they will get the information for which they are looking. Use of the Internet also encourages higher-level computer skills.

Homebound Individuals. The network is a huge boon to people who are homebound. Many housewives with small children report that it is an important source of contact with other adults. It allows elderly individuals to complete some business transactions and office visits without having to leave their homes. BEV is presently trying to develop a technology that will allow an audio/video feed between elderly individuals and their doctors. Many routine checkups for elderly individuals could then be accomplished without office visits.

Distance Learning. Like homebound individuals, handicapped children who have difficulty getting to school and children in remote communities would benefit from access to distance learning.

Parent-Teacher Communication. The network has great potential to ease communication between parents and teachers. Rather than having to set up meetings, much routine correspondence or updating can be done by both parties on their own schedules.

Economic Benefits. The network has attracted some industry growth in Blacksburg, and there is anecdotal evidence of an increase in the business activity of the businesses on-line. None of the BEV staffers were aware of studies weighing economic costs and benefits of the network, however.

Television Substitute. The network can act as an interactive entertainment substitute for the television.

Drawbacks of Network. The drawbacks to the network include that it makes it easier for radical or racist groups to organize, that it increases the amount of information people must process day to day, and that it makes it easier for "jerks" to be irritating because the barriers to interfering with other peoples' conversations are extremely low.

Privacy/Security Issues. BEV's basic policy is one of noncensorship. BEV staffers take a laissez-faire attitude to the network. They tell people about the range of material that is on the network and let them make their own informed decisions. So far there have been no problems with racist or otherwise bigoted language on the network. Users at the library have pulled down pornographic materials and used adult chat rooms. As above, the library's policy has been one of noninterference. In fact, the network is often self-regulating. One example was given of a person who put an irritating message out on the World Wide Web and got so many incensed messages in response that it overloaded his local server and caused his Internet provider to kick him off the system.

At least one project official thinks the hype about the lack of network security is misdirected. He feels, for example, that it is far safer to send a credit card number over the network than it is to give your credit card to a waiter at a restaurant. Most hackers on the net are not trying to "rip off" the individual user. Instead, they are going to target larger institutions. Moreover, hardware providers, such as Netscape communications, and Internet providers are less than a year away from developing encryption mechanisms that will make the whole security debate academic.

Ideas for Expansion. BEV staffers see themselves as a catalyst for change rather than shapers of the direction that change will take. They want to present people with this information and communication resource, get them excited about it, and let groups decide on their own how to use it. They feel expansion should be demand-driven. The presence of the K–12 schools on the network is being increased because of the initiative of a VT faculty member. The range of interactive government services on-line is being increased through the efforts of individuals at City Hall.

Technical/Financial Problems in Gearing Up. As they gear up, BEV officials are planning to hand off their dial-up access for all nonuniversity members to private companies (90 percent of support costs are related to dial-up access). With a modem connection, there are 11 potential failure points as compared with 2 on a T-1 line.

Recommendations

For Other FreeNets. Recommendations included maintaining a focus on the community, based on the belief that local is better. Furthermore, BEV officials stressed that quality, rather than quantity, of information is critical—information that is useful ("good, meaty stuff") is better than having information available just for the sake of having it there. That said, they also recommended having a variety of services. With a variety of services on-line, and avoiding "killer applications," the network will generate a critical mass more quickly because there will be something for everyone.

As a further recommendation related to community involvement. BEV officials believe that successful communities are ones with a responsive local government, an active citizenry, and a healthy commercial sector. Electronic communities are no different. They will do better if they involve all of these organizations.

By focusing on high-demand individuals (i.e., high-resource individuals) in the community and getting them on-line, more demand will be generated. Several people gave an analogy to the introduction of the telephone: Telephone companies gave phones to doctors because they thought this would encourage other people to buy phones. K–12 teachers are high-resource individuals for many families; doctors and health care providers are high-resource individuals for the elderly; the business community is high-resource for almost everybody.

If only underserved groups are targeted, they will not have the richer network access they would if they were involved in a broader-based community initiative. Targeting just underserved groups may not lead to the critical mass necessary to get the network operating.

To Government. To generate demand, BEV organizers believe that the best thing the state and federal governments can do is to get as much information and as many services on-line as possible. Increasing the ease of access to the government will increase demand for on-line services and drive down prices. The government can also increase demand by increasing the number of access points, by putting kiosks at the post office, and by helping schools to get Internet access. Children need to learn about this technology when they are young because they will be using it their entire lives. By increasing access points, the government can help to stimulate demand and bring prices down.

The library model of access is better than others because one of the most difficult things to manage is end-user support. At a library, one technically competent person can be responsible for training and support. Deregulation of the telecommunications market will also bring prices down. A BEV recommendation to policymakers is to allow communities to self-regulate content.

Abramsohn, J., "Helping the Homebound," *The Wall Street Journal*, Section R18-19, June 19, 1995.

Anderson, Robert H., Norman Z. Shapiro, Tora K. Bikson, and Phyllis H. Kantar, *The Design of the MH Mail System*, RAND, N-3017-IRIS, 1989.

Arnbak, J., B. Mitchell, W. Neu, K. Neumann, and I. Vogelsang, *Network Interconnection in the Domain of ONP: Study for DG XII of the European Commission*, European Commission, Brussels, 1994.

Attewell, Paul, "Computer-Related Skills and Social Stratification," presentation to the workshop *Universal Email: Prospects and Implications*, RAND, 1994.

Attewell, Paul, "Skill and Occupational Changes in US Manufacturing," in Paul Adler (ed.), *Technology and the Future of Work*, Oxford University Press, New York, 1992.

Baran, Paul, et al., On Distributed Communications: Vol. I. Introduction to Distributed Communications Networks, RAND, RM-3420-PR , 1964.

Baran, Paul, et al., On Distributed Communications: Vol. II. Digital Simulation of Hot Potato Routing in a Broadband Distributed Communications Network, RAND, RM-3103-PR, 1964.

Baran, Paul, et al., On Distributed Communications: Vol. III. Determination of Path-Length in a Distributed Network, RAND, RM-3758-PR, 1964.

Baran, Paul, et al., On Distributed Communications: Vol. IV. Priority Precedence and Overload, RAND, RM-3638-PR, 1964.

Baran, Paul, et al., On Distributed Communications: Vol. V. History of Alternative Approaches and Comparisons, RAND, RM-3097-PR, 1964.

Baran, Paul, et al., On Distributed Communications: Vol. VI. Mini-cost Microwaves, RAND, RM-3762-PR, 1964.

Baran, Paul, et al., On Distributed Communications: Vol. VII. Tentative Engineering Specifications and Preliminary Design for a High Data Rate Distributed Network Switching Mode, RAND, RM-3763-PR, 1964.

Baran, Paul, et al., On Distributed Communications: Vol. VIII. The Multiplexing Station, RAND, RM-3764-PR, 1964.

Baran, Paul, et al., On Distributed Communications: Vol. IX. Security, Secrecy, and Tamper Free Considerations, RAND, RM-3765-PR, 1964.

Baran, Paul, et al., On Distributed Communications: Vol. X. Cost Estimate, RAND, RM-3766-PR, 1964.

Baran, Paul, et al., On Distributed Communications: Vol. XI. Summary Overview, RAND, RM-3767-PR, 1964.

Baran, Paul, et al., On Distributed Communications: Vol. XII. Weak Spots and Proposed Patches in the Digital Distributed Communications System, RAND, RM-5067-PR, 1966.

Baran, Paul, et al., *On Distributed Communications: Vol. XIII. Semi-Automated Layout of Networks for "Real World" User Locations for the Digital Distributed Communications System*, RAND, RM-5174-PR, 1967.

Benjamin, R. I., and J. Blount, "Critical IT Issues: The Next 10 Years," *Sloan Management Review*, Vol. 33, 1992, pp. 7–20.

Berlin, Eric, and Andrew Kantor, "The Surfboard," *Internet World*, July 1995.

Bikson, T. K., "Organizational Trends and Electronic Media," *American Archivist*, Vol. 57, No. 1, 1994, pp. 48–68. Also available from RAND as RP-307.

Bikson, T. K., "Understanding the Implementation of Office Technology," in Robert Kraut (ed.), *Technology and the Transformation of White Collar Work*, Erlbaum Associates, Hillsdale, New Jersey, 1986, pp. 155–176. Also available from RAND as N-2619-NSF.

Bikson, T. K., and J. D. Eveland, "Integrating New Tools into Information Work: Technology Transfer as a Framework for Understanding Success," in D. Langford et al. (eds.), *People and Technology in the Workplace*, National Academy Press, Washington, D.C., 1991. Also available from RAND as RP-106.

Bikson, T. K., and J. D. Eveland, "The Interplay of Work Group Structures and Computer Support," in R. Kraut, J. Galegher, and C. Egido (eds.), *Intellectual Teamwork*, Erlbaum Associates, Hillsdale, New Jersey, pp. 245–290, 1990. Also available from RAND as N-3429-MF.

Bikson, T. K., and J. D. Eveland, *New Office Technology: Planning for People*, monograph, Work in America Institute's Series on Productivity, Pergamon Press, New York, 1986.

Bikson, T. K., and E. J. Frinking, *Preserving the Present: Toward Viable Electronic Records*, Sdu Publishers, The Hague, 1993. Parts of this book are available from RAND as RP-257.

Bikson, T. K., and S. A. Law, *Global Preparedness and Human Resources: College and Corporate Perspectives*, RAND, MR-326-CPC, 1994.

Bikson, T. K., and S. A. Law, "Electronic Mail Use at the World Bank: Messages from Users," *The Information Society*, Vol. 9, No. 2, 1993, pp. 89–124.

Bikson, T. K., S. A. Law, M. Markovich, and B. T. Harder, "On the Implementation of Research Findings in Surface Transportation,"

Research Results Digest, Vol. 207, June 1995. Also available from RAND as RP-432.

Bikson, T. K., J. D. Goodchilds, L. Huddy, J. D. Eveland, and S. K. Schneider, *Networked Information Technology and the Transition to Retirement: A Field Experiment*, RAND, R-3690-MF, 1991.

Bikson, T. K., B. E. Quint, and L. L. Johnson, *Scientific and Technical Information Transfer: Issues and Options*, RAND, N-2131-NSF, 1984.

Bloomberg Business News, "On the Internet Without a PC," *New York Times*, October 4, 1995, p. D2.

BoardWatch, "BoardWatch 100 Readers' Choice Contest Results," September 1994, pp. 28–33.

Bollen, Kenneth A., "Political Democracy and Measurement Traps," *Studies in Comparative International Development*, Vol. 25, No. 1, Spring 1990, pp. 7–24.

Boone, Peter, *Politics and the Effectiveness of Foreign Aid*, London School of Economics and Center for Economic Performance, November 1994.

Borden, Bruce S., R. Stockton Gaines, and Norman Z. Shapiro, *The MH Message Handling System: User's Manual*, RAND, R-2367-AF, 1979.

Borenstein, N. S., "MIME: A Portable and Robust Multimedia Format for Internet Mail," *Multimedia Systems*, Vol. 1, Springer-Verlag, New York, 1993, pp. 29–36.

Branscomb, Anne, *Who Owns Information? From Privacy to Public Access*, Basic Books, New York, 1994

Branscomb, Lewis M., and Brian Kahin, "Standards Processes and Objectives for the National Information Infrastructure," *Information Infrastructure and Policy*, Vol. 4, No. 2, 1995, pp. 87–106.

Brodsky, Ira, "Wireless World," *Internet World*, July 1995, pp. 34–41.

Builder, Carl H., "Is It a Transition or a Revolution?" *Futures*, March 1993, pp. 155–167.

Builder, Carl H., and Steven C. Bankes, *Artificial Societies: A Concept for Basic Research on the Societal Impacts of Information Technology*, RAND, P-7740, 1991.

Builder Carl H., and Steven C. Bankes, *The Etiology of European Change*, RAND, P-7693, 1990.

Bunn, Julie Ann, and Paul A. David, "The Economics of Gateway Technologies and Network Evolution: Lessons from Electricity Supply History," *Stanford Center for Economic Policy Research Discussion Paper*, 1988.

Business Week, "Dangerous Living in Telecom's Top Tier," September 12, 1994, p. 90.

Carroll, Chuck, "Development of Integrated Cable/Telephony in the United Kingdom," *IEEE Communications Magazine*, Vol. 33, No. 8, August 1995, pp. 48–50, 55–60.

Central Intelligence Agency (CIA), *World Fact Book*, 1993.

Cheek, M., "Computer Telephony Integration," *IEEE Computer*, June 1995.

Clark, Don, "U.S. Plans No Action Against Microsoft Before Launch of Windows 95 System," *Wall Street Journal*, August 9, 1995, p. A3.

Clinton, William H., "Remarks by the President in Live Telecast to Russian People," Ostankino TV Station, Moscow, Russia, January 14, 1994. (Text also available via FTP from info.tamu.edu in the directory /.data/politics/1994/tele.0114)

Coase, Ronald, "The Federal Communications Commission," *Journal of Law and Economics*, Vol. 2, October 1959, pp. 1–40.

Cocchi, R., D. Estrin, S. Shenker, and L. Zhang, "Pricing in Computer Networks: Motivation, Formulation and Example," *IEEE/ACM Transactions on Networking*, 1993.

Computer Science and Telecommunications Board (CSTB), National Research Council, *Realizing the Information Future: The Internet and Beyond,* National Academy Press, Washington, D.C., 1994.

Crocker, David, "Making Standards the IETF Way," *StandardView,* Vol. 1 No. 1, 1993. Available at http://www.isoc.org/standards/crocker-on-standards.html.

Cross-Industry Working Team (XIWT), "An Architectural Framework for the National Information Infrastructure," 1995a. Available at http://www.cnri.reston.va.us/xiwt.

Cross-Industry Working Team (XIWT) "Nomadicity in the NII," 1995b. Available at http://www.cnri.reston.va.us/xiwt.

Culnan, M. J., and M. L. Markus, "Information Technologies," in F. M. Jablin, L.L.L. Putman, K. H. Roberts, and L. W. Porter (eds.), *Handbook of Organizational Communication,* Sage Publications, Newbury Park, California, 1987, pp. 420–444.

Current Population Survey, October 1989 and 1993: School Enroll-ment [machine-readable data file], conducted by the Bureau of the Census for the Bureau of Labor Statistics, Bureau of the Census [producer and distributor], Washington, D.C., 1990 and 1994.

Dahl, Robert A., *Polyarchy: Participation and Opposition,* Yale University Press, New Haven, Connecticut, 1971.

Denning, Dorothy E., and Herbert S. Linn (eds.), *Rights and Responsibilities of Participants in Networked Communities,* Computer Science and Telecommunications Board (CTSB), National Academy Press, Washington, D.C., 1994

Digital Information Group, *Online Factbook,* Stamford, Connecticut, 1992.

Dubrovsky, V. J., S. Kiesler, and B. N. Sethna, "The Equalization Phenomenon: Status Effects in Computer-Mediated and Face-to-Face Decion Making Groups," *Human-Computer Interaction,* Vol. 6, 1991, pp. 119–146.

Dunlop, Charles, and Rob Kling, "Social Relationships in Electronic Communities," in Charles Dunlop and Rob Kling (eds.), *Com-*

puterization and Controversy: Value Conflicts and Social Choices,
Academic Press, San Diego, California, 1991.

"E-electioneering," *The Economist,* June 17, 1995, pp. 21–23.

Electronic Mail and Messaging Systems (EMMS), *Newsletter,* April 3, 1995, p. 3.

Electronic Mail and Messaging Systems, *Newsletter,* February 6, 1995, p. 3.

Electronic Mail and Messaging Systems, *The EMMS Messaging Industry Overview,* 1994.

Eng, P. "Big Business on the Net? Not Yet," *Business Week,* June 26, 1995, pp. 100–101.

Eveland, J. D., and T. K. Bikson, "Work Group Structures and Computer Support: A Field Experiment," in *ACM Transactions on Office Information Systems,* Vol. 6, No. 4, 1988, pp. 354–379. Also available from RAND as N-2978-MF.

Eveland, J. D., and T. K. Bikson, "Evolving Electronic Communication Networks: An Empirical Assessment," *Office: Technology and People,* Vol. 3, 1987, pp. 103–128.

Eveland, J. D., Anita Blanchard, William Brown, and Jennifer Mattocks, "The Role of 'Help Networks' in Facilitating Use of CSCW Tools," *The Information Society,* Vol. 11, No. 2, 1995, pp. 113–130.

Eveland, J. D., M. L. Markus, S. A. Law, D. M. Manual, and B. Stecher, "Case Studies of Technology Use in Adult Literacy Programs," Final Report to the Science, Education and Transportation Program, Office of Technology Assessment, U.S. Congress, Report No. PB 93-163905, August 1992.

Feldman, M. S., "Electronic Mail and Weak Ties in Organizations," *Office: Technology and People,* Vol. 3, 1987, pp. 83–101.

Finholt, Thomas, and Lee Sproull, "Electronic Groups at Work," *Organization Science,* Vol. 1, 1990, pp. 41–64.

Finholt, T., L. Sproull, and S. Kiesler, "Communication and Performance in Ad Hoc Task Groups," in R. Kraut, J. Galegher, and C. Egido (eds.), *Intellectual Teamwork: Social and Technological Foundations of Cooperative Work*, Erlbaum Associates, Hillsdale, New Jersey, 1990, pp. 291–325.

Firestone, Charles M., and Jorge R. Schement (eds.), *Toward an Information Bill of Rights and Responsibilities*, Communications and Society Program, The Aspen Institute, Washington, D.C., 1995.

Fisher, Francis D., "What the Coming Telecommunications Infrastructure Could Mean to Our Family," in *A National Information Network: Changing Our Lives in the 21st Century*, The Aspen Institute, Institute for Information Studies, Queenstown, Maryland, 1992.

Ganley, Gladys D., "Power to the People via Personal Electronic Media," *The Washington Quarterly*, Spring 1991, pp. 5–22.

Gattiker, U. E. "Computer Skills Acquisition: A Review and Future Directions for Research," *Journal of Management*, Vol. 18, No. 3, September 1992, pp. 547–574.

Gillett, Sharon, "Connecting Homes to the Internet: An Engineering Cost Model of Cable vs. ISDN," Thesis submitted to the Center for Technology, Policy and Industrial Development, MIT, Cambridge, Massachusetts, 1995.

Goldman, Sachs & Co., *Communacopia*, July 1992.

Gonzalez, Sean, "Mail Services for Hire," *PC Magazine*, April 25, 1995.

Gottlieb, Gidon, "Nations Without States," *Foreign Affairs*, May/June 1994, pp. 100–112.

Gross, N., "Kiss That Old Patient Logbook Goodbye," *Business Week*, June 26, 1995.

Havighurst, Robert J., "Social Roles, Work, Leisure, and Education," in C. Eisdorfer and M. P. Lawton (eds.), *The Psychology of Adult Development and Aging*, American Psychological Association, Washington, D.C., 1973.

Helliwell, John F., *Empirical Linkages Between Democracy and Economic Growth*, National Bureau of Economic Research, Working Paper No. 4066, Cambridge, Massachusetts, 1992.

Hess, Robert, "Pippin Faces Delays," *MacWeek*, Vol. 9, No. 25, June 19, 1995, p. 1.

Hesse, B., L. Sproull, S. Kiesler, and J. Walsh, "Computer Network Support for Science: The Case of Oceanography," unpublished manuscript, Carnegie Mellon University, Pittsburgh, Pennsylvania, 1990.

Hill, G. Christian, "Talking Technology," *Wall Street Journal*, June 19, 1995a, p. R33.

Hill, G. Christian, "The Myth of Multimedia," *Wall Street Journal*, June 19, 1995b, p. R6.

Hills, Michael T., "Carrier Pricing Increases Continue," *Business Communications Review*, February 1995, p. 32.

Holland, Kelley, and Amy Cortese, "The Future of Money," *Business Week*, June 12, 1995, pp. 66–78.

Huber, Peter, "Geodesic Network: 1987 Report on Competition in the Telecommunications Industry," U.S. Department of Justice, Washington, D.C., 1987.

Huff, C., L. Sproull, and S. Kiesler, "Computer Communication and Organizational Commitment: Tracing the Relationship in a City Government," *Journal of Applied Social Psychology*, Vol. 19, 1989, pp. 1371–1391.

Huntington, Samuel P., "The Clash of Cultures," *Foreign Affairs*, Summer 1993, pp. 22–49.

Huntington, Samuel P., "Will More Countries Become Democratic?" *Political Science Quarterly*, Vol. 99, No. 2, Summer 1984, pp. 193–218.

Information Computer Communications Policy 23, *Universal Service and Rate Restructuring in Telecommunications*, Organisation for Economic Co-Operation and Development, Paris, 1991.

Inkeles, Alex, et al., "Introduction: On Measuring Democracy," *Studies in Comparative International Development*, Vol. 25, No. 1, Spring 1990, pp. 3–6.

"Internet Costs and Interconnection Agreements," in Gerald Brock (ed.), *Towards a Competitive Telecommunications Industry: Selected Papers from the 1994 Telecommunications Policy Research Conference*, Lawrence Erlbaum Associates, Hillsdale, New Jersey, 1995.

Johnson, Leland L., *Common Carrier Video Delivery by Telephone Companies*, RAND, R-4166-MF/RL, 1992a.

Johnson, Leland L., *Telephone Company Entry into Cable Television: Competition, Regulation, and Public Policy*, RAND, MR-102-RC, 1992b.

Johnson, Leland L., *Telephone Assistance Programs for Low-Income Households: A Preliminary Assessment*, RAND, R-3603-NSF/MF, 1988.

Johnson, Leland L., and Deborah R. Castleman, *Direct Broadcast Satellites: A Competitive Alternative to Cable Television?* RAND, R-4047-MF/RL, 1991.

Johnson, Leland L., and David P. Reed, *Residential Broadband Services by Telephone Companies? Technology, Economics, and Public Policy*, RAND, R-3906-MF/RL, 1990.

Jouet, J., P. Flichy, and P. Beaud, *European Telematics: The Emerging Economy of Words.* North-Holland, Amsterdam, 1991.

Kaplan, Roger (ed.), *Freedom Review*, Vol. 25, No. 1, January/February 1994.

Kedzie, Christopher R., "A Brave New World or a New World Order?" in Sara Kiesler (ed.), *Research Outposts on the Information Highway*, Erlbaum Associates, Hillsdale, New Jersey, forthcoming (1996).

King, John L., and Kenneth L. Kraemer, "Information Infrastructure, National Policy, and Global Competitiveness," *Information Infrastructure and Policy*, Vol. 4, 1995, pp. 5–28.

Klein, H. K., "Grassroots Democracy and the Internet: The Telecommunications Policy Roundtable—Northeast USA (TPR-NE)," *Internet Society: INE '95 Proceedings*, 1995. Available at http://inet.nttam.com/HMP/PAPER/164/ txt/paper.txt.

Koschat, M. A., P. Srinagesh, and L. J. Uhler, "Efficient Price and Capacity Choices under Uncertain Demand: An Empirical Analysis," *Journal of Regulatory Economics*, Vol. 7, 1995, pp. 5–26.

Kraut, Robert E., "Electronic Mail and Organizational Knowledge: Media Use in a Global Corporation," seminar presented at RAND, November 19, 1993.

Kraut, R. E., and L. A. Streeter, "Satisfying the Need to Know; Interpersonal Information Access," in E. Diaper (ed.), *Human Computer Interaction, Interact '90* Cambridge, England, 1990, pp. 909–915.

Kraut, R. E., S. Dumais, and S. Koch, "Computerization, Productivity and Quality of Work-Life," *Communications of the ACM*, Vol. 32, 1989, pp. 220–239.

Krueger, Alan, "Why Computers Have Changed the Wage Structure: Evidence from Microdata, 1984–1989," *Quarterly Journal of Economics*, Vol. 108, No. 1, February 1993, pp. 33–61.

Law, S. A., T. K. Bikson, and E. Frinking, "UN UNESIS Phase 1 Report: User Requirements Study," final report to the Organisation for Economic Co-Operation and Development, Paris, January 1995.

Levin, Norman D, *Prisms & Policy: U.S. Security Strategy After the Cold War*, RAND, MR-365-A, 1994.

Lewis, Peter, "A Traffic Jam on the Data Highway," *New York Times*, February 2, 1994a, p. D1.

Lewis, Peter H., "On the Internet, Dissident's Shots Heard 'Round the World," *New York Times*, June 5, 1994b, p. 18.

Lipschutz, Robert P., "Extending E-Mail's Reach," *PC Magazine*, April 25, 1995.

Lipset, Seymour Martin, "Some Social Requisites of Democracy: Economic Development and Political Legitimacy," *American Political Science Review*, No. 53, 1959, pp. 69–105.

Lipset, Seymour Martin, Kyoung-Ryung Seong, and John Charles Torres, "A Comparative Analysis of the Social Requisites of Democracy," *International Social Science Journal*, Vol. 45, May 1993, pp. 155–175.

Lynch, Daniel, and Rose Marshall, *The Internet System Handbook*, Addison-Wesley, Reading, Massachusetts, 1993.

Lytel, David, "The Impact of Minitel Upon French Politics," in M. Bilezikian and M. Sarde (eds.), *Communication and Media in Contemporary French Culture*, Georgetown University Conference on Communication and Media in Contemporary French Culture, Washington, D.C., 1989.

Lytel, David, *Media Regimes and Political Communication: Minitel and the Co-evolution of Democracy and Interactive Media in France*, Ph.D. dissertation, Cornell University, Ithaca, New York, 1992.

MacKie-Mason, Jeffrey K., and H. R. Varian, "Some Economics of the Internet," Working Paper, Department of Economics, University of Michigan, Ann Arbor, Michigan, 1993

MacWeek, July 10, 1995, p. 30.

Maddala, G. S., *Limited-Dependent and Qualitative Variables in Econometrics*, Cambridge University Press, Cambridge, England, 1983.

Maier, Charles S., "Democracy and Its Discontents," *Foreign Affairs*, Vol. 73, No. 4, July/August 1994, pp. 48–64.

The Maloff Company, *1994–1995 Internet Services Provider Marketplace Analysis*, February 1995.

Malone, T. W., J. Yates, and R. I Benjamin, "Electronic Markets and Electronic Hierarchies," *Communications of the ACM*, Vol. 30, No. 6, 1987.

Markus, M. L., "Toward a 'Critical Mass' Theory of Interactive Media: Universal Access, Interdependence and Diffusion," *Communication Research*, Vol. 14, 1987, pp. 491–511.

Markus, M. L., T. K. Bikson, M. El-Shinnaway, and L. L. Soe, "Fragments of Your Communication: Email, Vmail, and Fax," *The Information Society*, Vol. 8, 1992, pp. 207–226.

Matrix Information and Directory Services, Inc., unpublished data, October 1993.

Michel, Caroline, "Electronic Commerce Services, 1993–1998: Facing the Global Information Highway," International Data Corporation, 1994.

Minoli, Daniel, *Video Dialtone Technology*, McGraw-Hill, Inc., New York, 1995.

Mitchell, Bridger, and Ingo Vogelsang, *Telecommunications Pricing: Theory and Practice*, Cambridge University Press, 1991.

Moran, J., "Computers Forge PEN Pal Link," *Los Angeles Times*, Section J5-J6, February 25, 1990.

Mueller, Milton, "Universal Service in Telephone History, A Reconstruction," *Telecommunications Policy*, July 1993.

Mueller, Milton, and Jorge Reina Schement, *Universal Service from the Bottom Up: A Profile of Telecommunications Access in Camden, New Jersey*, Rutgers University Project on Information Policy, Rutgers University School of Communication, 1995. Available at http://www.ba.com/reports/rutgers/ba-title.html.

Muller, Edward N., and Mitchell A. Seligson, "Civic Culture and Democracy: The Question of Causal Relationships," *American Political Science Review*, Vol. 88, No. 3, September 1994.

Multimedia Week, "General Instrument Joins Microwave to Establish Standard for Interactive Television Settop Systems," Vol. 4, No. 19, May 8, 1995.

Multimedia Week, "Microsoft Launches Partnership Program in Bid to Set Operating System Standard for Interactive TV," Vol. 4, No. 20, May 15, 1995.

National Academy Press, *Information Technology in the Service Society: A Twenty-First Century Lever*, Computer Science and Telecommunications Board (CSTB), Washington, D.C., 1994.

Negroponte, N., *Being Digital*, Knopf, New York, 1995a.

Negroponte, N., "Affordable Computing," *Wired*, July 1995b, p. 192.

Nelson, R. R., E. M. Whitener, and H. H. Philcox, "The Assessment of End-User Training Needs," *Communications of the ACM*, Vol. 38, No. 7, July 1995.

Newman, Denis, "School Networks: Delivery or Access," in Elliot Soloway (ed.), *Communications of the ACM*, Special Issue on Technology in K–12 Education, Vol. 36, No. 5, 1993, pp. 49–51.

New York Times, "Computer Gap Worries Blacks," 25 May 1995.

NNSC Report on the Internet, untitled, September 25, 1989.

Noam, Eli M., "NetTrans Accounts: Reforming the Financial Support System for Universal Service in Telecommunications," draft, September 1993.

Organisation for Economic Co-Operation and Development (OECD), *Universal Service and Rate Restructuring in Telecommunications*, Information Computer Communications Policy series, Paris, 1991.

Park, R. E., and B. M. Mitchell, *Optimal Peak-Load Pricing for Local Telephone Calls*, RAND, R-3404-1-RC, 1987.

Pitroda, Sam, "Development, Democracy, and the Village Telephone," *Harvard Business Review*, November-December 1993.

Pitta, J., "Oracle Unveils 3 Inexpensive Net Terminals," *Los Angeles Times*, October 6, 1995, p. D1.

Pool, Ithiel de Sola, *Technologies of Freedom*, The Belknap Press of Harvard University Press, Cambridge, Massachusetts, 1983.

Press, Larry, "Technetronic Education: Answers on the Cultural Horizon," in Elliot Soloway (ed.), *Communications of the ACM*, Special Issue on Technology in K–12 Education, Vol. 36, No. 5, 1993, pp. 17–22.

Probe Research, *Facsimile and Voice Services*, February 15, 1994.

Putnam, Robert D., "Bowling Alone: America's Declining Social Capital," *Journal of Democracy*, Vol. 6, No. 1, January 1995.

Putnam, Robert D., *Making Democracy Work: Civic Traditions in Modern Italy*, Princeton University Press, Princeton, New Jersey, 1993.

Quarterman, John S., and Carl-Mitchell Smoot, "What Is the Internet, Anyway?" *Matrix News*, Vol. 4, No. 8, August 1994.

Quinn, James B., *Intelligent Enterprise*, Free Press, New York, 1992.

Rheingold, Howard, "The Great Equalizer," *Whole Earth Review*, Summer 1991, pp. 5–11.

Rockart, J., and J. Short, "The Networked Organization and the Management of Interdependence," in Michael Scott-Morton (ed.), *The Corporation of the 90s*, Oxford Press, New York, 1991.

Rogers, E. M., *Diffusion of Innovation* (3rd ed.), Free Press, New York, 1983.

Ronfeldt, David, *Institutions, Markets and Networks: A Framework About the Evolution of Societies*, RAND, DRU-590-FF, 1993.

Ronfeldt, David, Cathryn Thorup, Sergio Aguayo, and Howard Frederick, *Restructuring Civil Society Across North America in the Information Age: New Networks for Immigration Advocacy Organizations*, RAND, DRU-599-FF, 1993.

Rose, M. T., *The Open Book: A Practical Perspective in OSI*, Prentice Hall, Englewood Cliffs, New Jersey, 1989.

Rothstein, Robert L., "Democracy, Conflict, and Development in the Third World," *The Washington Quarterly*, Spring 1991, pp. 43–63.

Rowen, Henry S., "The Tide Underneath the 'Third Wave,'" *Journal of Democracy*, Vol. 6, No. 1, January 1995, pp. 52–64.

Schifter, Richard, "Is There a Democracy Gene?" *The Washington Quarterly*, Summer 1994, pp. 121–127.

Schimpp, Michele Wozniak, *A.I.D. and Democratic Development: A Synthesis of Literature and Experience*, Agency for International Development, Center for Development Information and Evaluation, May 12, 1922.   Also available via FTP from gaia.info.usaid.gov0/promoting_demo/docs/iss_brief/ibdemoc.txt.

Schrage, M., "Information Age Passes Up Gold by Ignoring Silver," *Los Angeles Times*, Section D1, p. 12, 1993.

Shapiro, Carl., "Theories of Oligopoly Behavior," Chapter 6 in Richard Schmalensee and Robert Willig (eds.), *Handbook of Industrial Organization*, North Holland, Amsterdam, 1988.

Shapiro, Norman Z., and Robert H. Anderson, *Toward an Ethics and Etiquette for Electronic Mail*, RAND, R-3283-NSF/RC, 1985. Available at http://www.rand.org/areas/r3283.html.

Shin, Doh Chull, "On the Third Wave of Democratization: A Synthesis and Evaluation of Recent Theory and Research," *World Politics*, No. 47, 1994, pp. 135–170.

Shiver, J. "Busting the Barriers to Cyberspace," *Los Angeles Times*, Section A1, p. 18, 29 May 1995.

Sirbu, Marvin A., "Telecommunications Technology and Infrastructure", in *A National Information Network: Changing Our Lives in the 21st Century*, The Aspen Institute, Institute for Information Studies, Queenstown, Maryland, 1992.

Soloway, Elliot, "Technology Education: Introduction," in Elliot Soloway (ed.), *Communications of the ACM*, Special Issue on Technology in K–12 Education, Vol. 36, No. 5, 1993, pp. 28–30.

Sproull, L., and Samer Faraj, "Atheism, Sex, and Databases: The Net as a Social Technology," *Workshop on Public Access to the Internet*, John F. Kennedy School of Government, Cambridge, Massachusetts, May 26–27, 1993.

Sproull, L., and S. Kiesler, "Computers, Networks and Work," *Scientific American*, Vol. 265, September 1991a, pp. 116–123.

Sproull, Lee, and Sara Kiesler, *Connections: New Ways of Working in the Networked Organization*, MIT Press, Cambridge, Massachusetts, 1991b.

Standing, Jonathan, "Sega to Give Saturn Game Player Access to Internet," *New York Times Syndicate* (a Web news service), September 12, 1995.

Starr, Harvey, "Diffusion Approaches to the Spread of Democracy in the International System," *Journal of Conflict Resolution*, Vol. 35, No. 2, June 1991, pp. 356–381.

Stasz, C. M., T. K. Bikson, J. D. Eveland, and J. Adams, *Assessing Benefits of the U.S. Forest Service's Geographic Information System: Research Design*, RAND, N-3245-USDAFS, 1991.

Stefferud, Einar, "Strategic Issues in Our E-Mail World," *Proceedings, Email World & WebWorld Conference*, Santa Clara, California, April 19–21, pp. B1-1 to B1-15, 1995.

Stefferud, E., and J. Pliskin, "To Tunnel or Translate, That Is the Question," in "Upper Layer Protocols, Architectures and Applications," *Proceedings of the IFIP TC6/WG6.5 International Conference on Upper Layer Protocols, Architectures and Applications*, Barcelona, Spain, North-Holland Elsevier Science B.V., The Netherlands, pp. 285–296, 1–3 June 1994.

Steinfield, Charles, Robert Kraut, and Lynn Streeter, "Markets, Hierarchies, and Open Data Networks," presented to the International Telecommunications Society, Gothenburg, Sweden, June 20–22, 1993.

Sterling, Bruce, "Triumph of the Plastic People," *Wired*, January 1995, pp. 101–158.

Streeter, Lynn A., Robert E. Kraut, Henry C. Lucas, and Laurence Caby, "The Impact of National Data Networks on Firm Performance and Market Structure," *Communications of the ACM*, in press.

Tessler, Lawrence, "Networked Computing in the 1990s," *Scientific American*, Vol. 265, September 1991, pp. 86–93.

Times Mirror, Times Mirror Center for The People & The Press, *Technology in the American Household,* Los Angeles, California, 1994

Toth, Victor, "Is Frame Relay Regulation Worth the Risks," *Business Communications Review,* March 1995.

United Nations Development Programme, *Human Development Report,* Oxford University Press, New York, 1993.

U.S. Congress, Office of Technology Assessment, *Making Government Work: Electronic Delivery of Federal Services,* OTA-TCT-578, U.S. Government Printing Office, Washington, D.C., September 1993.

Vail, Theodore, *AT&T Annual Report,* 1910.

Vail, Theodore, *AT&T Annual Report,* 1907.

van de Donk, W.B.H.J., I.Th.M. Snellen, and P. W. Tops, *Orwell in Athens: A Perspective on Informatization and Democracy,* IOS Press, Amsterdam, 1995.

Vittoro, Vince, "Portability without Politics," *America's Network,* May 15, 1995, pp. 42–44.

Vogelsang, Ingo, and Bridger M. Mitchell, *Telecommunications Competition: The Last 10 Miles,* MIT Press and AEI Press, 1996.

Vu, C., J. Esquea, L. Brooks, P. Bunyaviroch, G. Cerise, A. Grossman, J. Hellerstein, M. Leighninger, M. Matteson, Y. Onishi, S. Stanley, and J. Tu, *Civic Networks in the United States,* Final Report, Prepared for the U.S. National Commission on Libraries and Information Sciences, Washington, D.C., May 1994.

Wall Street Journal, "MCI to Offer E-Mail Service in Calling Plan," November 11, 1994, p. B3.

Ware, Willis, "The New Faces of Privacy," *The Information Society,* Vol. 9, No. 3, July–September 1993

Watson, Russell, John Barry, Christopher Dickey, and Tim Padgett, "When Words Are the Best Weapon," *Newsweek,* February 27, 1995, pp. 36–40.

Williams, L. "Computer Gap Worries Blacks," *New York Times*, Section B1, p. 4, 1995.

Williamson, O. E., "Transaction Cost Economics," in Richard Schmalensee and Robert Willig (eds.), *Handbook of Industrial Organization*, Chapter 3, North Holland, Amsterdam, 1988.

Winther, Mark, *Personal Messaging Services Forecast: On-Ramps to the Information Highway*, Link Resources Corporation, 1994.

World Bank, *World Bank Development Report*, The World Bank, Washington D.C., 1991.

"World Telecommunication Development Report 1994," International Telecommunications Union, 1994.

Yupeng, Pan, "IT & Telecom Keys to Promoting China's Economic Reform," *Transnational Data and Communications Report*, November/December 1992, pp. 19–24.

UNIVERSAL ACCESS TO E-MAIL
FEASIBILITY AND SOCIETAL IMPLICATIONS

Robert H. Anderson, Tora K. Bikson, Sally Ann Law, Bridger M. Mitchell

What if e-mail were as ubiquitous as telephones, TVs, and VCRs, so that literally *everyone* were on-line, accessible by e-mail, and able to send messages to bulletin boards, news groups, friends, family, and colleagues? Is this technically feasible? If so, at what cost? What would be the personal and societal benefits resulting from "universal access to e-mail?"

UNIVERSAL ACCESS TO E-MAIL provides some answers to these questions.

E-mail has swept the communications and information world, providing instantaneous global information and data exchange. However, this revolution has not altered one fundamental feature: An information elite still exists, made up of those with access to and knowledge about computers and e-mail. The diverging trends in access based on income and education are placing significant groups of current and next-generation U.S. citizens at a serious disadvantage in relevant job-related skills and in access to social programs and information. As e-mail becomes more pervasive, those information haves may leave the have-nots further behind, unless concerted efforts are made to provide all citizens with access to the technology.

UNIVERSAL ACCESS TO E-MAIL gives serious consideration to closing the access gap. This comprehensive study details the benefits—on the personal as well as global level—of e-mail access. It urges the nation to support a U.S. policy of universal access and addresses the technical and economic aspects of putting such a policy into operation.

ISBN 0-8330-2331-4

52000

9 780833 023315

MR-650-MF